IMAGES
of America

OSWEGO TOWNSHIP

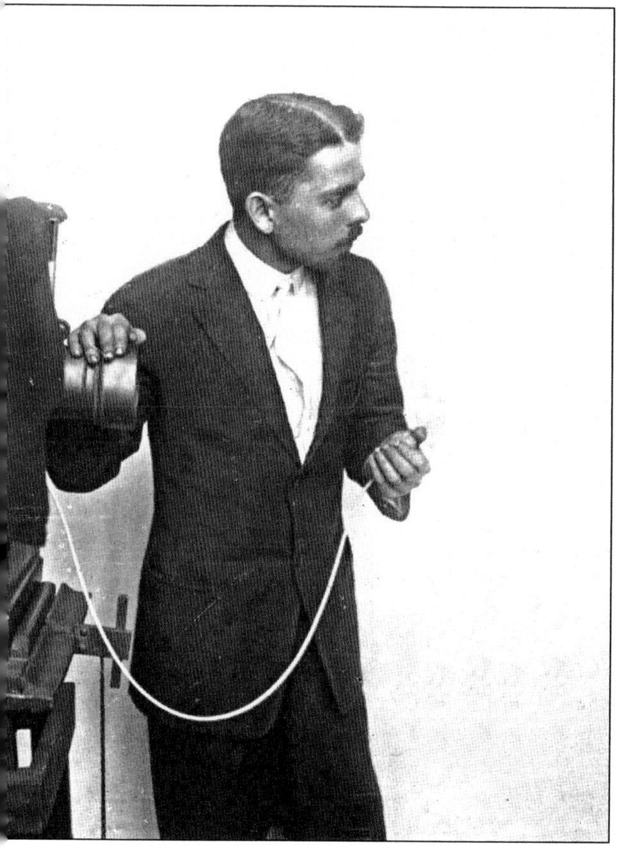

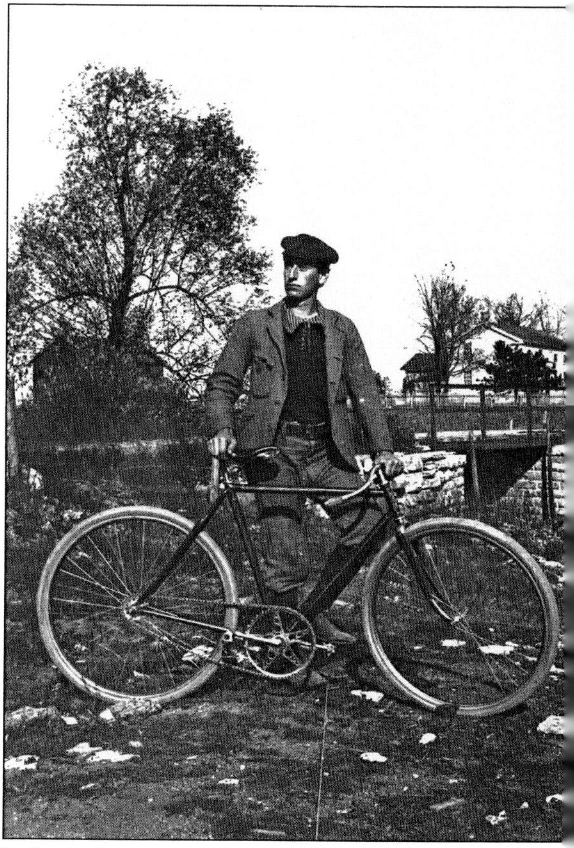

In the late 1800s and early 1900s, Oswego was lucky to have two pioneer photographers who recorded life in and around Oswego Township. Dwight Smith Young (left) worked professionally until the 1930s, while Irvin Haines (right) was an inspired amateur. Both are shown here in self-portraits, Young's snapped in his studio, while Haines took his along Wolf's Crossing Road just outside Oswego.

On the cover: It may be hard to believe one's grandparents and great-grandparents were once young and carefree, but this photograph proves that having fun is not a recent invention. On a sunny day in the 1890s, from left to right, Mae Barrett, Amy Effie Parkhurst, and Clara Minkler took a stroll along Waubonsie Creek in Oswego. Fortunately, someone was available to capture this delightful image as the three friends enjoyed a day together. (Courtesy of the Little White School Museum Collection.)

IMAGES
of America

OSWEGO TOWNSHIP

Oswegoland Heritage Association
Roger A. Matile, Editor

ARCADIA
PUBLISHING

ISBN 978-0-7385-5208-8

Published by Arcadia Publishing
Charleston SC, Chicago IL, Portsmouth NH, San Francisco CA

Printed in the United States of America

Library of Congress Catalog Card Number: 2007941494

For all general information contact Arcadia Publishing at:
Telephone 843-853-2070
Fax 843-853-0044
E-mail sales@arcadiapublishing.com
For customer service and orders:
Toll-Free 1-888-313-2665

Visit us on the Internet at www.arcadiapublishing.com

To Oswego's pioneer photographers, Irvin Haines and Dwight S. Young; to photographer Homer Durand; and to Oswego historians Mary Cutter Bickford and Paul Shoger, without whose work so much of Oswego Township's rich history would have been lost.

Contents

Acknowledgments

The last—and so far only—history of Oswego Township was published to commemorate the community's 1983 sesquicentennial. Since then, the Oswegoland Heritage Association's Little White School Museum has collected thousands of priceless historical photographs that illustrate the community's long and fascinating history. To create this volume, volunteers mined those collections during a period of months, choosing the best from among a myriad of images. Many of the photographs subsequently picked for this volume have never before been published. In fact, many have never been seen outside family photograph albums.

Also invaluable and offering indispensable insight on Oswego Township people, places, and activities during the past 150 years was the museum's newspaper collection, including the *Kendall County Courier*; the *Kendall County Record*; the *Oswego Herald*; the *Oswego Ledger*; and the *Ledger-Sentinel*.

Helping during our regular Thursdays and Saturdays at the museum was assistant director Bob Stekl, and lending valuable assistance on Saturdays was volunteer Stephanie Just. Museum assistants Mary Therriault and Pat Torrance also lent their assistance and expertise at critical times.

Also lending a hand at critical times was Dennis Buck of the Aurora Historical Society and Glenn Young, a former heritage association board member and grandson of pioneer Oswego photographer Dwight Young.

While we all did our bit, without the museum's resources this work would have been impossible. The museum, housed in Oswego's former Methodist Episcopal Church and beloved one-time elementary school, is a unique cooperative venture of the non-profit Oswegoland Heritage Association, which maintains and operates the museum and archives; the Oswegoland Park District, which provides essential financial, physical, and moral support; and the Oswego School District, which still owns the building. Without the firm backing of all three, preservation of Oswego Township's rich heritage could not continue. To all of them go our thanks.

And finally, a special and heartfelt thanks to my wife, Sue, who has managed to be understanding as I spent so many weekends and evenings completing *Oswego Township*.

—Roger Matile, editor

INTRODUCTION

When the extended Pearce clan, brothers John, Walter, and Daniel, their brother-in-law, William Wilson, and their families, rolled up to the east bank of the Fox River in the spring of 1833, they probably had every intention of making permanent homes on the claims they had staked the previous fall.

Daniel Pearce and Wilson settled on land that eventually became the original village of Oswego, Pearce claiming land that makes up today's Fox Bend Golf Course, and Wilson building his cabin near the busy modern intersection of Illinois Route 25 and U.S. Route 34.

But as it turned out, only brothers Daniel and Walter chose to occupy their claims for the rest of their lives. John and Wilson soon moved a few miles west to modern Little Rock Township, where they built a mill. They left Illinois in the early 1840s to homestead west of the Mississippi.

Thus began a pattern that continues to this day, with newcomers arriving and some deciding to stay, making Oswego Township their new home, while others choose to stay for varying lengths of time before moving on to other homes in other areas.

The Pearces left their homes in Ohio in what became known ever after as the Year of the Early Spring. According to the pioneers, the snow left early that year, the prairies dried out more quickly than usual, and grass quickly greened up providing necessary fodder for the pioneers' teams of draft horses and yokes of oxen. That fortunate accident of nature resulted in the area's first—but far from last—development rush.

The rest of the 1830s were some of the most exciting times in Oswego Township's history. Lewis B. Judson and Levi F. Arnold laid out the village on land first claimed by Wilson, calling it Hudson. Arnold opened the first store in town. Stagecoach service started soon after, and the town was granted its post office in January 1837, which the post office department for some reason named Lodi. Arnold was named the first postmaster, and later that year voters in town—meaning male property owners during that era—decided to select a permanent name. In the end, they chose neither Hudson nor Lodi. Instead, Oswego won by a single vote.

Government surveyors worked their way through the area the next year, finally paving the way for land sales a few years later.

Thanks to its position as a stagecoach crossroads, Oswego grew quickly. Settlers arrived from New England, the old Middle Colonies, and from foreign countries including Scotland, Germany, and England to take advantage of the rich prairie soil.

In 1841, the Illinois General Assembly created Kendall County and made Yorkville the county seat. But in 1845, Oswego boosters engineered a vote on the county seat's location, which

Oswego won. In 1859, voters, tired of making long journeys in the day of horse and buggy travel, approved moving it back to Yorkville. The Civil War prevented the immediate construction of a new courthouse, but in June 1864 the county records were finally removed to Yorkville where they have remained ever since.

After losing the county seat, Oswego's growth slowed to a trickle. It no longer needed the three hotels that catered to those doing their county business in town, and most of the legal and government professionals that made the county run moved to Yorkville. Then in 1867, a devastating fire destroyed the main business block on the east side of Main Street, including the majestic National Hotel.

The Oswego of the 1870s until the middle of the 1950s relied on its status as the market town for the large, and rich, surrounding agricultural area rather than on the status of its professionals. The arrival of the Fox River Valley Railroad in 1870 (the Chicago, Burlington and Quincy tracks had bypassed the village two miles to the west two decades earlier) and the Aurora, Elgin and Yorkville Railway's construction in 1900 helped keep the village moving forward, however slowly. Children were born, educated, and grew up in town. They went off to fight in World War I and World War II, while their mothers, fathers, brothers, and sisters stayed home and volunteered with Civil Defense, the home guard, and the Red Cross.

When World War II ended, servicemen and women came home looking to start new families. In a remarkable bit of serendipity, two major industrial concerns, Western Electric, the manufacturing arm of AT&T, and Caterpillar Tractor, decided to locate industrial plants in the township just as developer Don L. Dise was beginning to develop the sprawling Boulder Hill subdivision. Fueled by the easy money provided by the G.I. Bill, the already strong postwar demand for new housing was accelerated by the housing needs of the thousands of workers the two huge manufacturing plants drew to the area. So began a time of profound change that continues to the present day.

From the first families farming the tallgrass prairie that produced such rich harvests to the pioneer business owners that followed, from teachers and students to circuit riding preachers, the history of Oswego Township has been made and recorded by the people who lived it. In the pages that follow, take a trip back through time and experience Oswego Township history in words and pictures.

One

Pioneer Days

Oswego Township pioneers often commented about how empty the prairie was when they arrived, but numerous Native American families and hardy frontiersmen were already in the area when the first "permanent" American settlers arrived in 1833.

Southeast of Oswego, David Laughton and his Potawatomi wife, Waish-kee-shah, and their son Joseph were living in what the settlers called the AuSable Timber, which is today part of Waa Kee Sha Park. A bit farther west, Peter Specie, a French Canadian, was living in the grove that bore his name. Waish-kee-shaw's reserve, granted in the Treaty of 1829, was some of the first land that could be legally sold in Oswego Township and became the basis for Daniel Townsend's sprawling agricultural and business empire. Specie, meanwhile, contracted with settlers to "break," or plow for the first time, the tough prairie sod. He also sold the first apple seedlings to future orchardist Smith Minkler, thus providing the basis for the development of the locally famed Minkler Apple.

Also living up and down the river in that year were the Potawatomi, Ottawa, and Chippewa families that made up part of the Three Fires Confederacy that had occupied the Fox Valley since the 1740s.

But within a few years, the area's Native American inhabitants had been removed west of the Mississippi, and a flood of new settlers arrived, both overland and on the Great Lakes. Typical was the trip taken by the group of families young James Sheldon Barber accompanied from Smyrna, New York, to Oswego. Arriving in December 1843, the group spent 35 days on the trail, traveling what they estimated to be 805 miles through Ontario, Michigan, Indiana, and Illinois.

Along with the American settlers, other immigrants from much farther away began arriving in the 1840s. Germans, Scots, and British families looking for new lives on the Illinois prairies soon arrived. The descendants of the Hafenrichters, Stewarts, Collins, and other European pioneers still live in Oswego Township today.

By the mid-1850s, the pioneer era in Oswego Township had ended, although those who were part of it never forgot that exciting time.

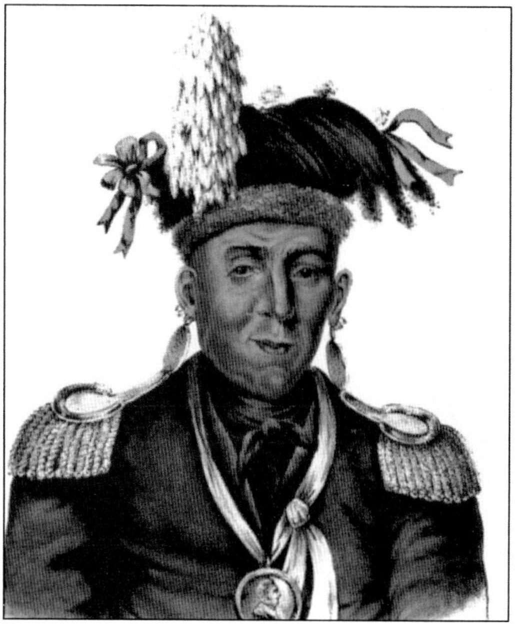

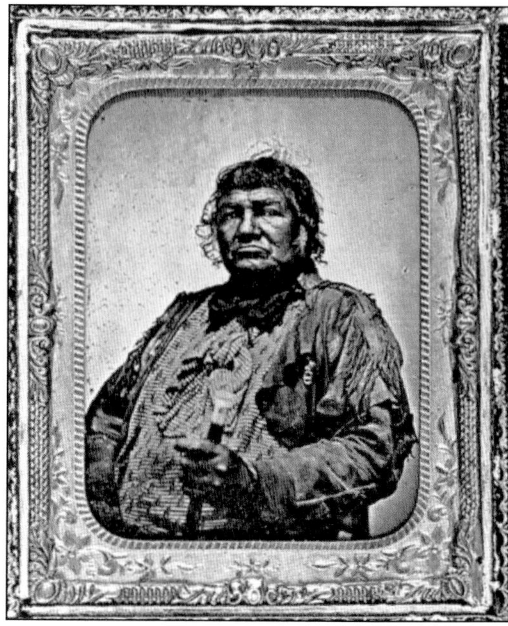

Waubonsee (left) was the war chief of the Prairie Potawatomi; Shabbona, an Ottawa, was a civil chief. Both were intimates of the Native American nationalist Tecumseh. Waubonsee reportedly maintained a favored camp along the creek that bears his name in Oswego. Although they supported the Americans during the Black Hawk War of 1832, they were forced west of the Mississippi in 1835 with the rest of their people.

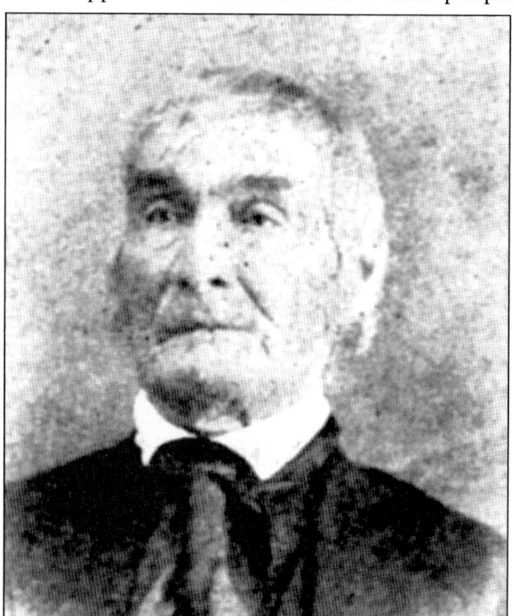

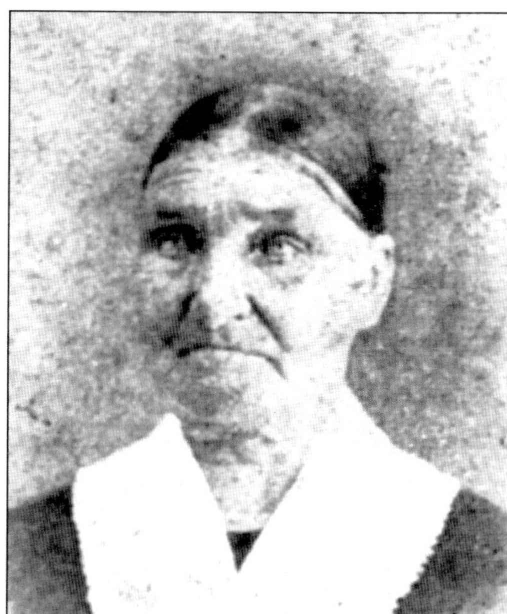

Daniel and Sarah Pearce arrived at Oswego with their extended family in 1833. They settled along Waubonsie Creek on what is today Fox Bend Golf Course. Daniel's brothers, John and Walter, staked claims on the west side of the Fox River, while their brother-in-law William S. Wilson, nearer Waubonsie Creek's mouth. Daniel and Sarah spent the rest of their lives on the land they claimed in 1833.

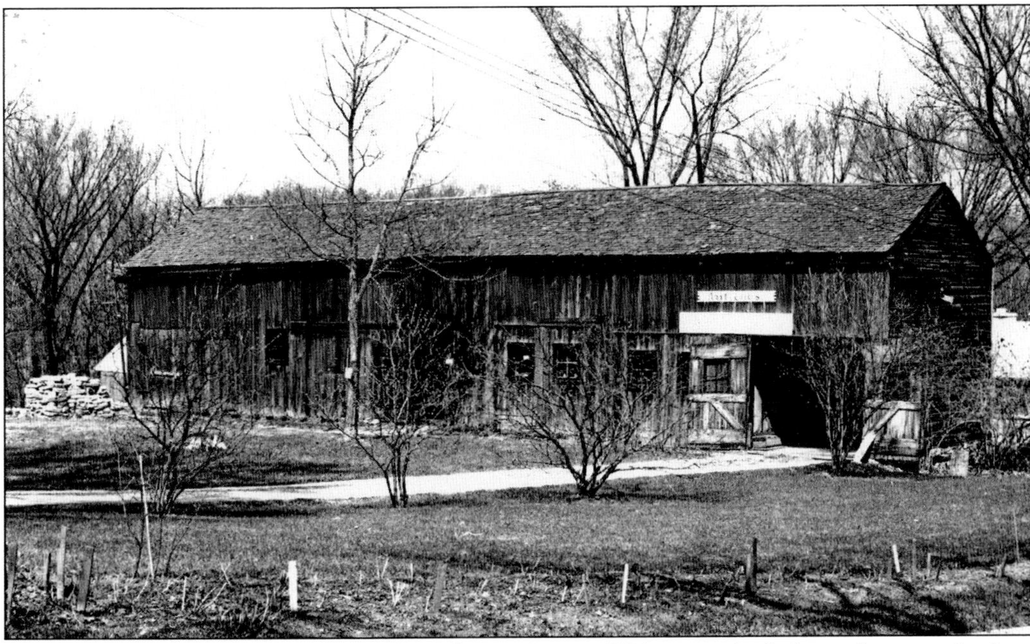

William Smith Wilson and his wife, Rebecca Pearce Wilson, staked their claim at the busy modern Oswego intersection of U.S. Route 34 and Illinois Route 25. Wilson is said to have built this barn along with his first home before leaving about 1836 with his brother-in-law Elijah Pearce to build a sawmill three miles north of modern Plano. The Wilsons eventually moved west to Missouri and then Kansas.

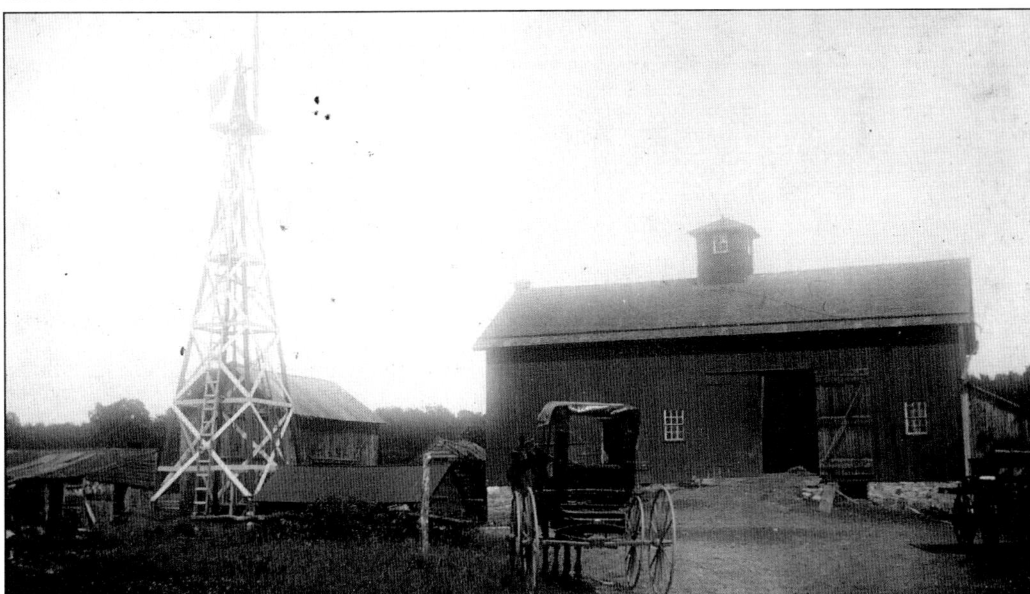

Smith G. Minkler, then just 18 years of age, arrived in Oswego Township with his parents, Peter and Betsy Minkler, in 1833. The Minklers pioneered the area round Specie Grove, where Smith built his farm, including the barn above. He was the Fox Valley's premier pioneer orchardist, developed the Minkler Apple from cuttings provided by Peter Specie, and was a founder of the Illinois State Horticulture Society.

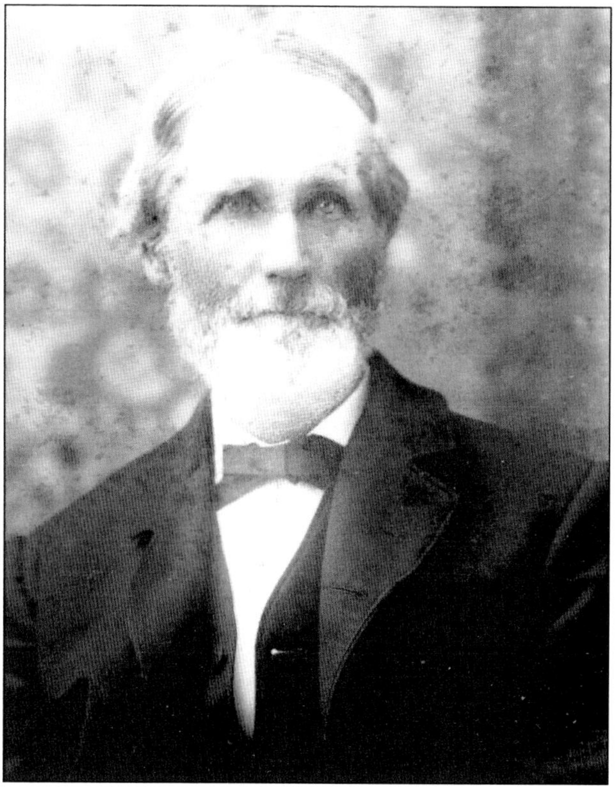

Lewis Brinsmaid Judson first saw Oswego while serving in the Michigan Militia during the Black Hawk War of 1832. Early in 1834, he apparently dispatched T. B. Mudget, probably his brother-in-law, to stake a claim of several hundred acres for him at what is now Oswego. Judson arrived later that year with his wife and took up his claim, which covered much of what is now Oswego.

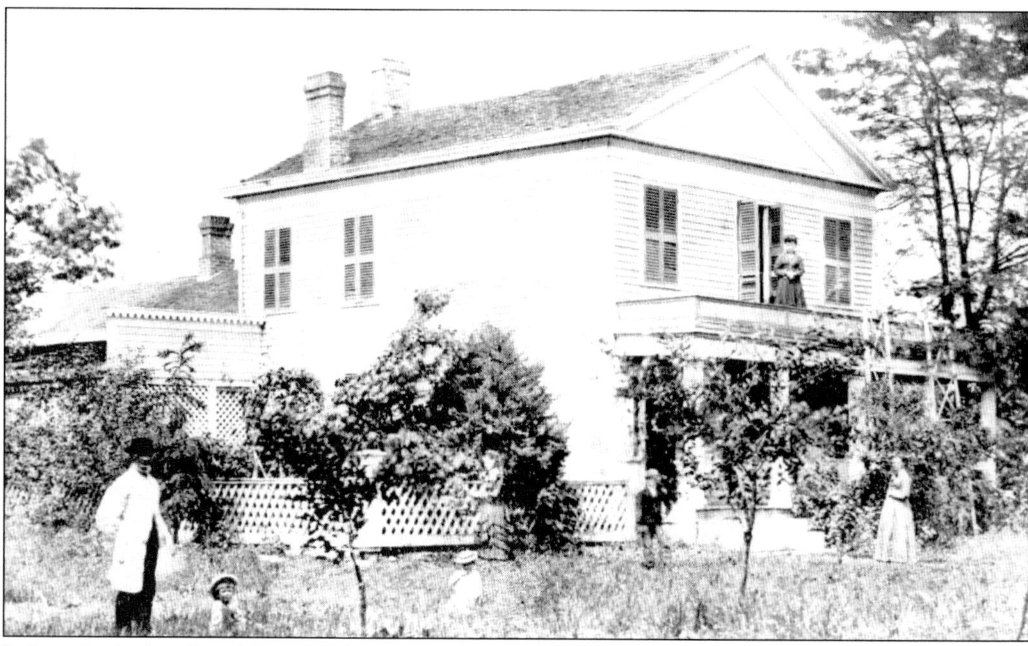

Judson built this Greek Revival house on what eventually became South Main Street in Oswego after he and Levi F. Arnold laid the village out in 1835. Judson was active in Oswego's civic and political life until 1872, when he moved to Aurora. The home was demolished by its most recent owner in February 2006.

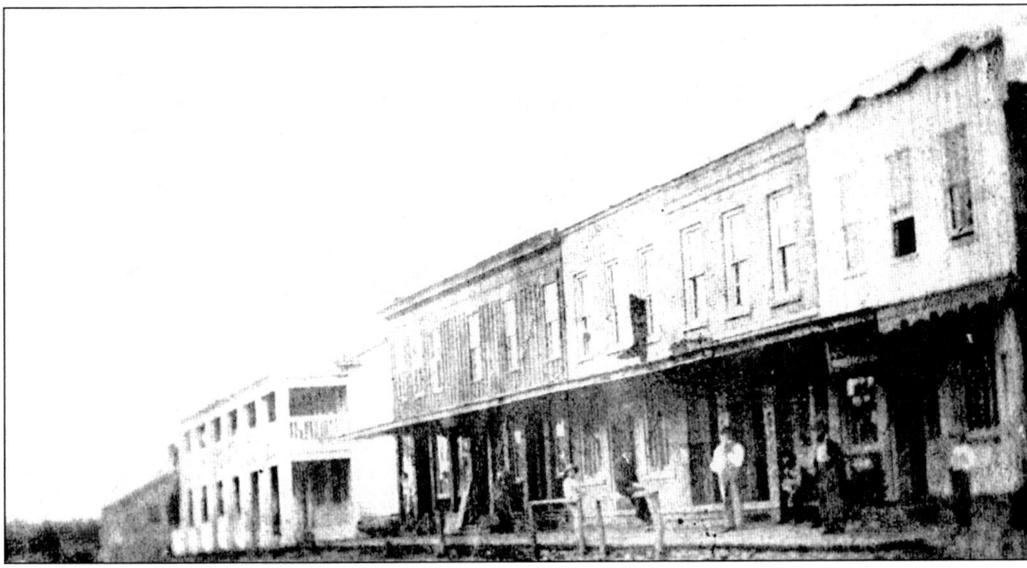

The east side of Main Street about 1865 boasted the stately columns of the National Hotel and several frame storefronts. Arnold's store and post office, the village's first, was located on the lot immediately to the right of the hotel. On February 9, 1867, all the buildings in this photograph were destroyed by fire.

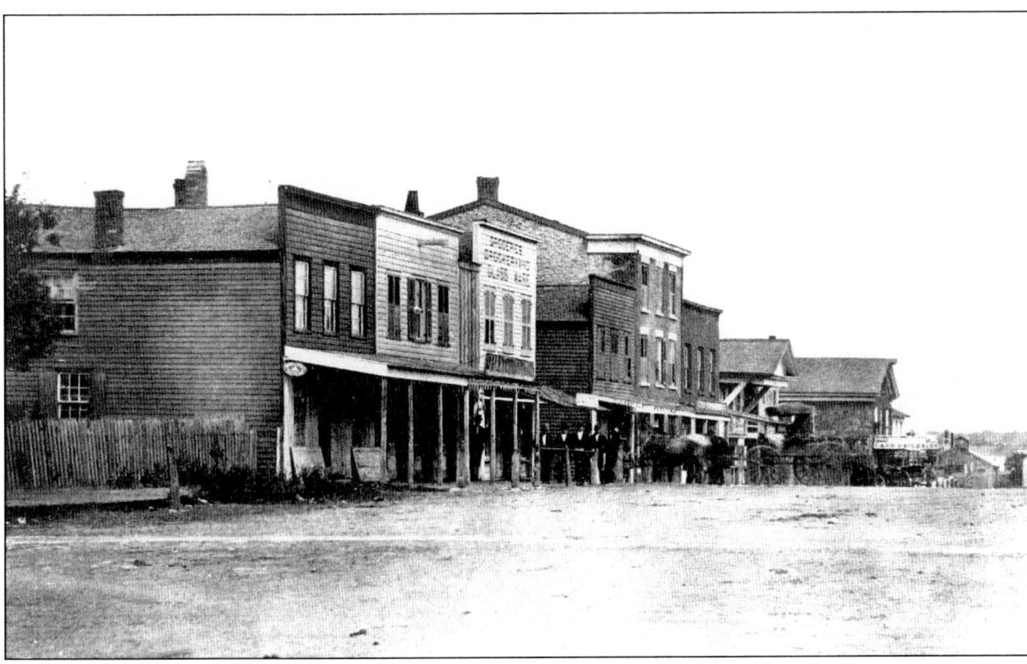

The west side of Oswego Main Street business district in the mid-1860s resembled towns in the Wild West. The only building still standing from this era is located at the right. Today, it houses the American Male and Company and Editions clothing stores.

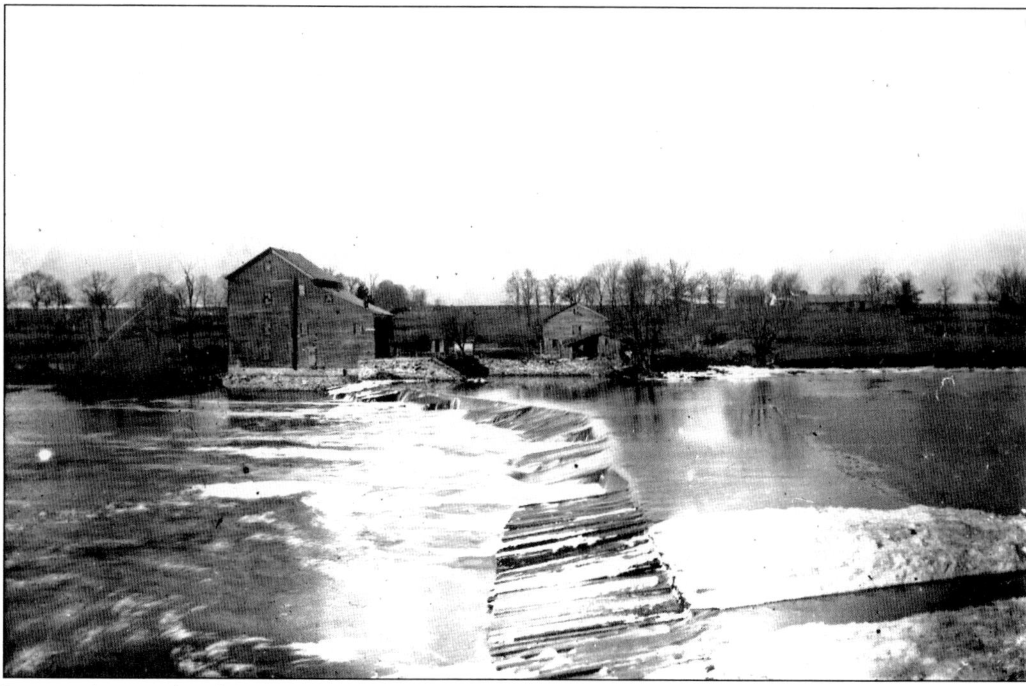

Just to the north of Oswego, millwrights quickly took advantage of the Fox River's hydraulic power. Merritt Clark's first small corn mill on the west side of the river was replaced in 1838 by Levi Gorton's more substantial gristmill and more permanent dam. The mill site is known today as Millstone Park.

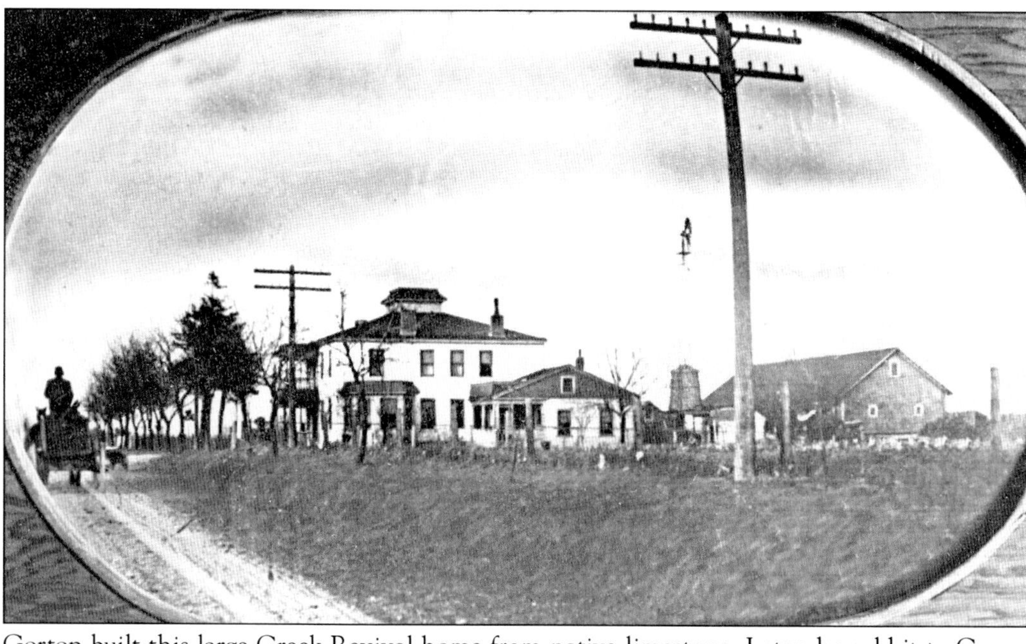

Gorton built this large Greek Revival home from native limestone. Later, he sold it to George Hopkins. The home, now sporting a row of classic columns supporting a portico added in the 1950s, still stands along Illinois Route 25 in Oswego, a testament to the area's growth during the pioneer era.

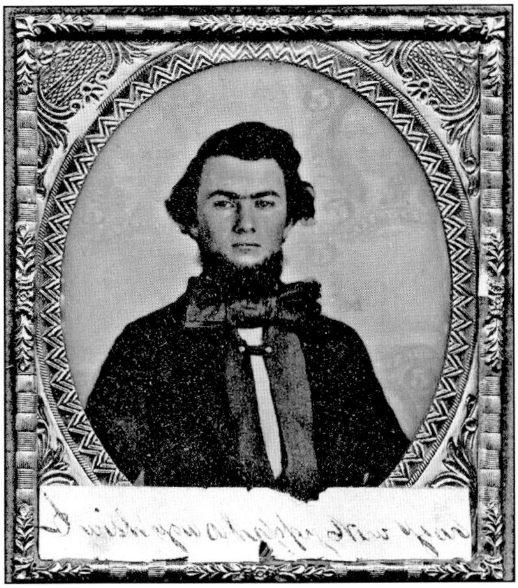

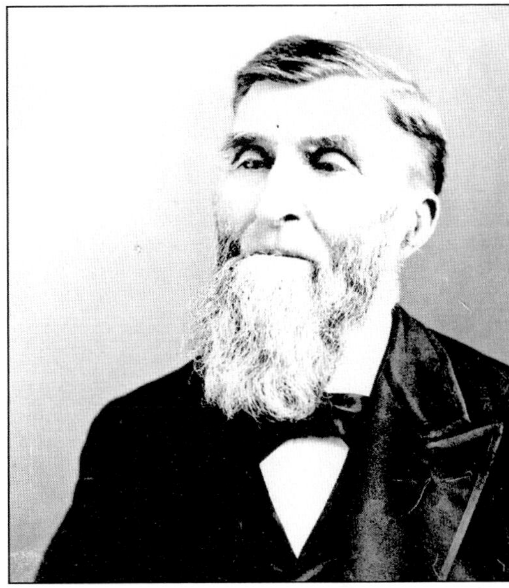

Cyrus Cass (left) and John Hem marked the kinds of settlers attracted to Oswego Township. Cass, a native of New Hampshire, arrived in 1843 with his wife, Mary. Hem, a stonemason by trade, and his wife, Margarethe, immigrated first to New York, and then to Illinois in 1843, where they bought 100 acres of land along today's Wolf's Crossing Road. According to family tradition, he helped build Gray's Mill in Montgomery.

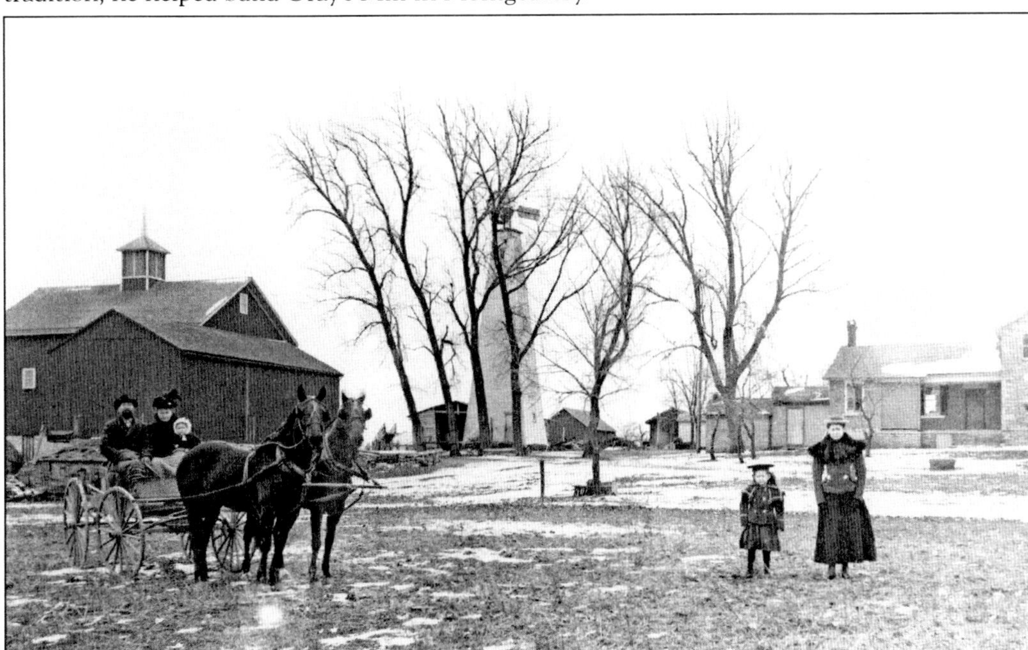

Standing outside at the John Hem Farmstead, three miles east of Oswego on Wolf's Crossing Road, in the winter of 1886 were, from left to right, Oliver O. Hem (John's son), Sarah Constantine Hem, Elda Hem (Smith), Bernice Hem (Schwantz), and Stella Hem (Pierce). The Hems, along with the Roths, Shogers, Burkharts, Hafenrichters, Haags, and other German families settled in a cluster along and near Wolf's Crossing Road.

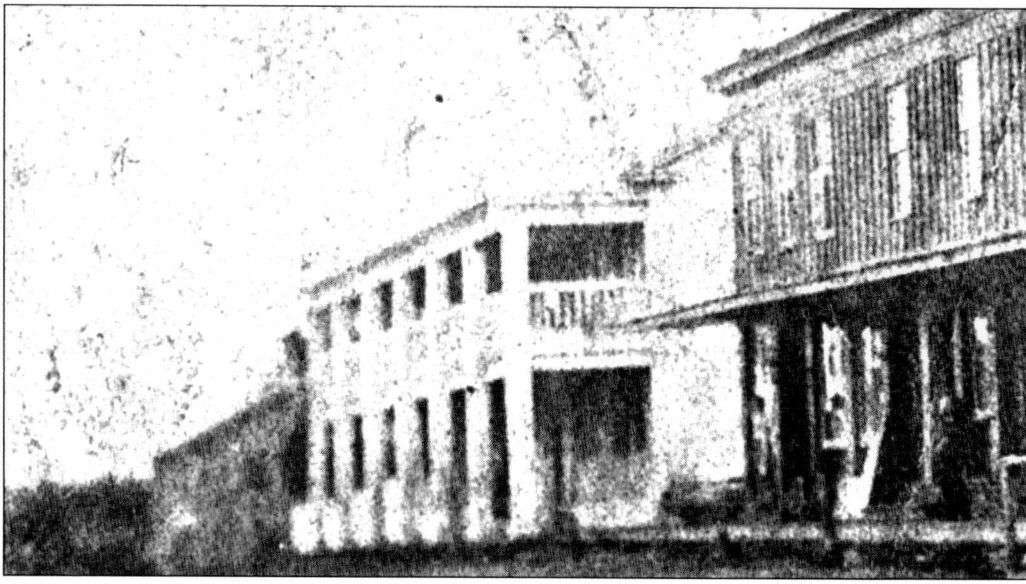

The National Hotel was Oswego's premier lodging place during the 1840s, 1850s, and 1860s. When the county seat moved from Yorkville to Oswego in 1845, the first term of the circuit court that year was held in the hotel. The hotel catered to the stagecoach trade, as well as those coming to Oswego for legal and government business.

COTILLION PARTY,

—AT THE—

NATIONAL HOTEL, OSWEGO, ILL.,

ON WEDNESDAY EVENING, NOV. 16th, 1864.

Yourself & Lady are respectfully invited.

MANAGERS.

A. B. HALL, Oswego. W. S. BEAUPRE, Aurora. C. H. PATRICK, Joliet.
J. D. KENADA, " T. SEELEY, Bristol. WM. COWDRY, "
L. KNOX, Bristol. L. O. LATHROP, Bristol. J. PLATT, Plattville.
G. HAPGOOD, Newark. H. E. BENNER, — — H. O. BINGHAM, Plainfield.

C. E, BEAUPRE, I. PEARCE, FLOOR MANAGERS.

Good Music in attendance.

TICKETS, $3.00, M. RICHARDS, Proprietor.

Not only was the National Hotel a successful business in the days of stagecoach travel, but it was also the social center of Oswego, hosting a variety of entertainments, from patriotic celebrations to the "Cotillion Party" advertised on this Civil War–era advertising card and hosted by hotel manager Marcius Richards.

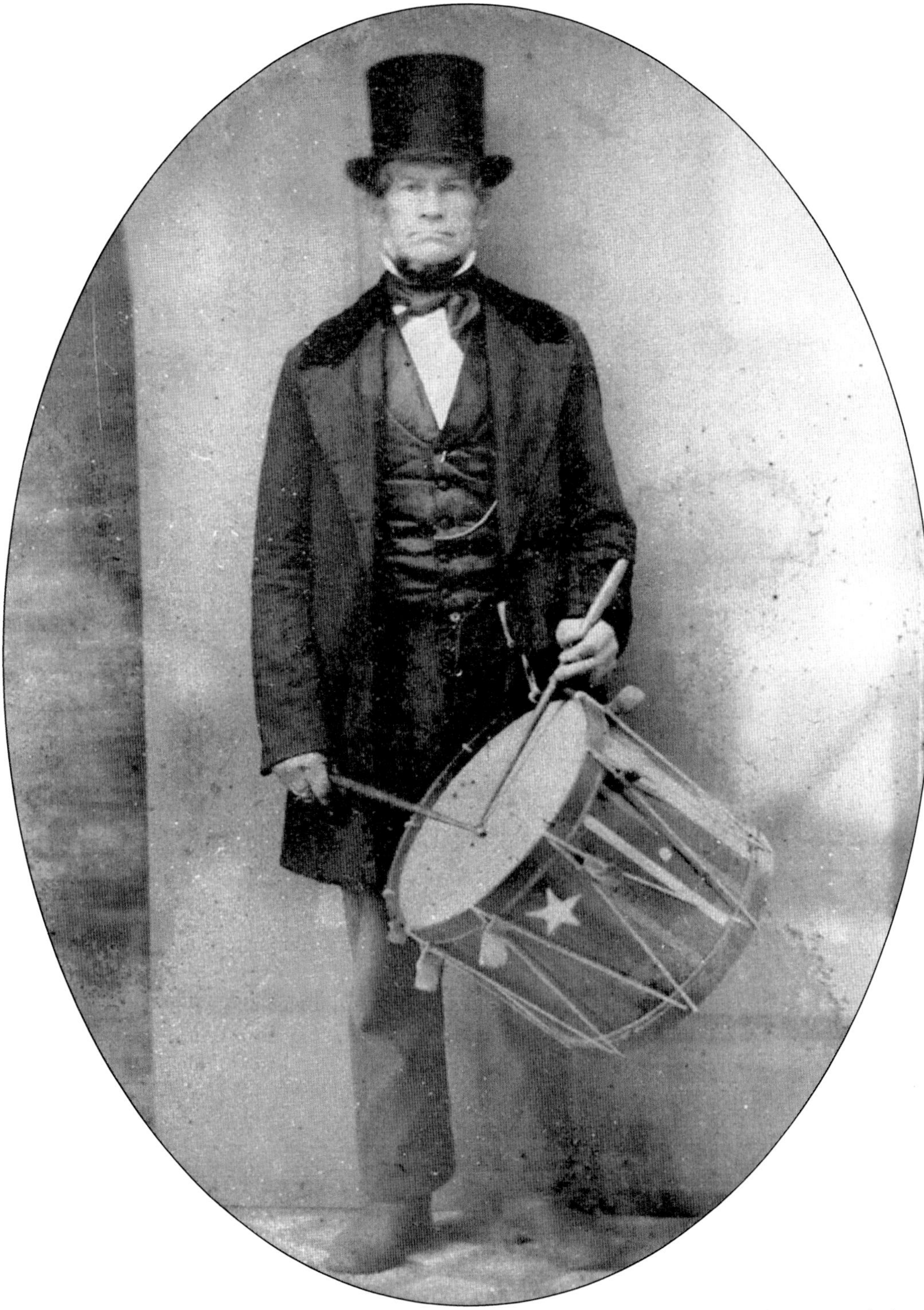

A cobbler by trade, Ezra Smith was also well-known in Oswego as a hotelkeeper and drum maker. Smith's drums were used by Oswego soldiers who marched off to the Civil War, and he gave patriotic concerts on national holidays.

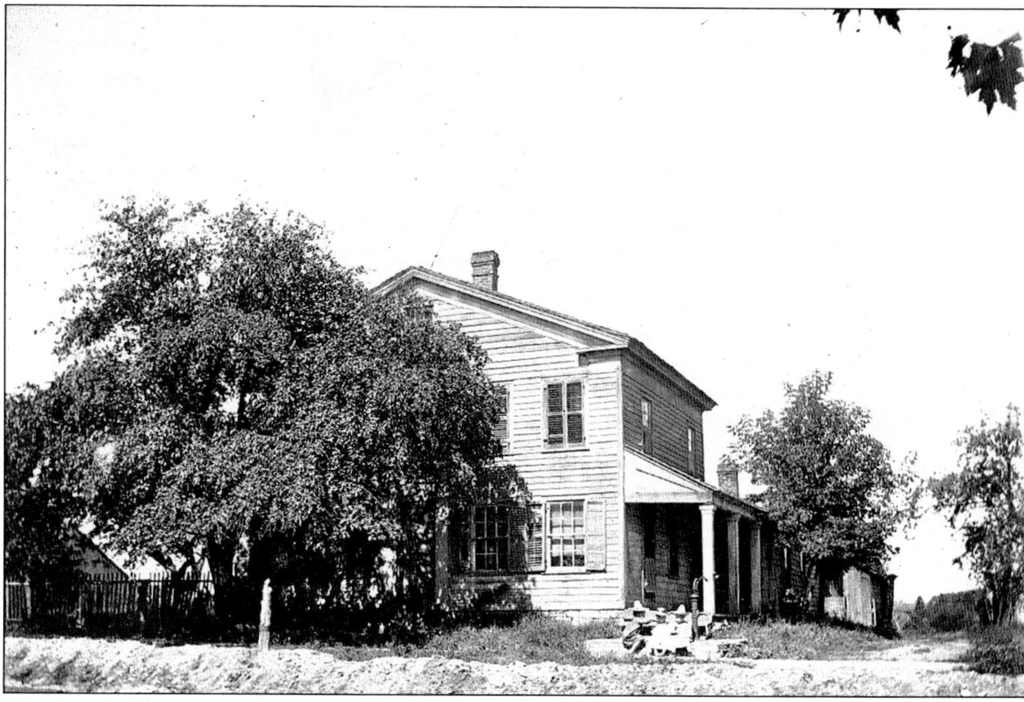

The Smith House hotel, operated by Ezra Smith and his wife, stood on south Main Street on the site occupied by today's Dari Hut. Smith operated his shoemaking business from the hotel, and it catered to the stagecoach trade. The old Chicago-Ottawa Trail ran down Main Street in front of the hotel.

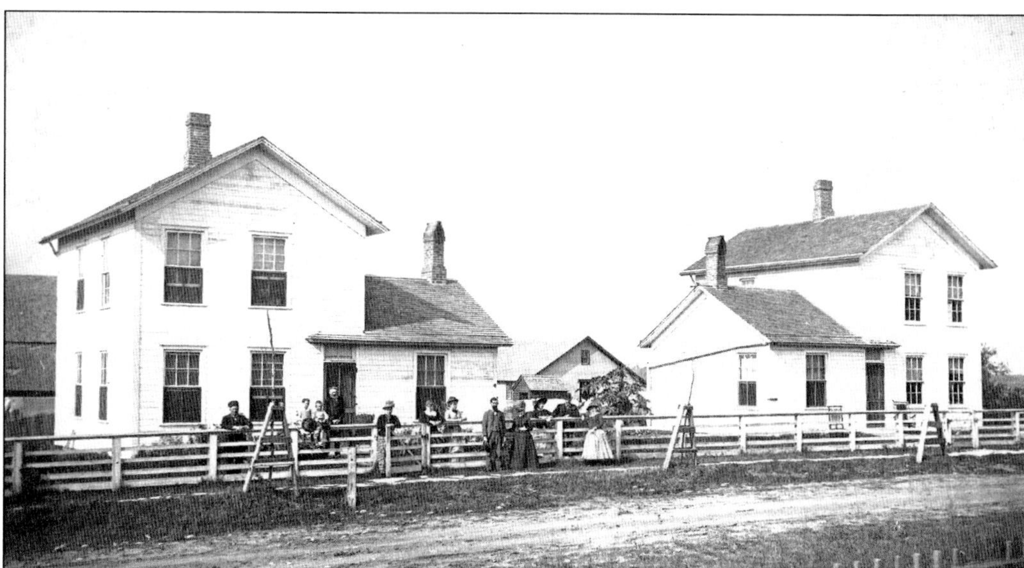

The Kendall House, at Jackson and Madison Streets, was Oswego's third hotel during its era as county seat and major stagecoach stop. Built by Wright Murphy and then operated by a succession of hoteliers, it was divided into two buildings in 1880, which were moved a short distance apart. While still a hotel, Sheriff Mathias Beaupre—who was, conveniently, also the hotelkeeper—used the upstairs of the building to house prisoners.

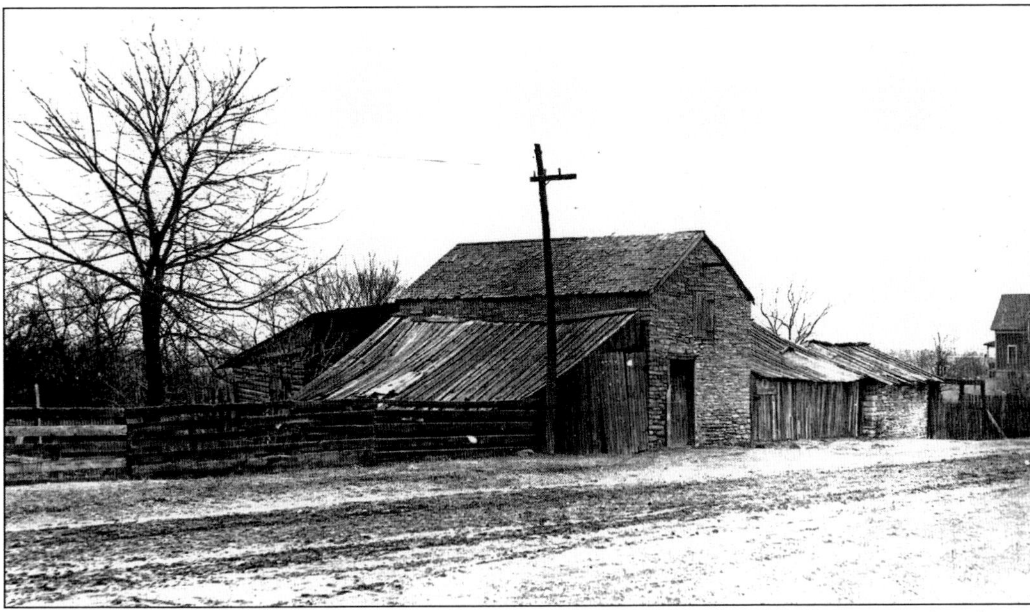

Teamster Josiah Smith reportedly built this stone barn and livery stable on what is today Illinois Route 25 immediately north of the U.S. Route 34 intersection. Smith housed both his wagons and teams in the rough-laid limestone building and shed additions.

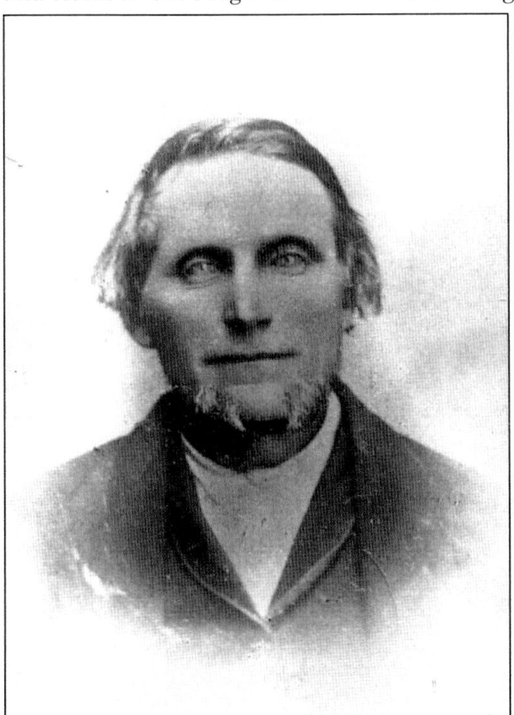

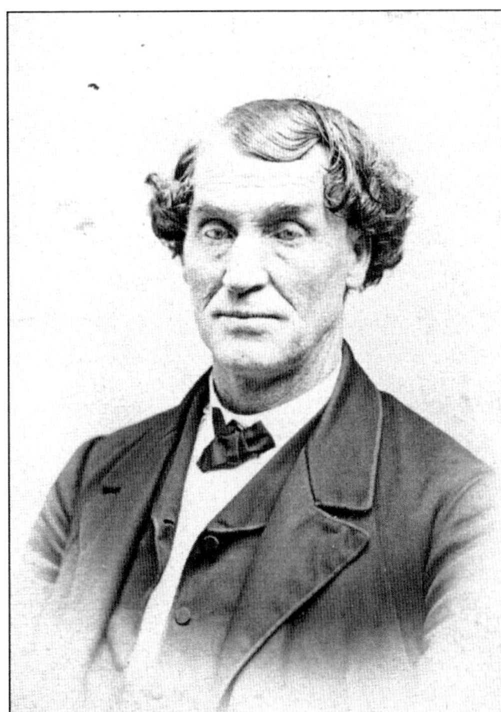

Josiah Smith (left) relied on local blacksmiths and wagon wrights to keep his business going, including William Hoze (right), a New Yorker who arrived in Oswego in 1840. Hoze's wagon shop employed carpenters, wood turners, and blacksmiths to turn out the wagons, carriages, and buggies Oswego Township residents needed in the town's early days.

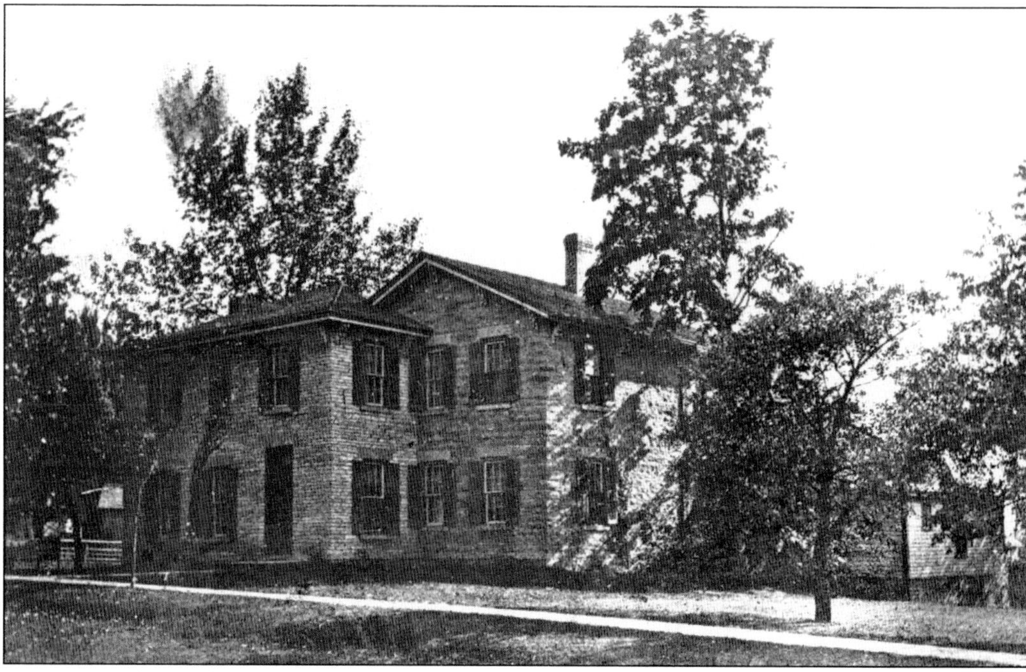

Wagon wright William Hoze built the original gable-roof portion to the right of this stately home at the corner of Washington and Monroe Streets in Oswego in the 1860s with (according to family tradition) limestone imported from Wisconsin, an indication his business was thriving. The hip-roofed addition, built from Joliet limestone, was added by John W. Cherry in the late 1800s.

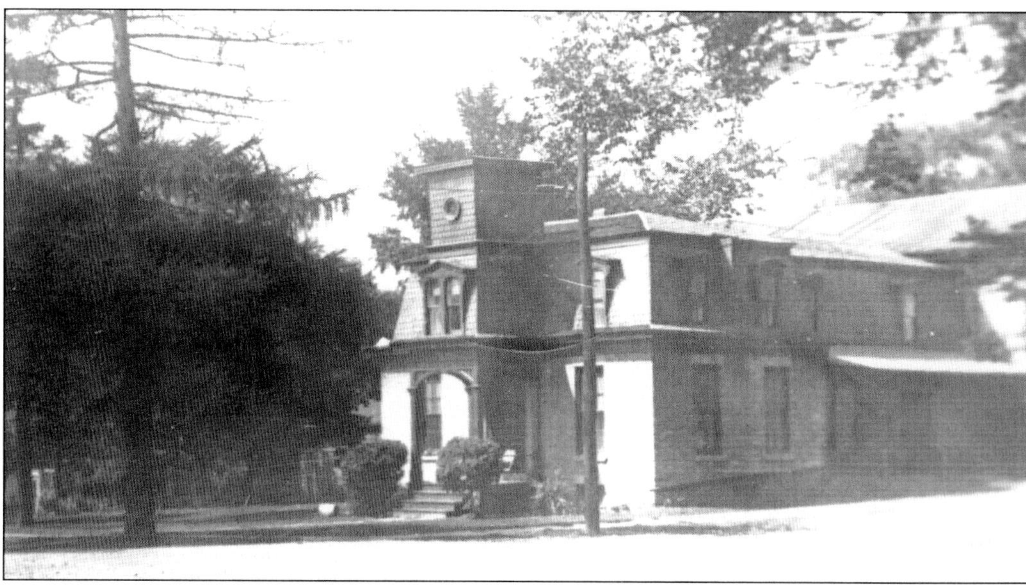

Oliver Hebert, another Oswego wagon wright, built this Second Empire–style residential addition to his wagon factory at Van Buren and Madison Streets in 1872. Hebert and his family originally lived in a portion of the two-story native limestone wagon shop. According to a brief note in the October 17, 1872, *Kendall County Record*, the new house "departed from the usual style of architecture and it will have quite a foreign look."

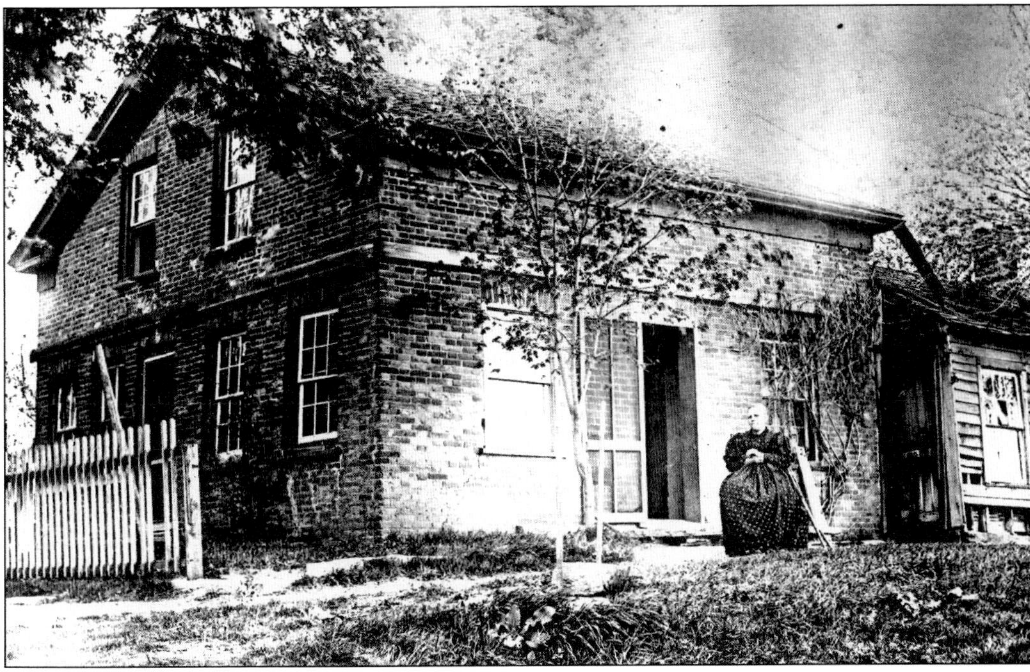

Margaret Phillips Young sits outside the brick home she and her husband, Oswego blacksmith John A. Young, owned at Main and Tyler Streets in Oswego. Young came to Oswego in 1841 with her parents, William and Margaret (Daved) Phillips. The brick home is typical of the substantial structures built by pioneer businessmen during Oswego's early years.

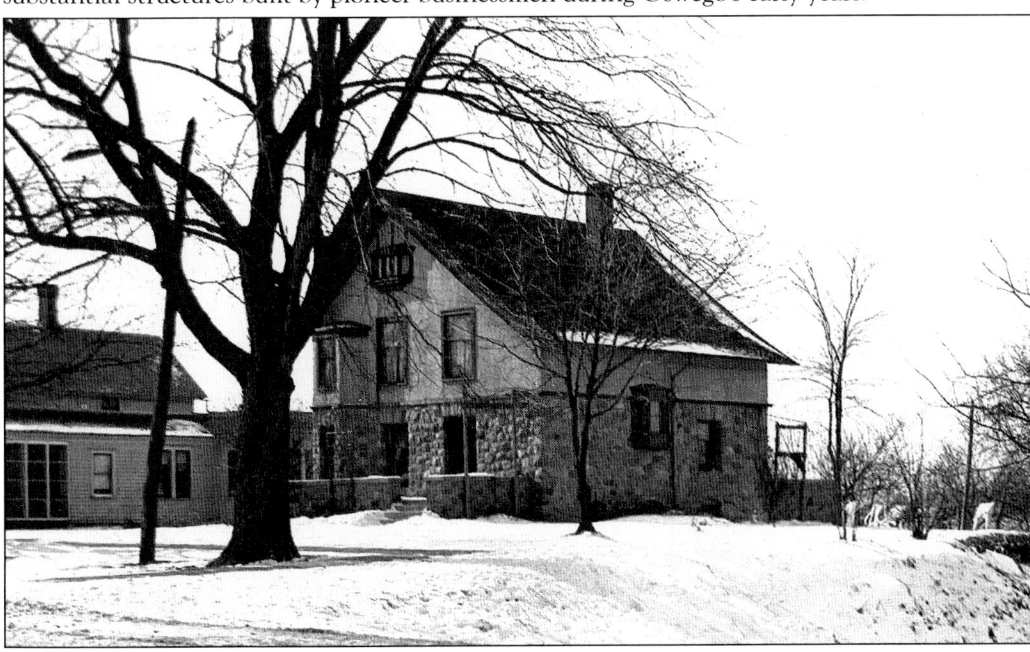

Margaret and John Young's son Lou C. Young built this shingle-style home to replace his parents' original brick home in a process of architectural evolution that continues in Oswego to the present day. It features a rustic stone first floor, and classic shingle touches including a balcony and eyebrow window.

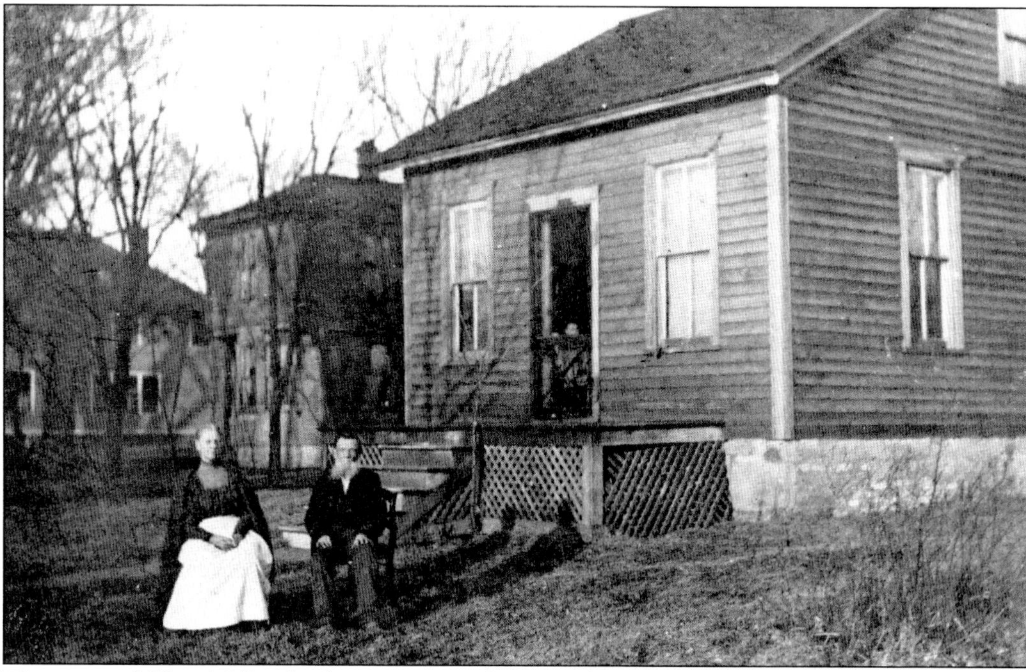

Thomas and Eliza Miller, both immigrants from England, sit outside their small house at the corner of Washington and Ashland Streets in Oswego sometime before the beginning of the 20th century. The small frame house was typical of the workers cottages that dotted Oswego during that era.

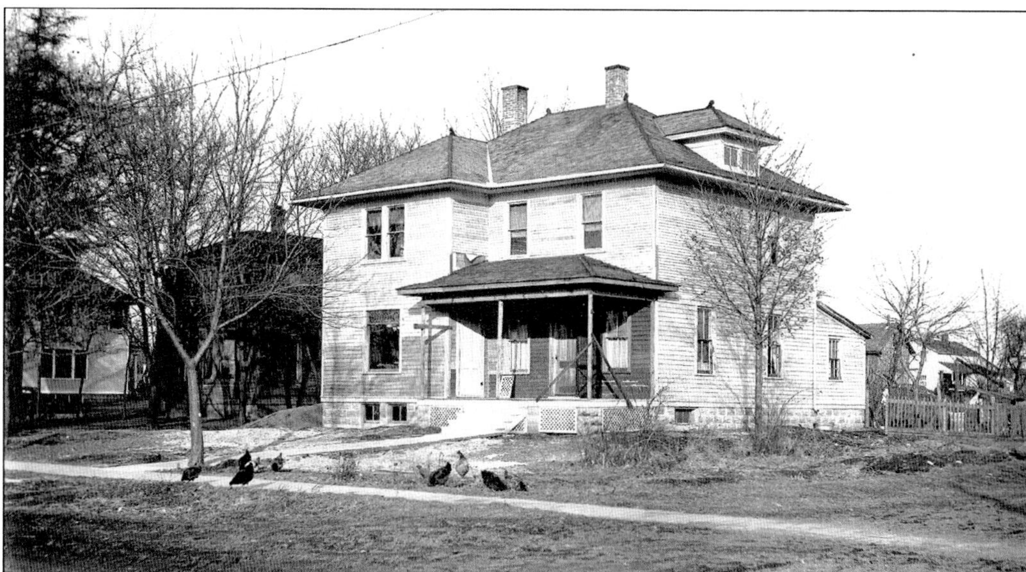

About 1914, photographer Dwight Young snapped this photograph of the reconstruction of the Miller's small home into a then fashionable hip-roofed foursquare by contractor Lou C. Young. The original first story of the home is covered by the front porch and features a significant addition to the left of the photograph, plus a full second story, illustrating the reuse and renovation of older structures in Oswego as its pioneer history faded.

Two

Tilling the Prairie

The majority of the pioneers who made the trek from their homes in the old eastern states were looking for good, cheap farmland. And they found it when they arrived along the banks of the Fox River.

The earliest settlers made claims but could not purchase the land until it had been surveyed and authorized for sale by the United States government. A five-man survey crew, led by James Reed, passed through what would one day become Oswego Township in the summer of 1838. Among the information they recorded was that Oswego had replaced Hudson as the name of the village along the Fox River. The land that Reed and his crew surveyed was not put up for sale until 1842, but provisions had been made for early settlers to acquire their claims. And although there were a few disputes, the system worked out by the government and the settlers themselves seemed to work.

Land cost $1.25 per acre, payable in gold at the Chicago Land Office. Then the prairie had to be broken, or plowed for the first time, at an additional cost of up to $1.50 per acre. Breaking prairie proved a good business for men like Peter Specie, the French Canadian who greeted the settlers when they arrived.

Farmers from New York, Vermont, New Hampshire, and even Ohio were astonished at the richness of the soil they found on the Illinois prairies. In the Oswego area, there was sufficient timber for pioneer farmers to build the homes, outbuildings, and rail fences they needed. In an 1844 letter to his parents back in New York, James Sheldon Barber noted that 10 acres of timber was sufficient for an 80-acre Oswego farm.

Some early arrivals, such as Daniel Townsend and Lewis Judson, bought up hundreds, and sometimes thousands, of acres of cheap land and then sold it to later arrivals. By 1843, good rolling prairie was selling for $10 to $15 per acre, a good return on a $1.25 investment.

The judgment of those early settlers was confirmed over the next several years, as Kendall County became one of the richest farming areas in the nation.

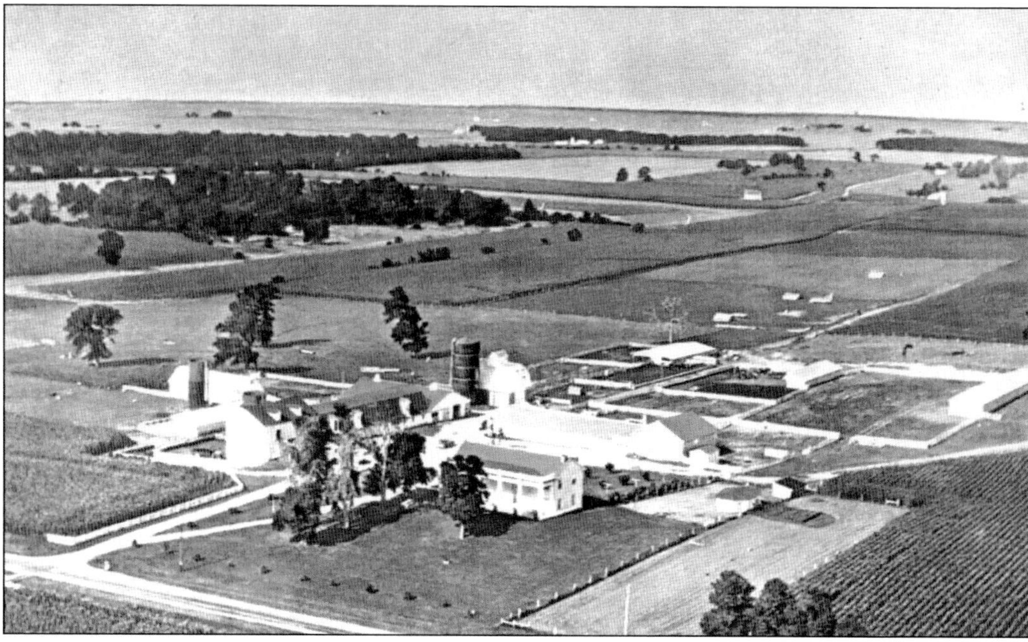

Isaac Townsend arrived from New York in 1835 and proceeded to buy up thousands of acres of land, starting with the Waish-kee-shaw and Mo-ah-way reserves. His son Daniel Townsend established this large farming and manufacturing enterprise on part of the land in the 1840s called the Na-Au-Say Steam Mill. The farm was later sold to Moses Cherry.

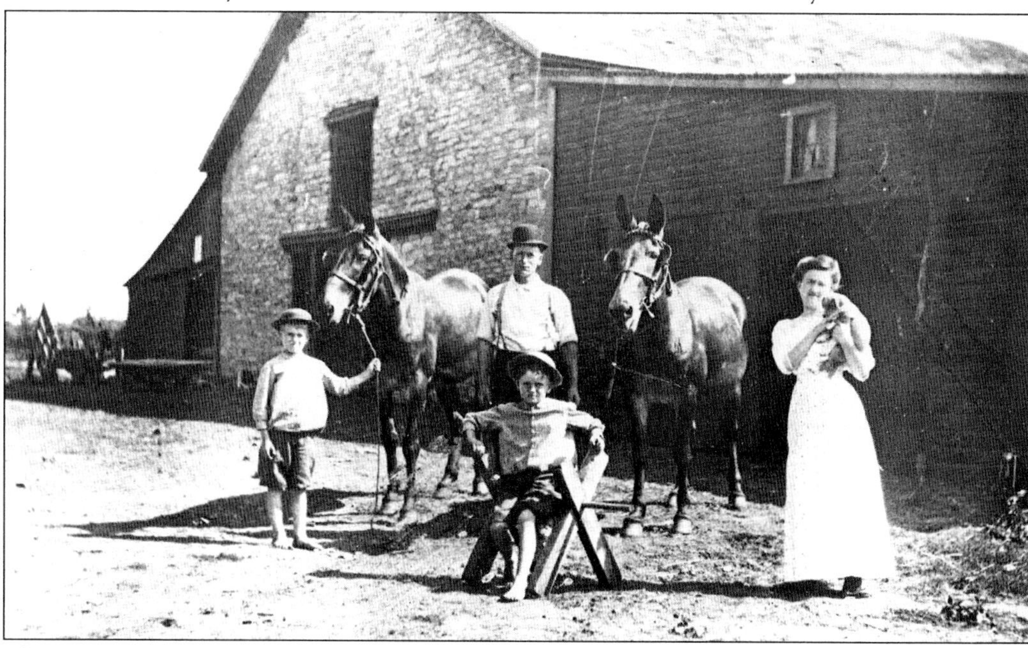

The Townsend Barn, a classic, Pennsylvania-style stone barn, may have been the site of the Townsend manufacturing operations. Above, standing in front of the Townsend Barn are, from left to right, Kenneth, Isaac, and Nellie Tripp, and seated is Norval Tripp. Although the rest of the farm buildings have been demolished to make way for a housing development, the historic barn is, as of 2008, still standing.

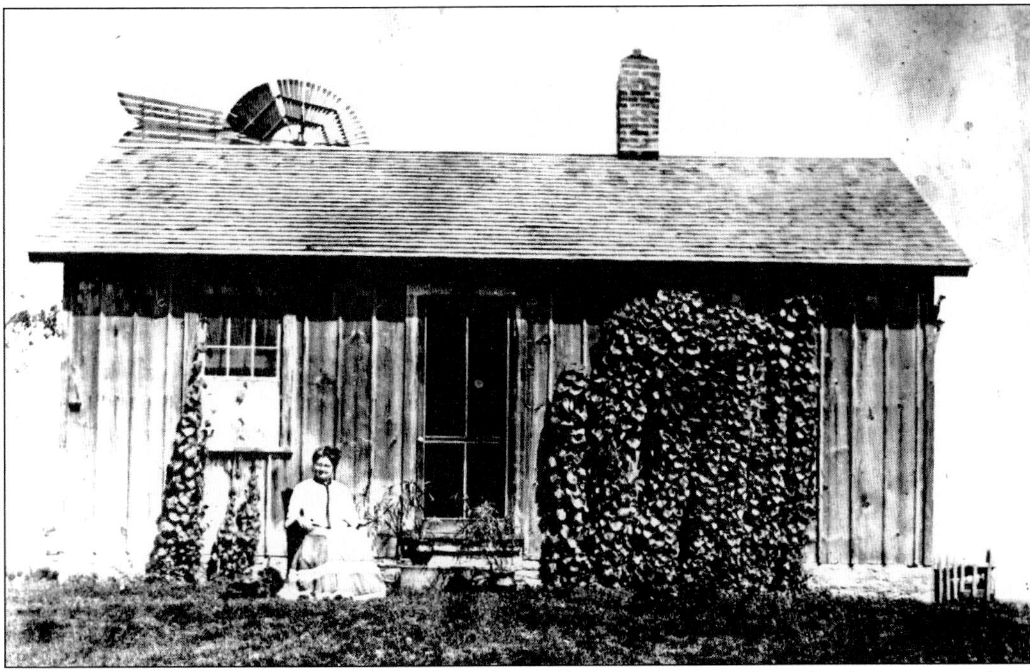

Harriet Cooney Cherry sits in front of her small farm home before the beginning of the 20th century. The small home, almost a cabin, with its small windows and board and batten siding, was typical of the earliest frame farm homes built on the Oswego Prairie.

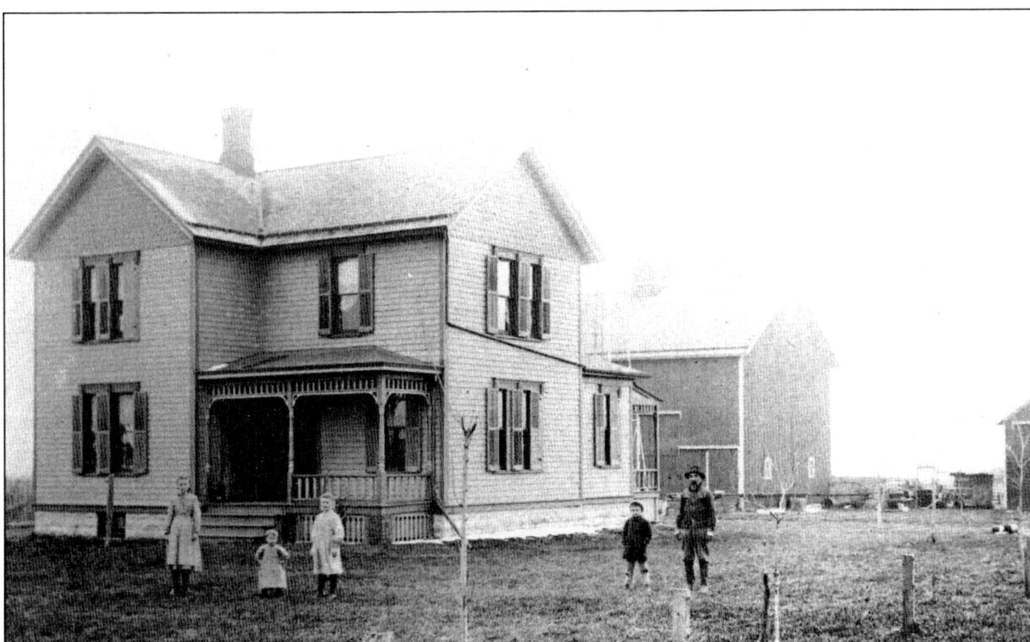

The Hafenrichter farm home on Roth Road east of Oswego illustrates the kind of large homes that began replacing smaller, original homes in the late 1800s. Sometimes, the old, small home was reused for hired help, or it was used as the basis for the new, larger home. Above, from left to right, Elsie, Nina, Eva, Robert, and John Hafenrichter stand in their home's front yard.

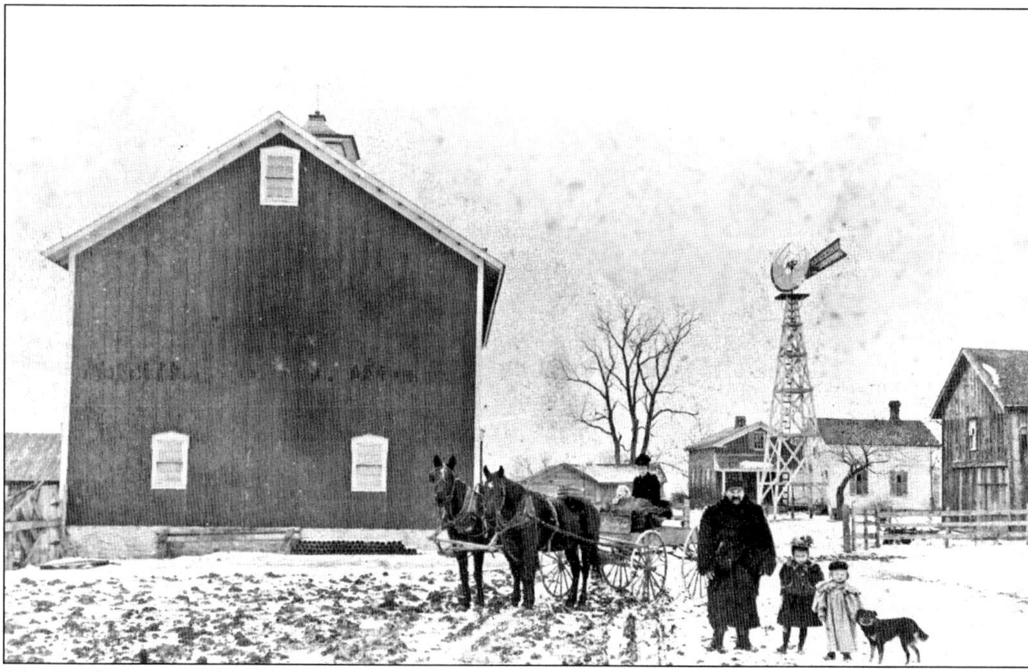

The Roth farmstead on Roth Road sports a large horse barn and a newer windmill in this 1899 photograph. Horses were the basis of agriculture—and personal transportation—until after the first quarter of the 20th century and required sufficient facilities for their care, breeding, and feeding. Above, Maude and Belle are ready to pull the buggy with Katherine and Raymond Roth as George, Edna, and Clayton Roth, and dog Rover look on.

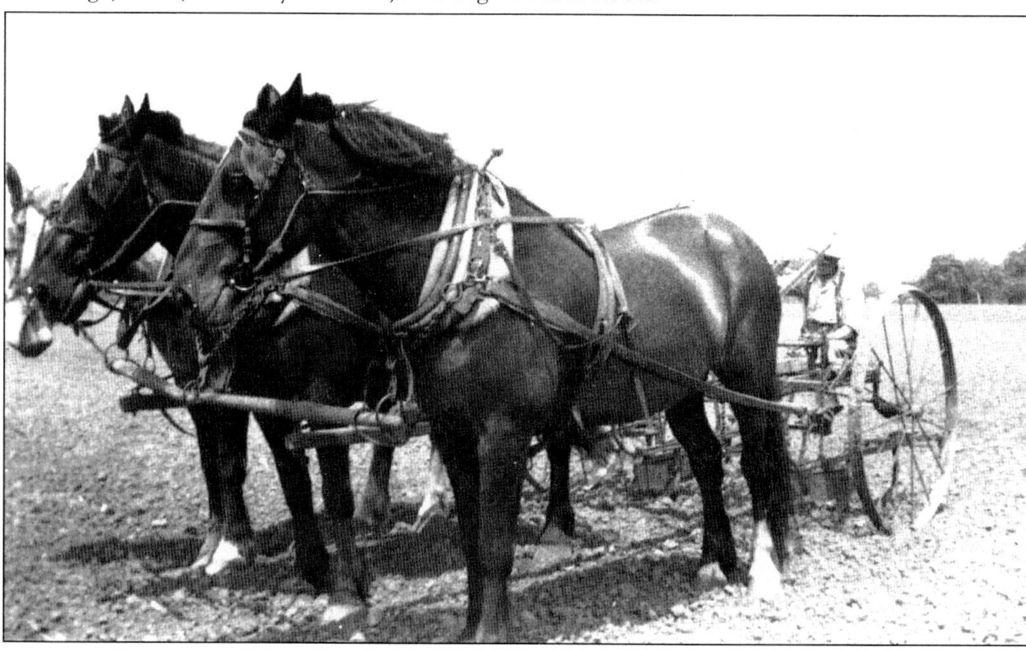

As late as the spring of 1943, George Hafenrichter was cultivating corn with a two-row "gopher," pulled with a three-horse hitch in a field along Wolf's Crossing Road just east of Oswego. The war years' fuel scarcity made the continued use of horses attractive to farmers.

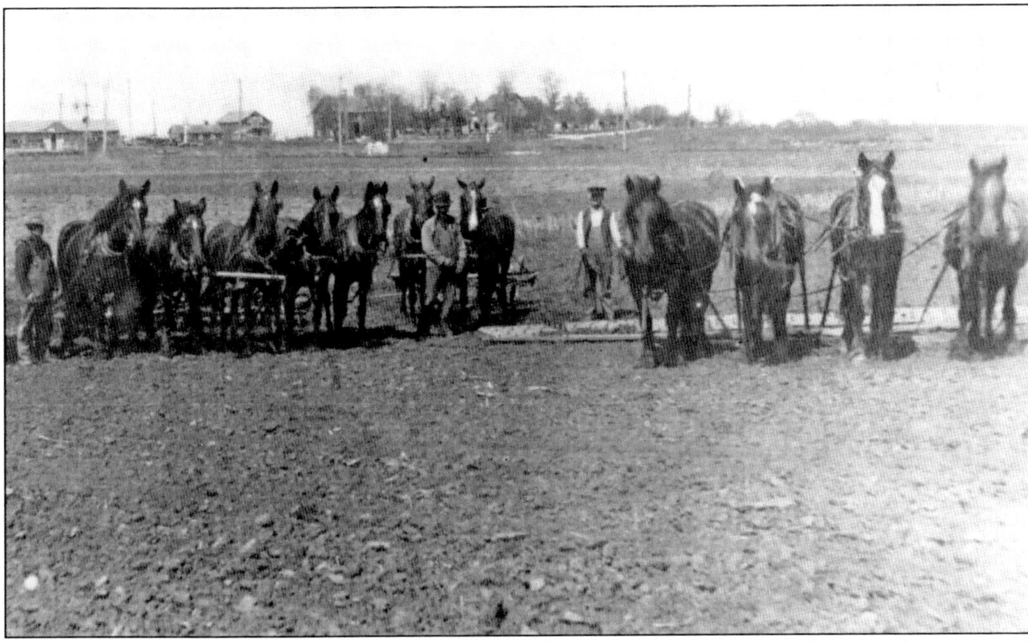

As illustrated in this 1911 photograph taken on the Harvey farm east of Oswego, farming took more than a single team. From left to right, Ed Harvey, L. Hinchman, and Alex Harvey take a breather while using 11 horses to pull drag harrows on the farm at Wolf's Crossing Road and modern U.S. Route 30.

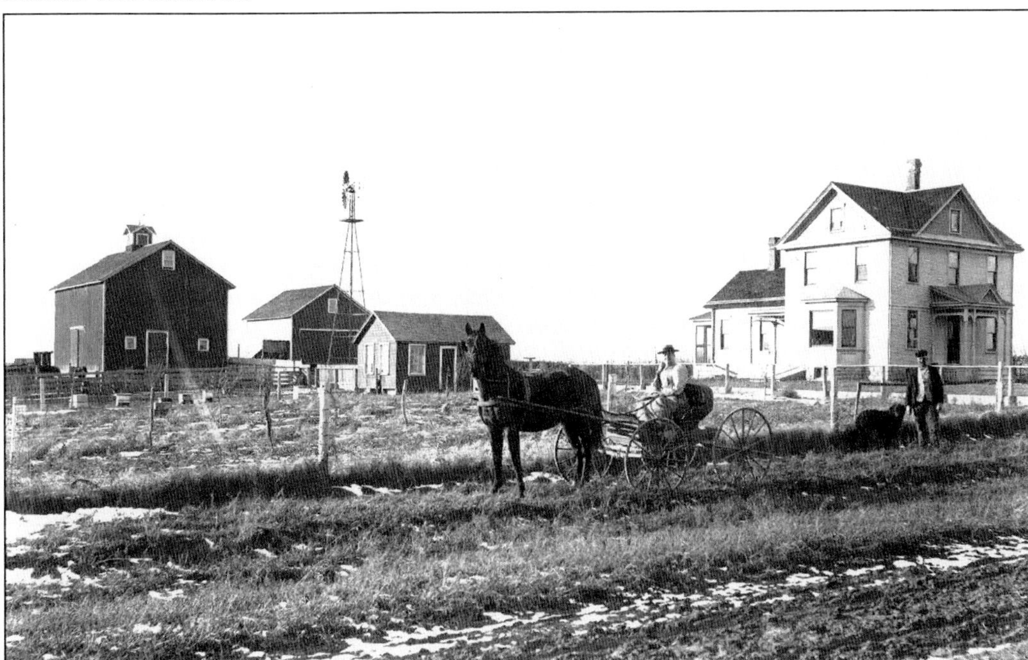

The layout of a typical Oswego Township farm is clearly illustrated in this photograph of the Otto Johnston farm on Stewart Road. Farm buildings were generally clustered for efficiency, with the windmill and well situated for easy access by livestock. Buildings were, if possible, placed east of the house so odors and dust would be diverted by the prevailing west winds.

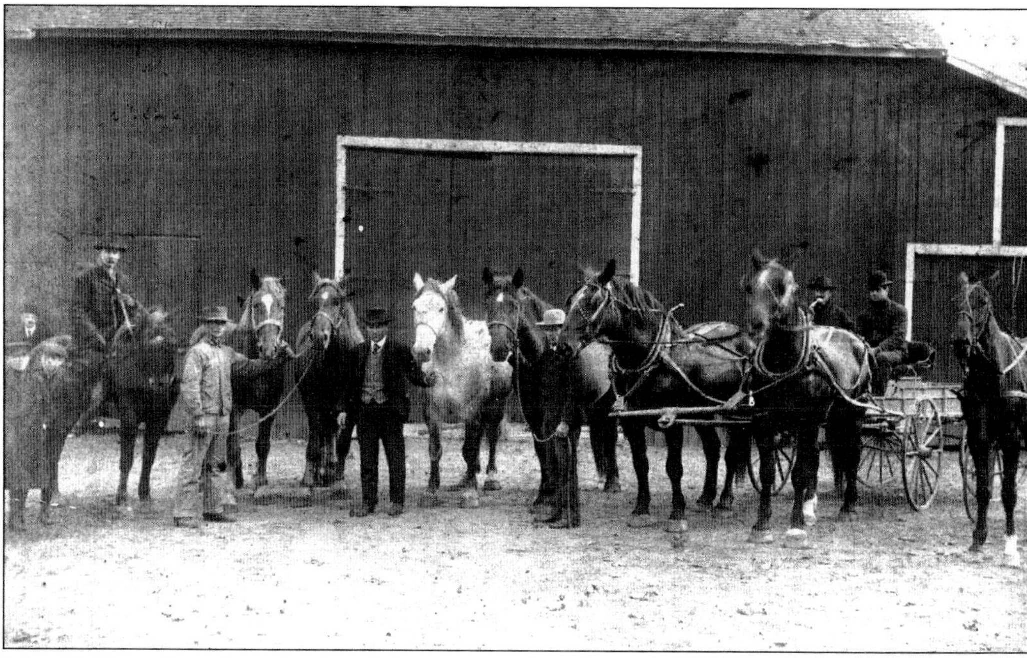

John D. Russell, on horseback at left, prepares for a horse sale at his farm on Grove Road in Oswego Township sometime in the early 1900s. Breeding and raising horses was serious business in the days of horse-powered farming. The powerful workhorses for sale can be identified by their large hooves and muscular legs.

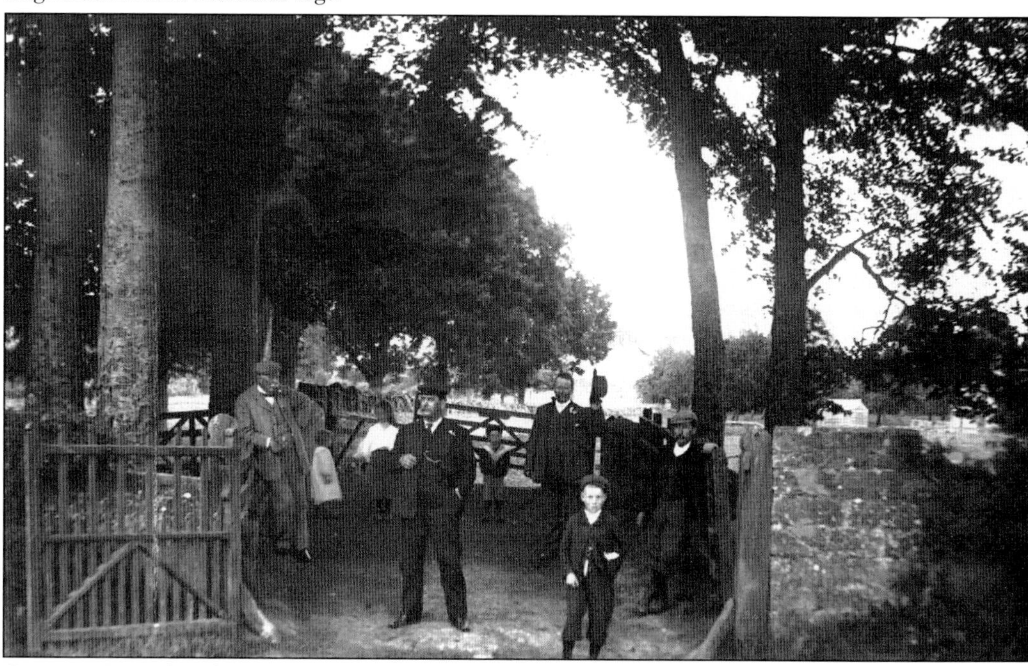

Oswego Township farmer George Collins, tipping his hat, is shown on a horse-buying trip to England in this photograph, probably taken about 1885. The Collins family had immigrated to the United States from England, and Collins returned periodically to purchase horses to improve the bloodlines of his stock.

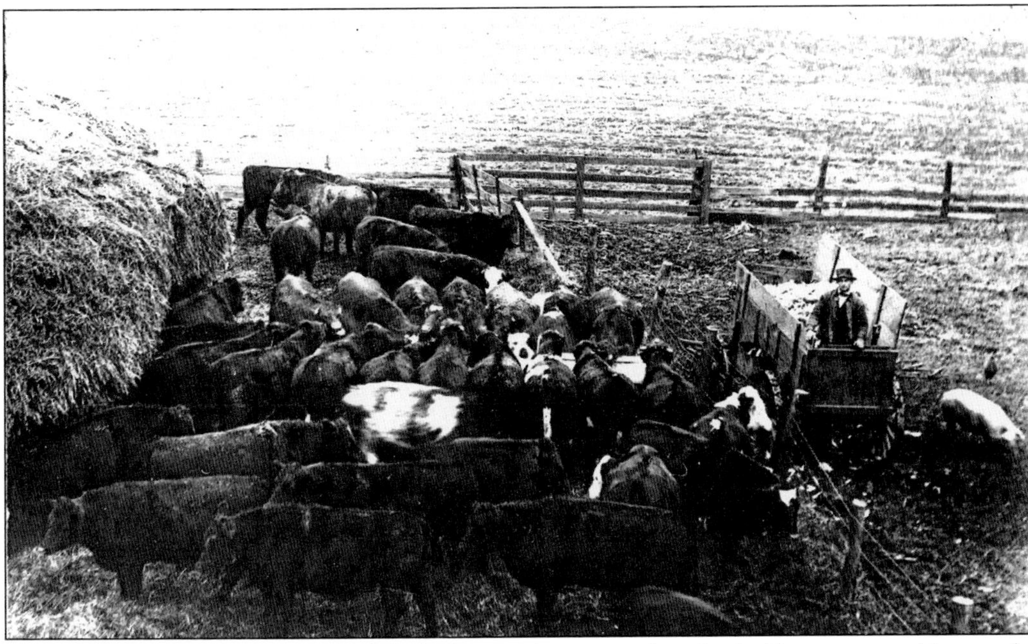

Oscar Shoger (standing in wagon) looks his cattle over as they feed off ear corn and hay at the Shoger farm just outside Oswego. In the days before good roads and stock trucks, livestock had to be driven into Oswego where they could be shipped out from the stockyards along South Adams Street. Today the Oswego Commons Shopping Center occupies the former Shoger Farm.

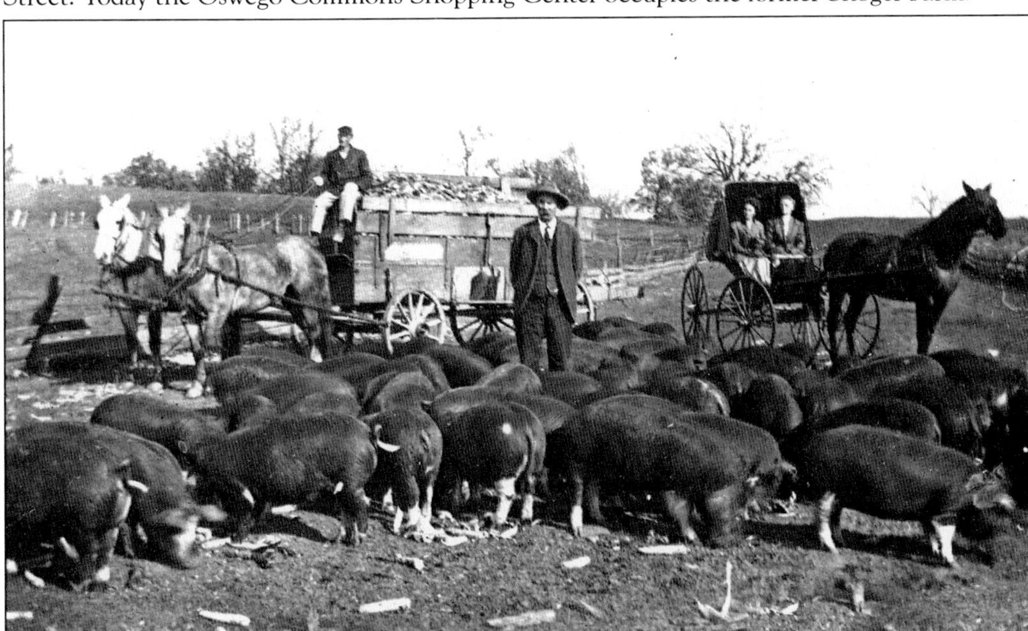

R. D. Gates (wearing hat) admires his feeder pigs at his Minkler Road farm, about 1895, as his wife and daughter look on from their buggy. The full wagon of picked corn and bare tree branches in the background suggest that the photograph was taken during the corn harvest season. Like cattle, pigs had to be herded to the railroad in Oswego in the days before motorized stock trucks.

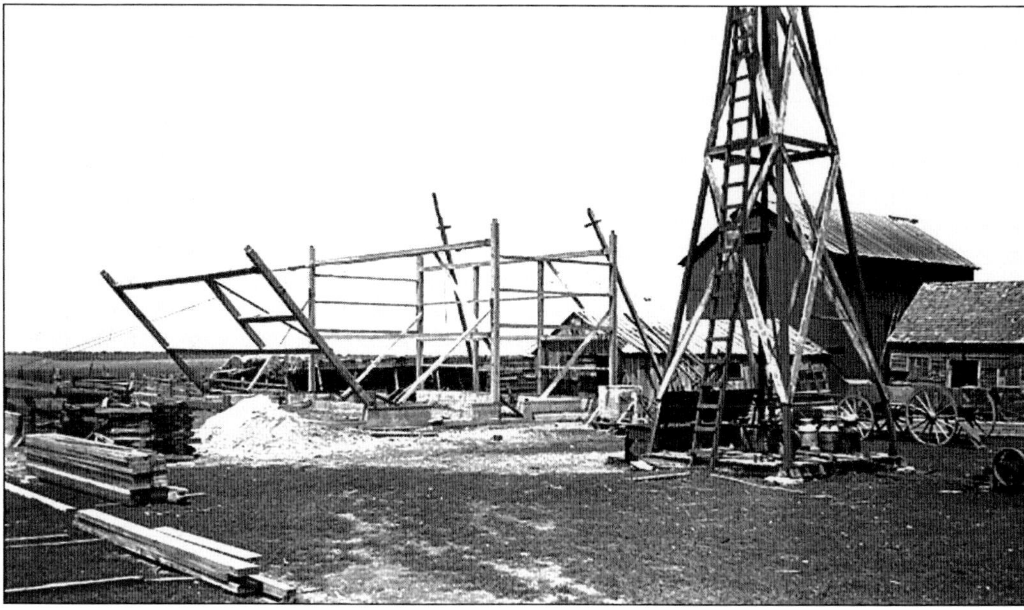

In the summer of 1912, Charles Sorg contracted with Lou C. Young to build a new gambrel roof barn on his farm, located on Harvey Road in Oswego Township. Young had his son Dwight take photographs as the construction of Sorg's barn progressed. In preparation for the barn raising on July 18, 1911, the frame was assembled on the ground in the order the individual members—called bents—would be raised into place. Young titled the photograph above "Two bents up, third bent half up," and the photograph below is labeled "Frame at quitting time, August 18, 1912." The series of photographs gives a unique look at barn-building techniques in the early 20th century.

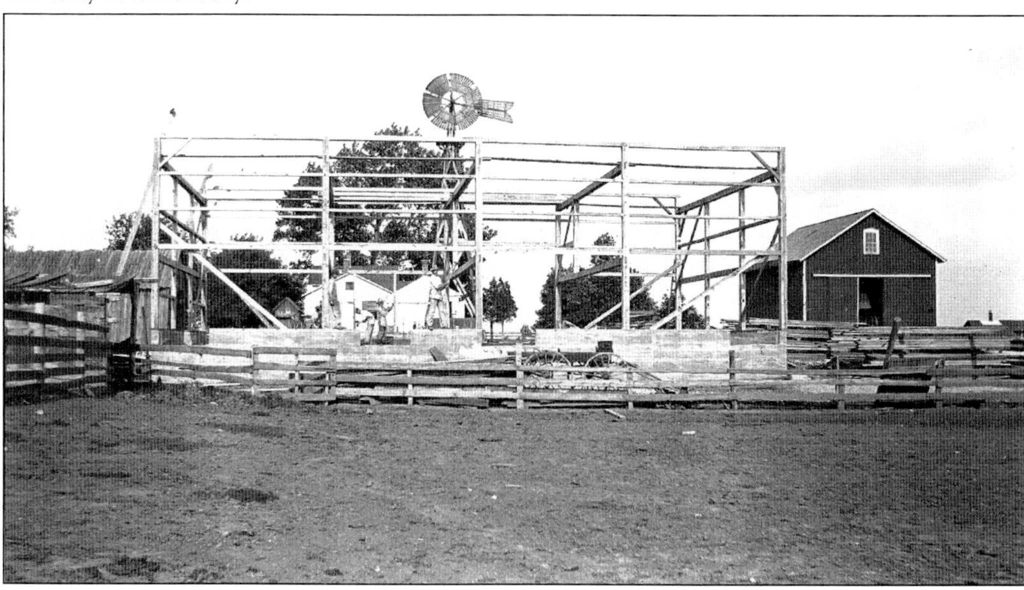

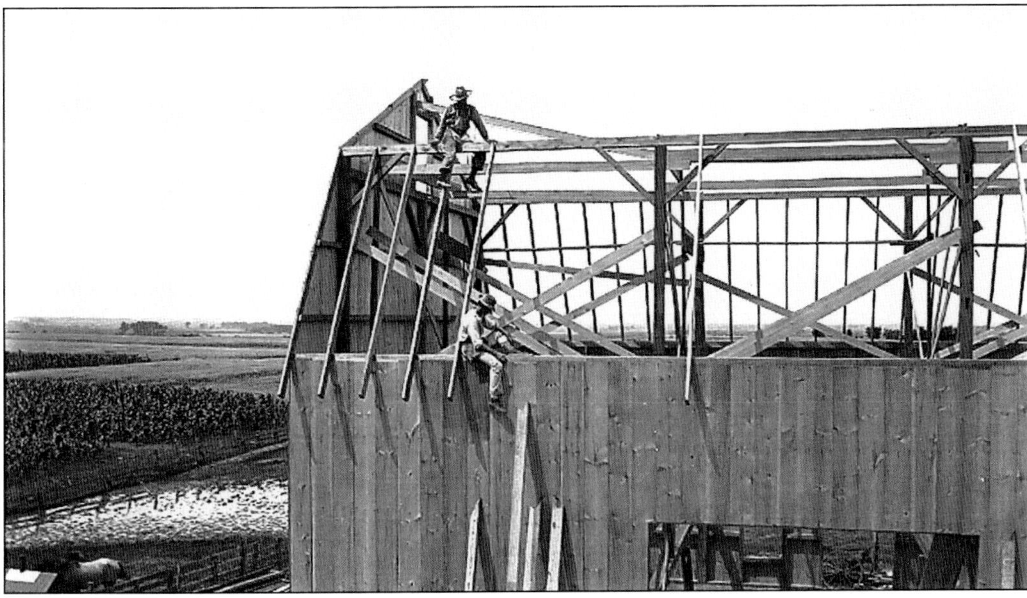

After the frame of Sorg's barn had been completed by Lou C. Young's construction crew, the vertical board siding was installed to increase the barn's stability, and then the roof trusses and rafters and the balance of the roof were installed. The photograph above is dated August 25, 1912. The photograph of Sorg's completed barn below, then nearly 76 years old, was taken in February 1988 by Lou C. Young's great-grandson Glenn Young. As of 2008, the barn is still standing, although like many other Oswego area farm buildings its fate is in doubt given the area's on-going development.

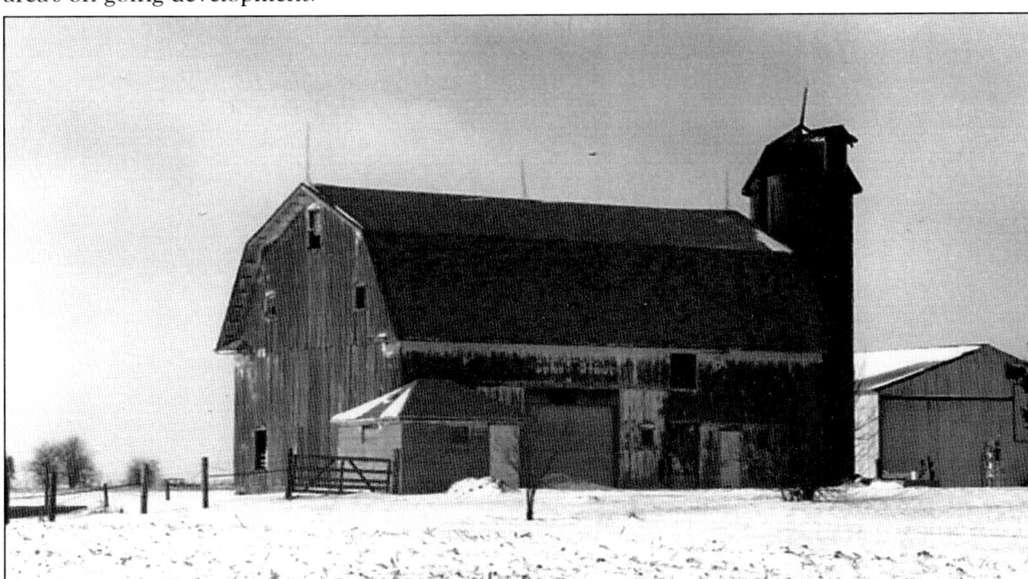

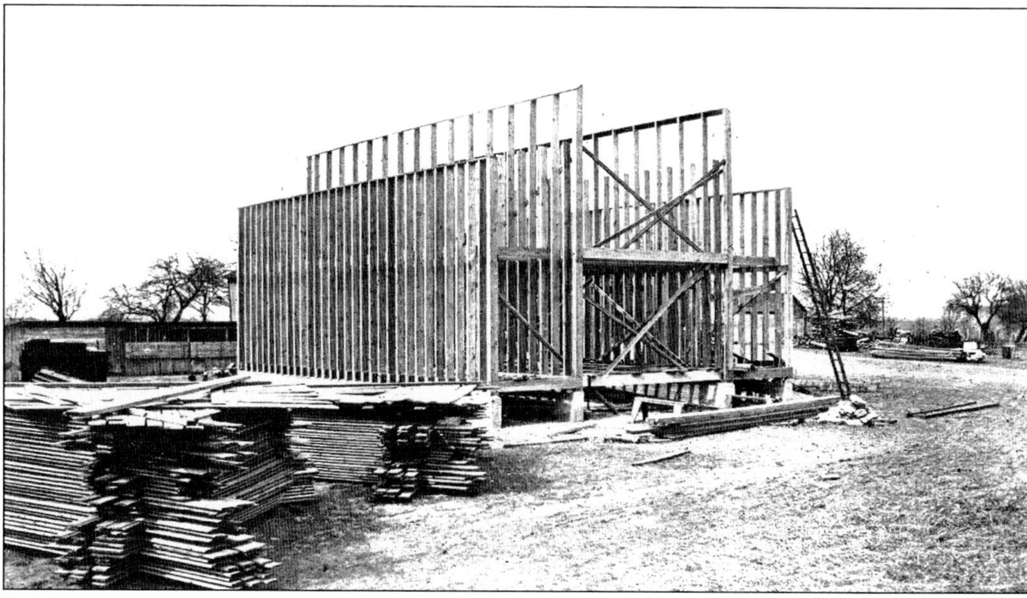

In the early spring of 1912, Lou C. Young had contracted with Robert Lippold to build a corn crib on his farm, located on the west side of the Fox River, south of Oswego. Unlike timber-framed barns, cribs were built using two-by-four and two-by-six lumber to create a "balloon" frame. In the photograph taken by Dwight Young above, the side bins and central alley have been formed and await the roof and siding.

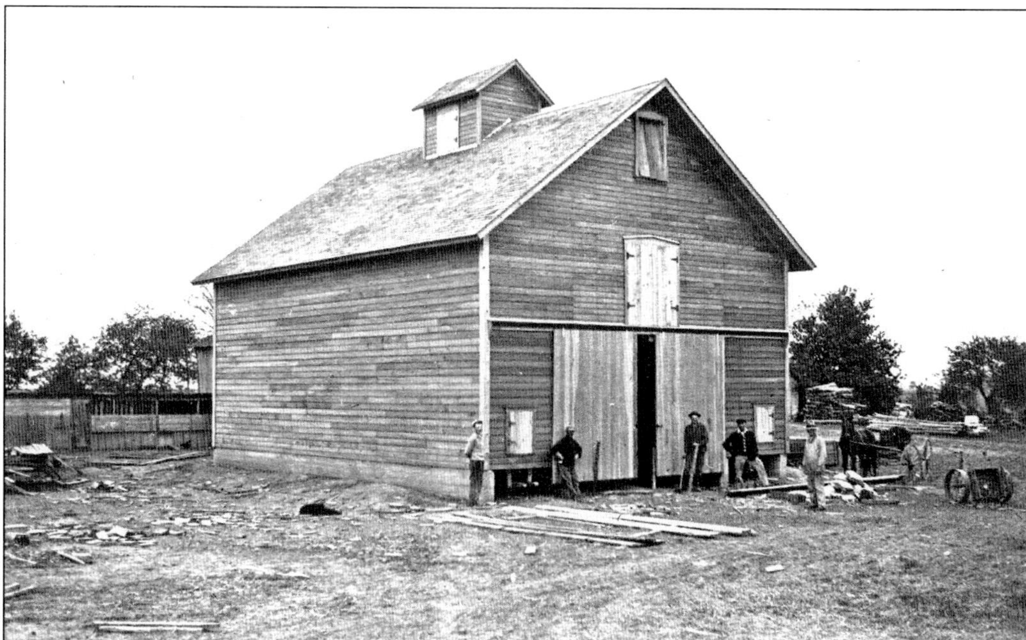

The completed Lippold corncrib is seen here in May 1912, with siding on the bins spaced about an inch apart. That allowed air to circulate around the handpicked ears of corn to naturally dry them and enhance preservation. The dried corn was shelled from the cob for use as livestock feed or for sale on the grain market. Modern mechanical combine harvesters both pick and shell corn, making cribs like this obsolete.

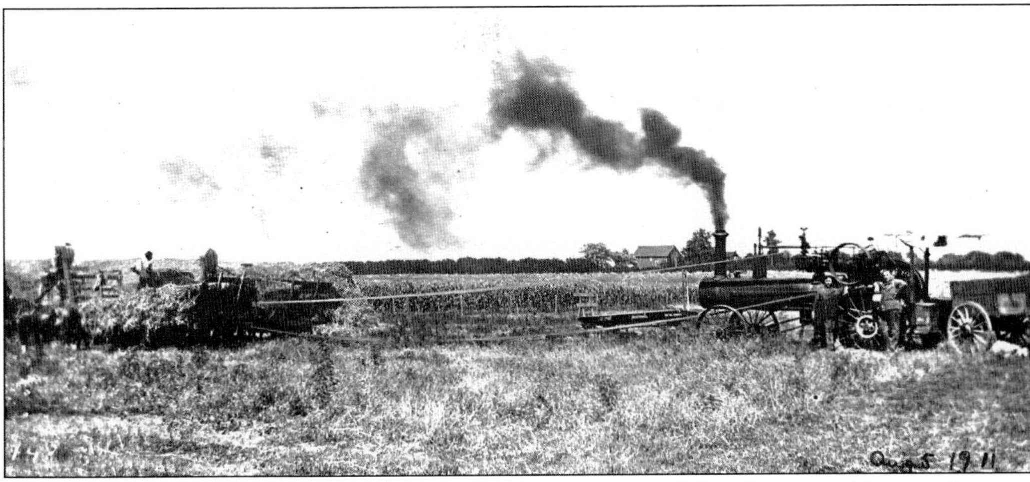

Grain such as oats, wheat, and barley required steam-powered threshing machines and several people to operate them. Here the East Oswego Threshing Ring is at work with the steam engine at right and the threshing machine at left. The machines were expensive, so groups—called rings—purchased them cooperatively. The ring's members then helped thresh each other's grain. Farmers traded off on the various jobs, except engineer, which was a skilled position.

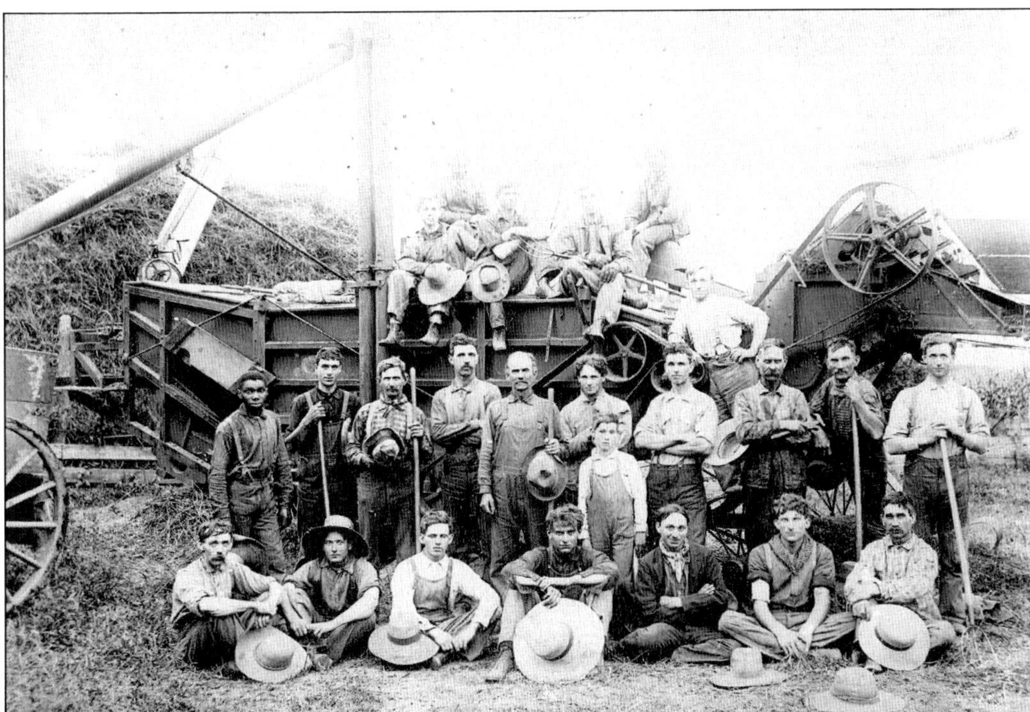

The Grove Road Threshing Ring poses after a hard day's work southeast of Oswego about 1905. When threshing season arrived everyone, from the richest farmers to the lowliest farm hand, pitched in. As the crew moved from farm to farm, wives were expected to provide the huge noon meals the workers required.

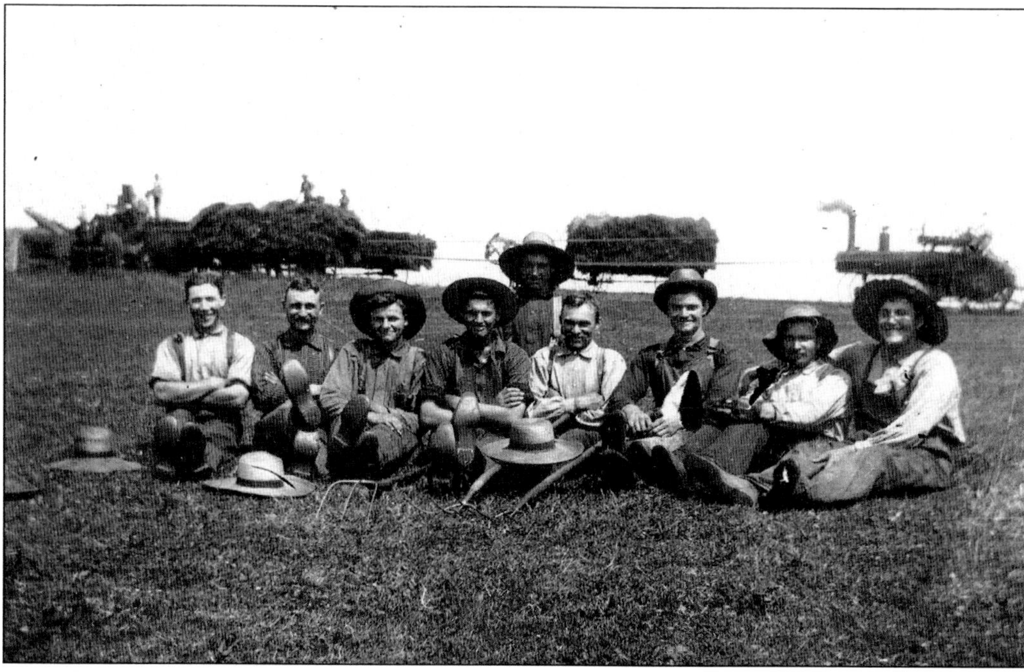

Part of the Harvey Threshing Ring takes a cheerful break for a photograph in 1906. Threshing season was not only a time of long hard days, for thresher men and their wives alike, but were also part of the area's social fabric. Wives cooperated to help produce the gigantic noon dinners for the crews that created some social time together, while their husbands and sons worked and relaxed together.

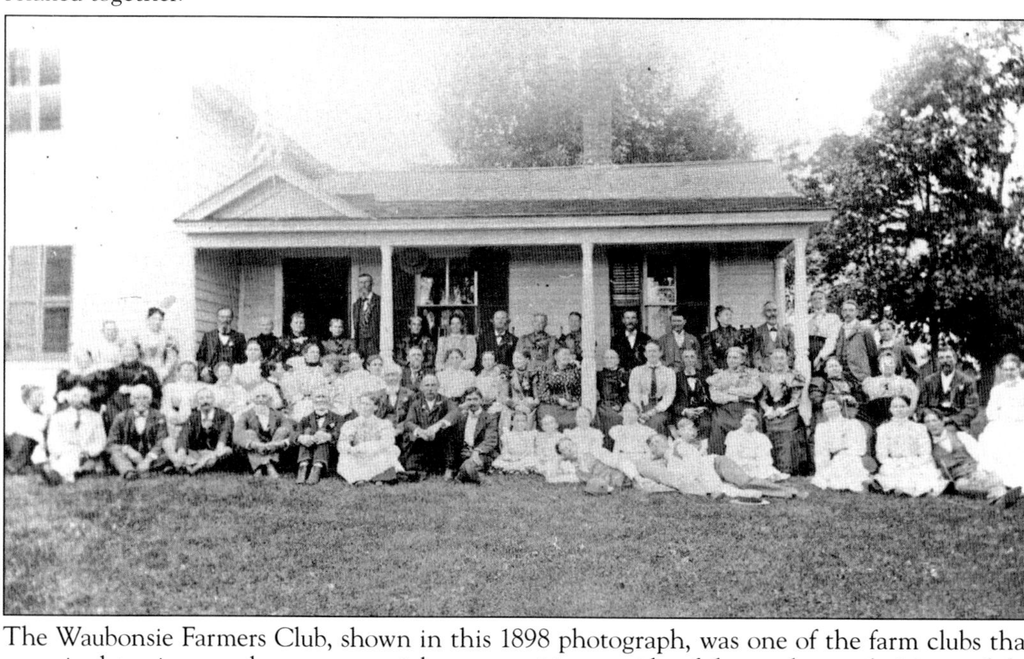

The Waubonsie Farmers Club, shown in this 1898 photograph, was one of the farm clubs that organized to give members some social opportunities outside of day-to-day work. Many of the clubs formed, such as this one and the Grove Road Farmers Club, had their genesis in the area's threshing rings.

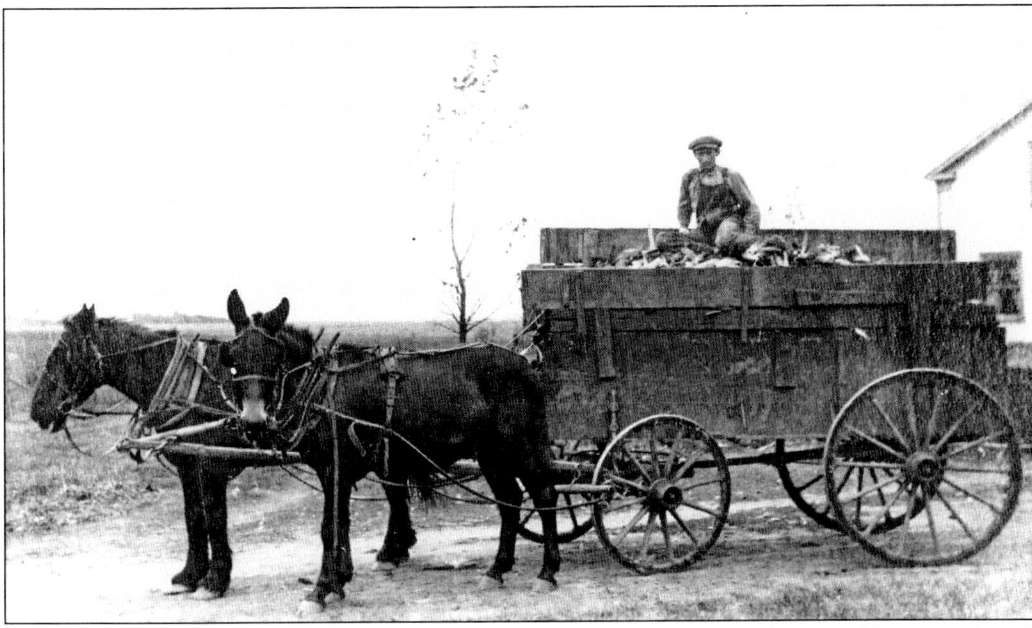

Lyle Shoger sits atop a full load of freshly picked corn about 1920. Well-trained horse and mule teams patiently pulled wagons along the corn rows as ears were picked by hand and thrown into the box, ricocheting off the bank board on the far side. Skilled huskers could work fast enough to keep an ear in the air at all times while moving down the row.

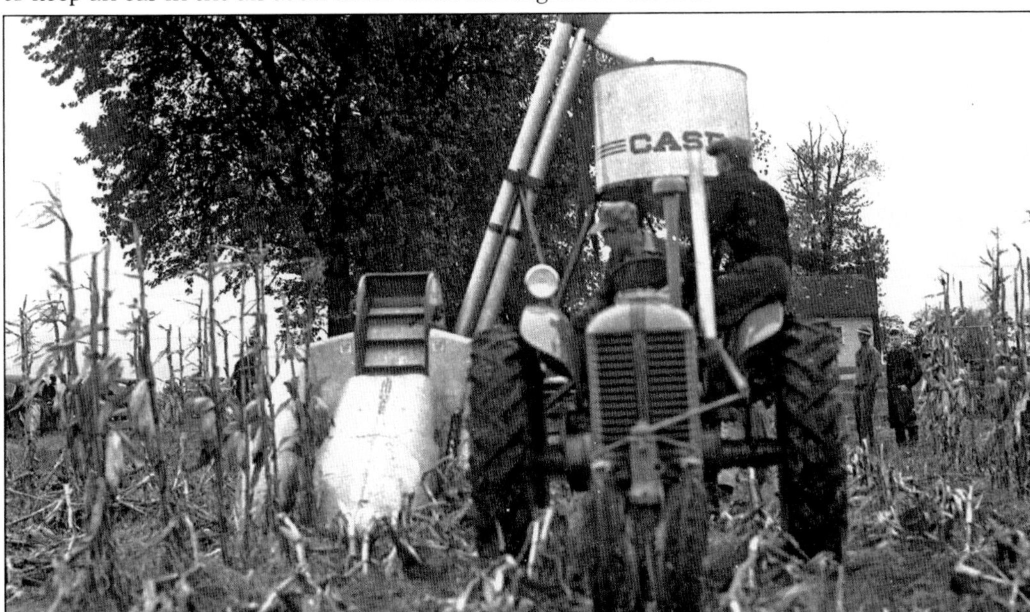

Both the invention and perfection of the farm tractor and improved equipment such as the corn picker increased farm productivity. The use of the two together increased productivity almost exponentially. In the image above, Graeme Stewart uses a Case tractor and corn picker in the 1930s on his Oswego Township farm, eliminating the need for labor-intensive hand picking and husking.

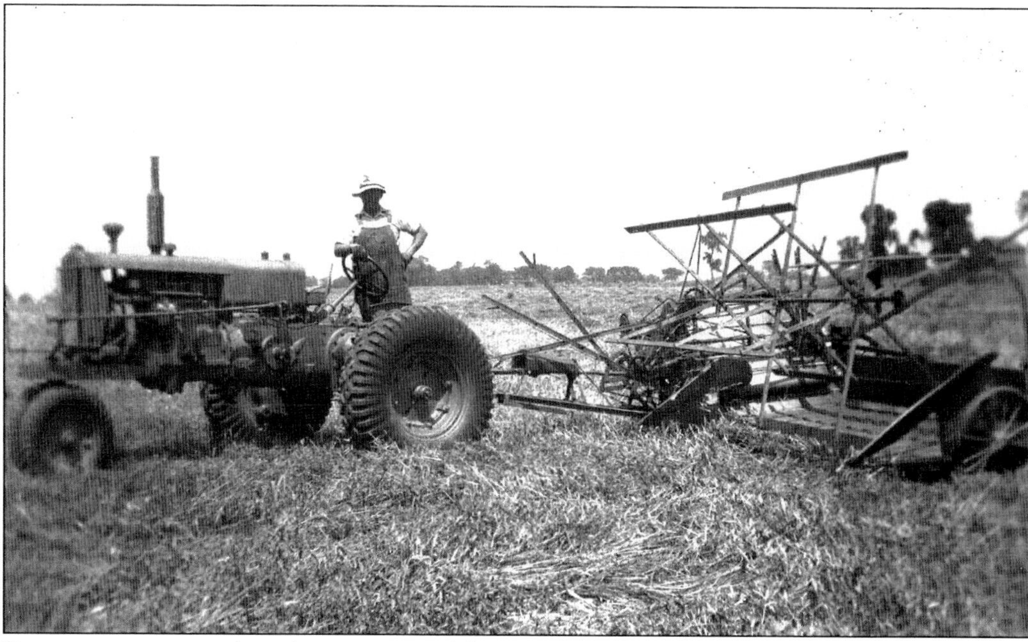

Farmers were not quick to throw away useful equipment. Graeme Stewart, above, uses his tractor to pull a binder, that cuts and binds "small grain" such as oats, barley, and wheat, into bundles for later threshing. Soon after this photograph was snapped, the binder-threshing machine method was permanently replaced by the tractor-pulled combine harvester that cut and threshed grain in one operation.

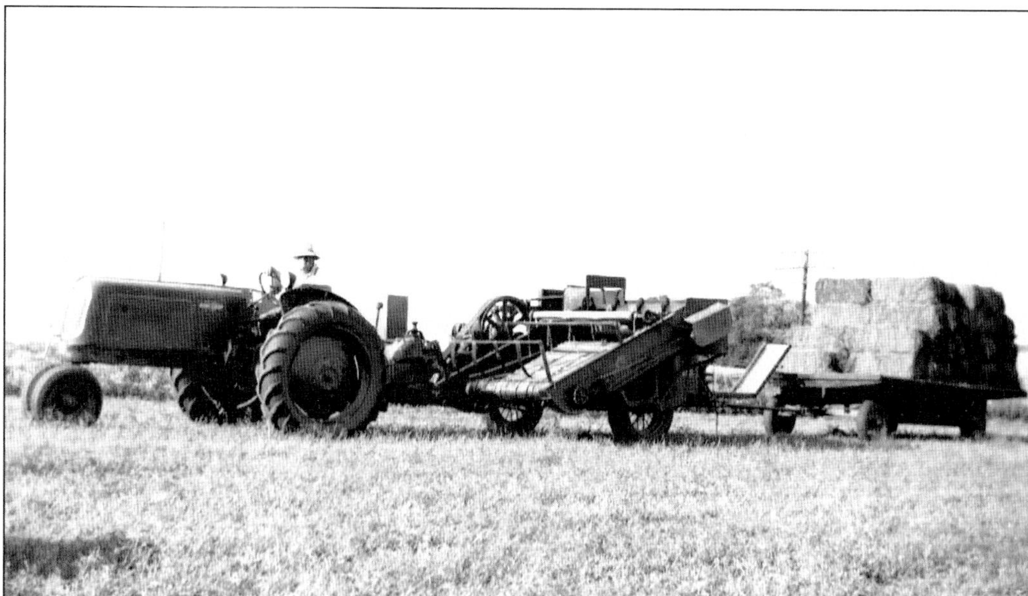

Russell Rink, with his Oliver tractor and hay bailer, is working along Wolf's Crossing Road east of Oswego in the 1940s. Bailers compressed the straw produced during grain harvests, as well as hay crops such as alfalfa, clover, and timothy, to be compressed into bales that were stored in the barn haylofts for later use as livestock feed and bedding, a more efficient and economical practice than building haystacks.

Three

Millers, Merchants, and Manufacturers

While farmers seeking a better life made up most of the area's earliest settlers, pioneer businessmen were not far behind.

Storekeepers were first to arrive, participating in the rapidly disappearing fur trade, followed closely by blacksmiths. But farmers had other requirements as well. Lumber was needed to build homes, outbuildings, and fences. Grain had to be ground into flour for both human and livestock consumption.

Lewis Judson and Levi Arnold laid out their new village, soon called Oswego, where the Fox River is at its narrowest and where old trails intersected. The river was not only narrow at Oswego; a ford across the shallow stream with a floor of smooth natural limestone had drawn travelers to the crossing for hundreds of years.

Arnold's store, the first in the new village, doubled as the first post office. It was quickly joined by taverns, the motels of the 1830s. One of the first was owned by Decolia Towle and was located at Main and Jefferson Streets where the Oswego Public Library today overlooks the old ford across the river, just above the mouth of Waubonsie Creek.

By 1838, U.S. government surveyor James Reed noted that Oswego boasted "20 wood buildings." The tiny hamlet was well on its way towards the growth that continues to this day.

But harder times were to come. The Chicago Burlington and Quincy Railroad bypassed Oswego two miles to the west in 1850. The county seat moved back to Yorkville in 1864. And then on February 9, 1867, a devastating fire struck the village, destroying the entire block on the east side of Main Street between Washington and Jackson Streets.

But the village bounced back, with a new brick business block to replace the one destroyed by the fire and a new iron bridge across the river. In 1870, the Ottawa, Oswego, and Fox River Valley Railroad reached downtown Oswego, connecting the town with the rest of the nation.

Growth was slow until the region's first real population boom in the 1950s. The second major boom, which started in the 1980s, continues today with Oswego's population nearing 30,000 in 2008.

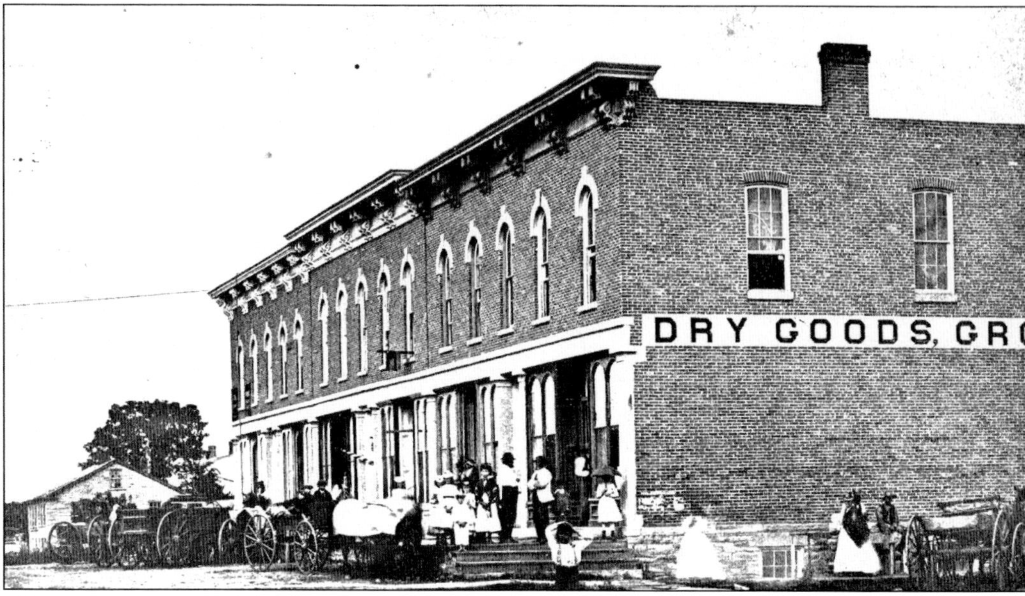

When the east side of the downtown business district burned early 1867, local businessmen lost no time in rebuilding. The result, finished late that year, was the "Brick Block" shown above with drug, hardware, grocery, and dry goods stores. The stately National Hotel, which stood immediately south of the business block, was not rebuilt.

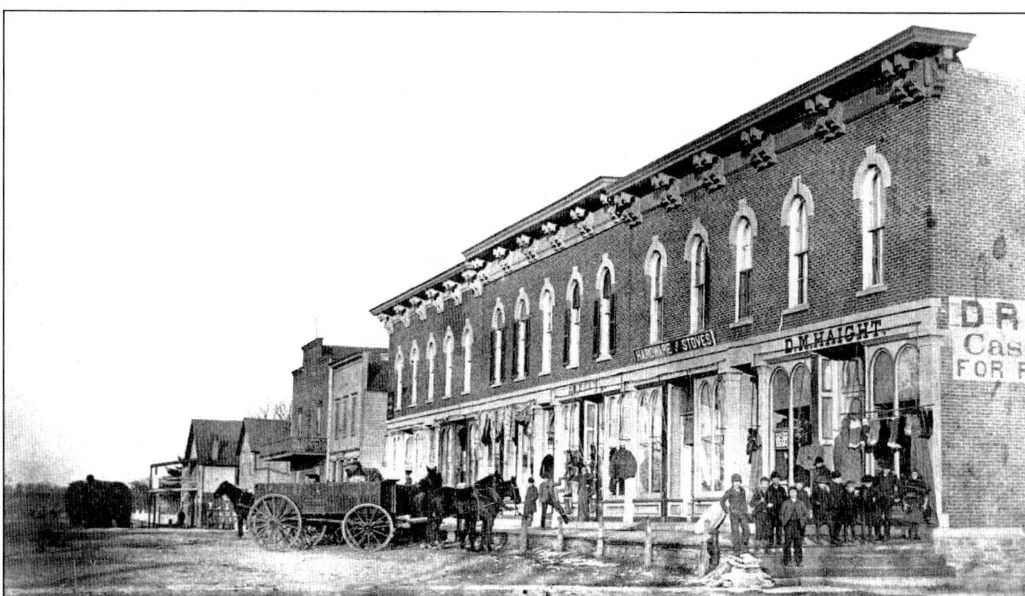

By the 1880s, buildings had filled in the site of the old National Hotel. The Star Roller Skating Rink's flagpole reaches toward the sky in this 1885 photograph. To its right is the Oswego Post Office built by postmaster Lorenzo Rank with his living quarters above the office. The old National Hotel horse barn is still standing on the corner of Main and Jackson Streets here, with the Shoger Livery Stable on the opposite corner.

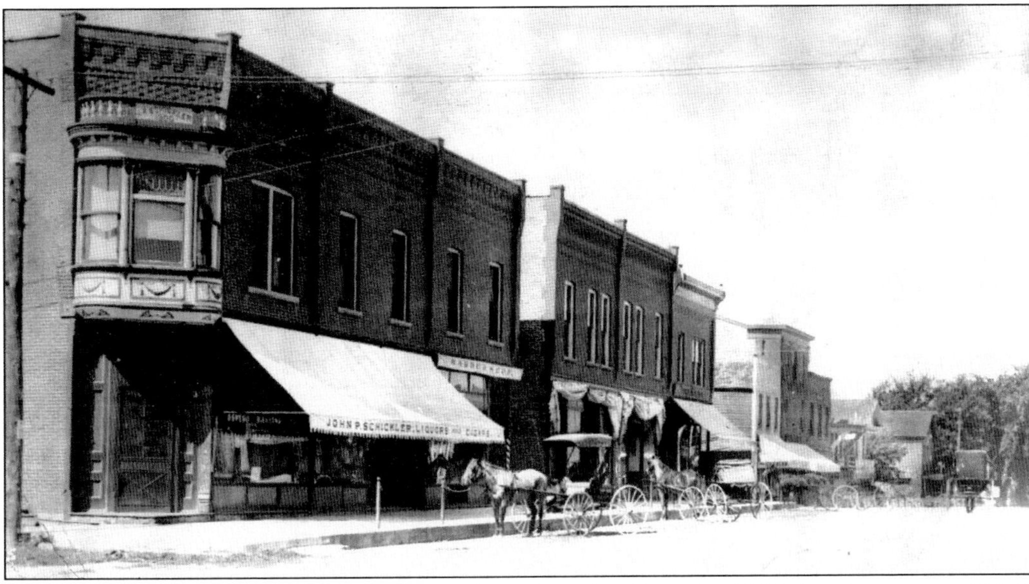

The west side of Main Street boasted a number of new buildings by 1905. On the corner of Main and Washington Streets, the Schickler Building housed John Schickler's retail businesses, with a cigar factory located in the basement. Next-door is Voss's Barber Shop. When the photograph was taken, the automobile era had yet to displace the horses tied up to hitching posts up and down the street.

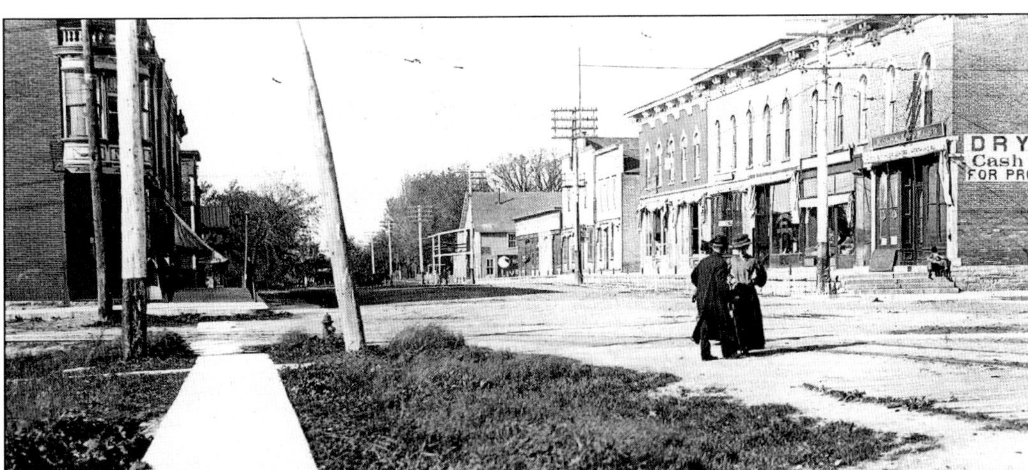

Photographer Daniel Bloss, who worked for several postcard publishers, created this literal snapshot in time at exactly 3:30 p.m. on June 5, 1910, according to his notation on the photograph. The cooler temperatures of the era are suggested by the clothing worn. By 1910, both telephone and electrical lines festooned downtown utility poles and the rails of the interurban trolley curve from Washington Street onto South Main Street.

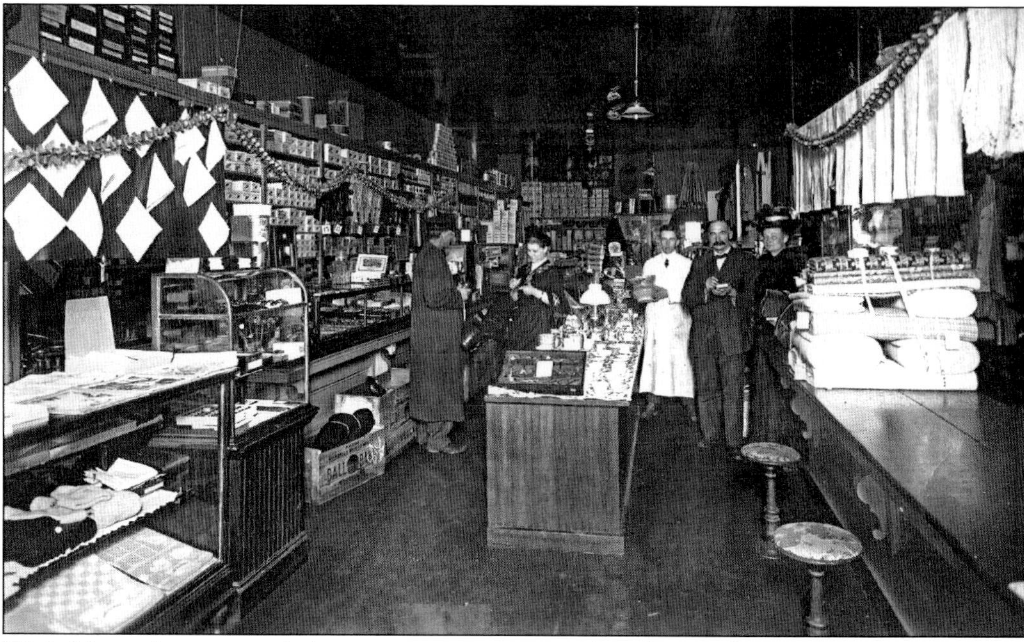

W. J. Morse (in moustache) waits on customers in his dry goods store on Main Street in downtown Oswego in 1902. The store's interior was typical of the stores in Oswego's Brick Block and offered dry goods for sale by the yard, buttons, and notions, along with decorations. Note the acetylene lamps hanging from the tongue and groove ceiling.

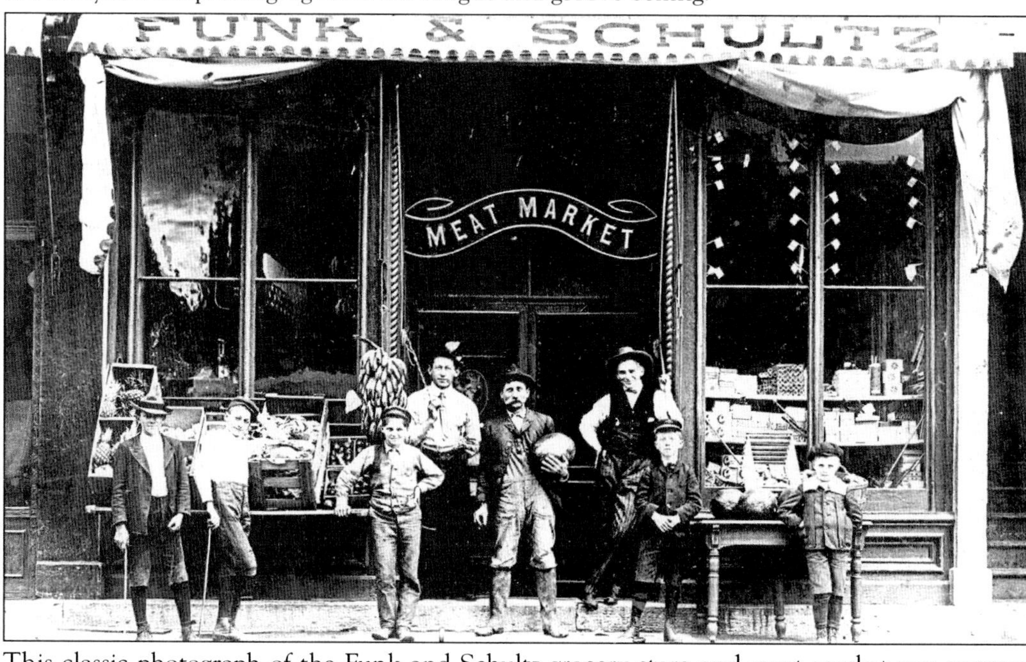

This classic photograph of the Funk and Schultz grocery store and meat market was snapped in 1909, probably around July 4. The store, located in the Brick Block on the east side of Main Street featured a cast-iron storefront and plenty of glass to let passersby see what was offered for sale inside. Charles Schultz (in hat and vest) was a downtown Oswego business owner for decades.

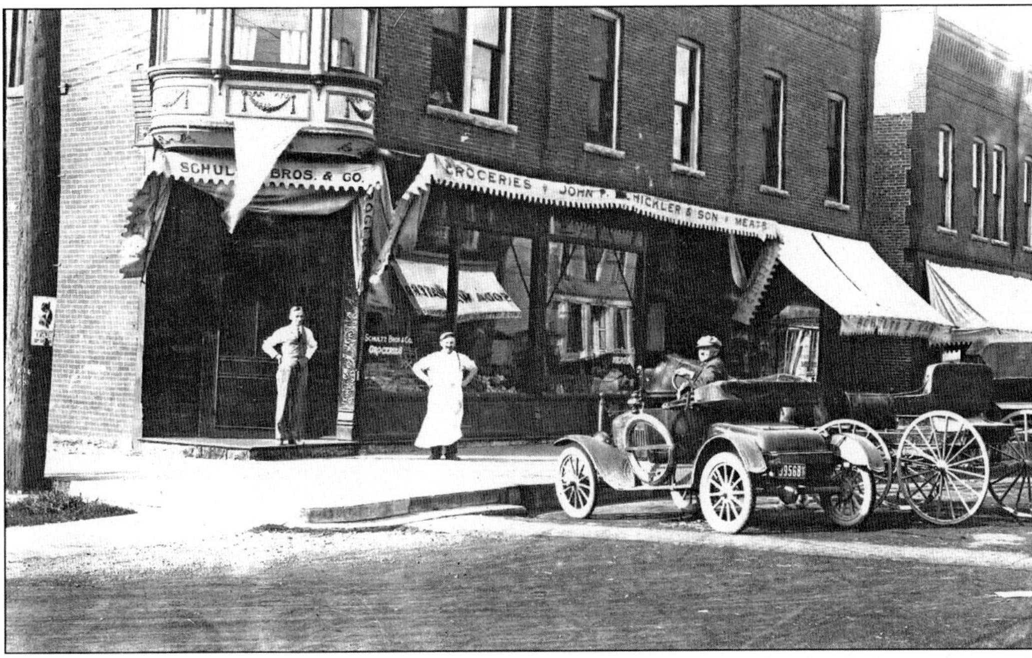

In December 1915, John Schickler sold his building to Charles and Richard Schultz, and in 1916, they opened their Schultz Brothers grocery and meat market. The event was celebrated with this photograph when the brothers had yet to replace the large awning across their store's front windows. Popular Model T Fords shared Oswego's business district with horses during that era.

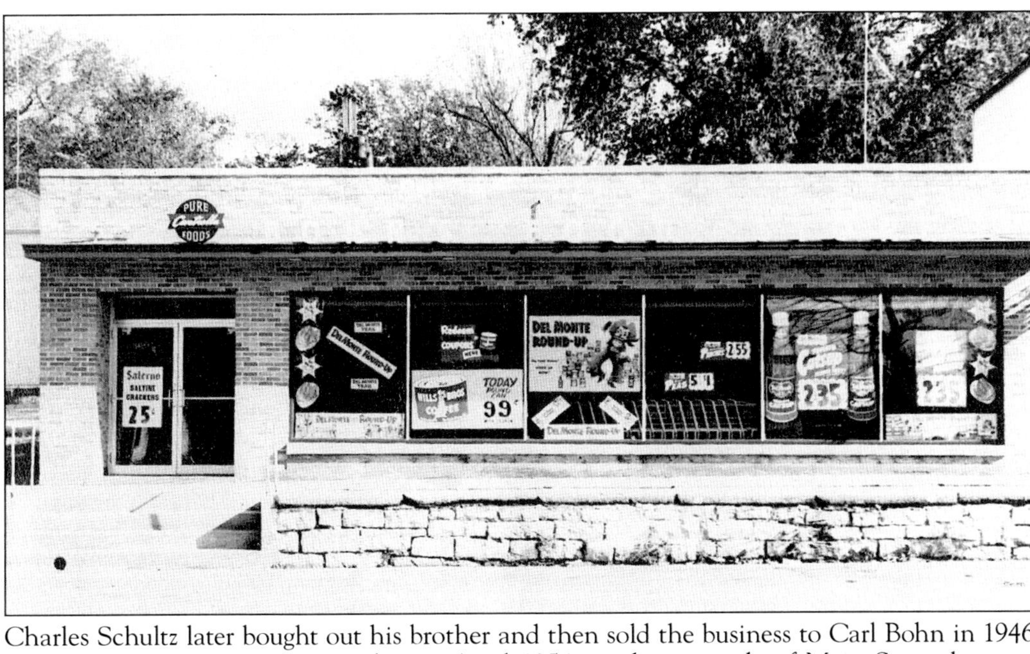

Charles Schultz later bought out his brother and then sold the business to Carl Bohn in 1946. Bohn opened this new supermarket in April 1954 on the east side of Main Street between Washington and Jackson Streets. Bohn's, operated by his son Kenneth at the time, closed in 1981, the last of Oswego's downtown grocery stores.

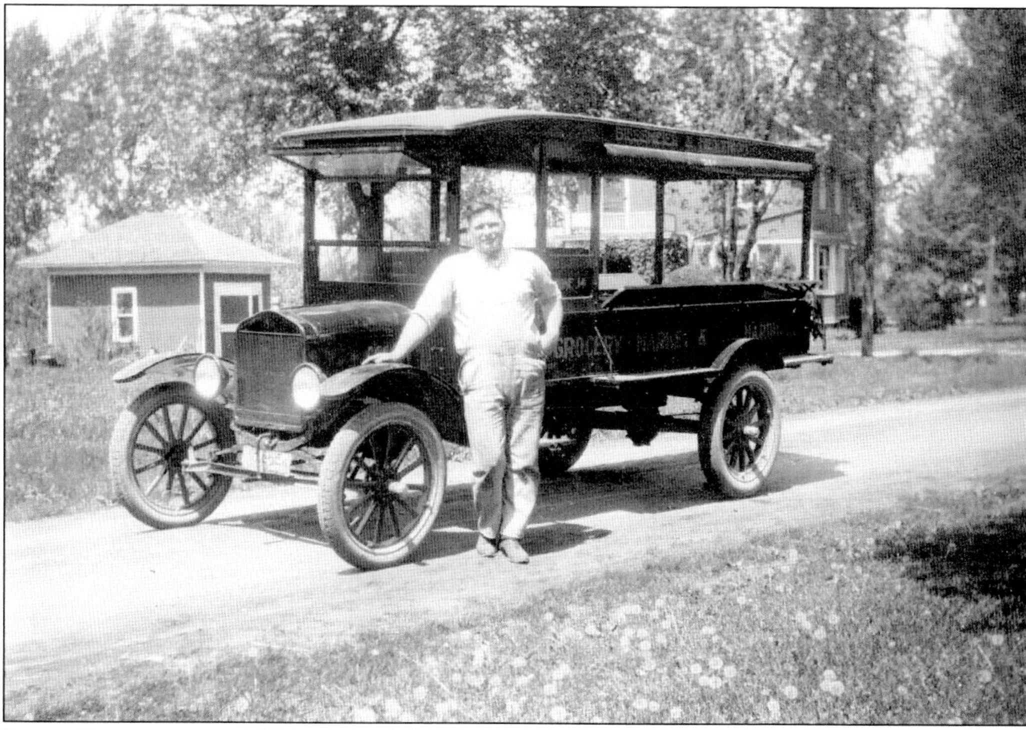

Benny Biesemeier proudly poses with his new delivery truck in 1920 after he and A. J. Hettrick bought out H. B. Read's grocery business. The store was located at 70 Main Street, next to Scott Cutter's drug store. Biesemeier later sold his business to Wayne Denny, who operated it until the 1970s, leaving Bohn's as the last downtown grocery store.

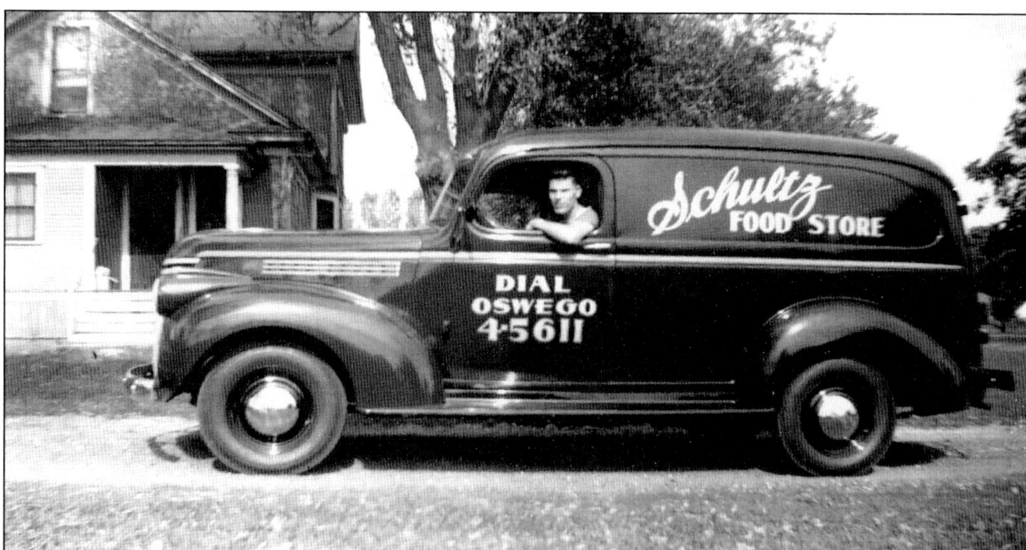

Ray Campbell delivered groceries for the Schultz Food Store during the 1940s. During that era, customers called in their orders by telephone and then accepted delivery, which was offered as a free service.

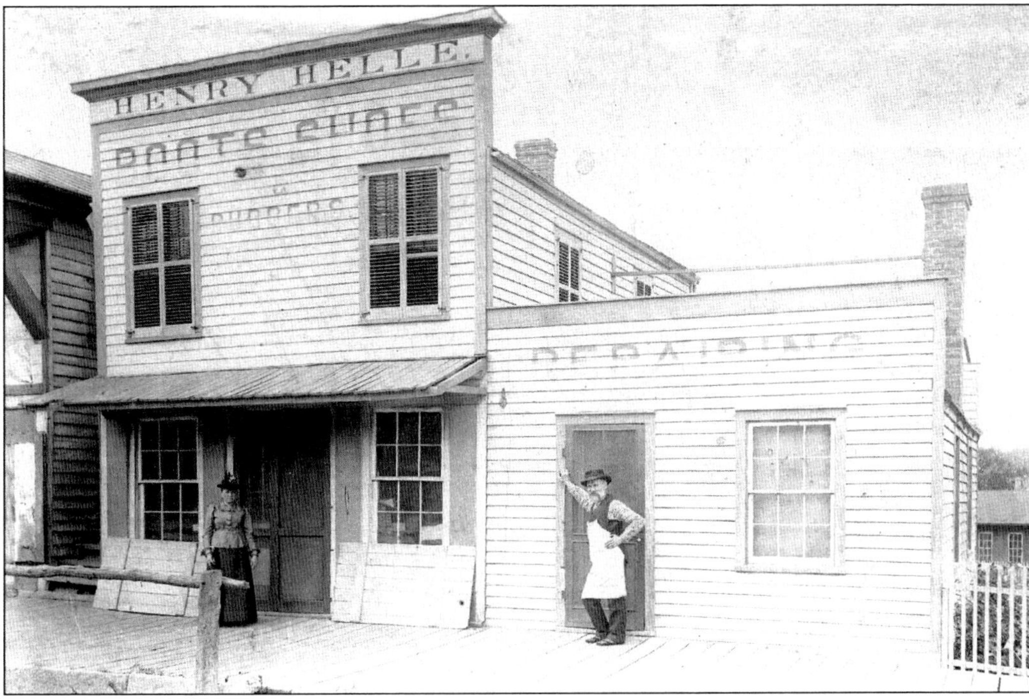

Henry Helle, a German immigrant, owned and operated his shoemaking business from this building at the corner of Main and Jackson Streets in downtown Oswego for decades. Helle and his wife, Margaret Bower Helle (standing near the door), lived in a home attached to the rear of the shoe shop. Margaret was a renowned gardener whose colorful perennials enlivened downtown Oswego.

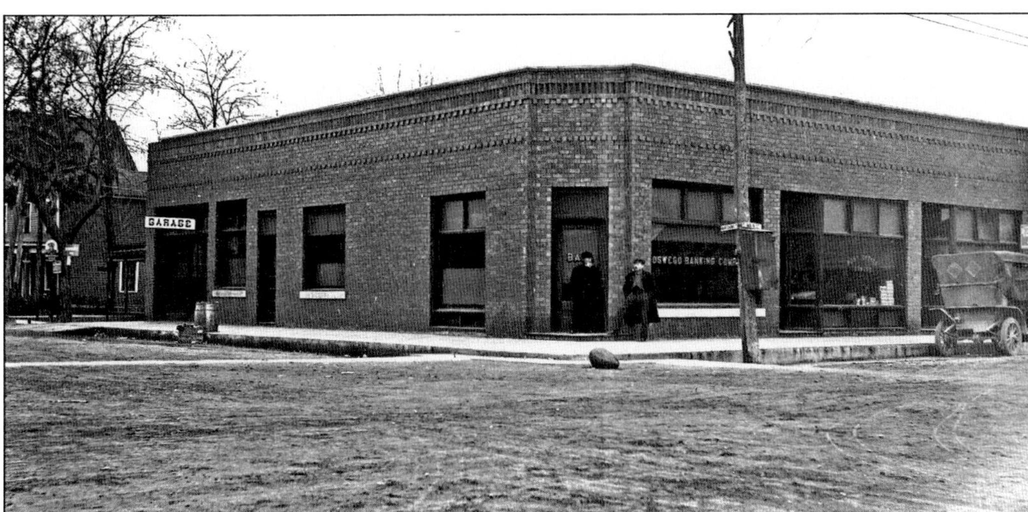

The Oswego State Bank was located on the corner in new Burkhart Block, photographed by Dwight Young in 1911 right after construction was finished. The bank was the community's first financial institution since Levi Hall's bank was destroyed by the depression of the 1890s. The building also housed the Oswego Post Office, the telephone exchange, and Oliver Burkhart's garage, which he first operated with Charles Shoger.

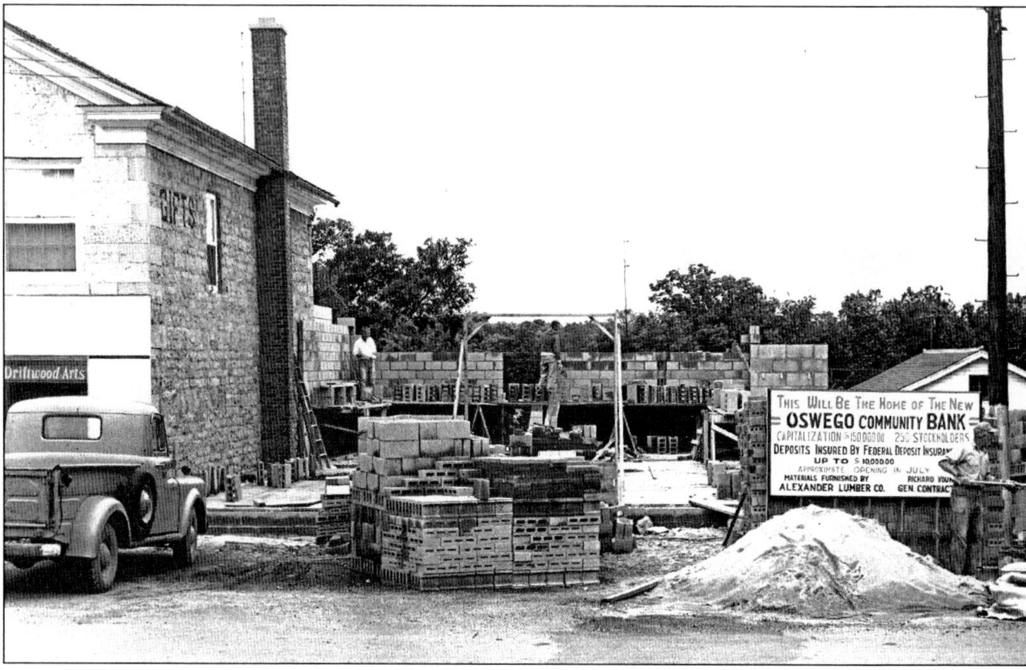

The Great Depression caused the Oswego State Bank to close in 1937, and depositors lost thousands of dollars. Not until 1958 did Oswego manage to establish another bank. That year, construction of the new Oswego Community Bank started at 25 Main Street in Oswego's downtown business district. Contractor Dick Young, seen above, takes a break on the scaffolding at rear while building the bank's back wall.

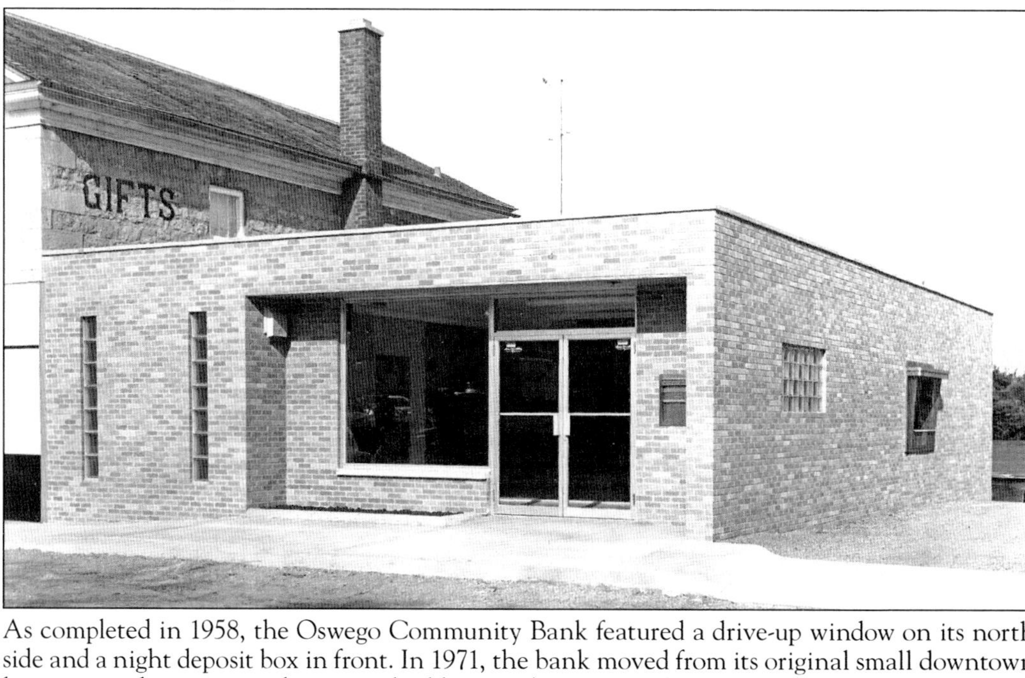

As completed in 1958, the Oswego Community Bank featured a drive-up window on its north side and a night deposit box in front. In 1971, the bank moved from its original small downtown location to their new, and current, building at the corner of Madison and Jackson Streets. A branch bank opened in the Boulder Hill Market in 1990.

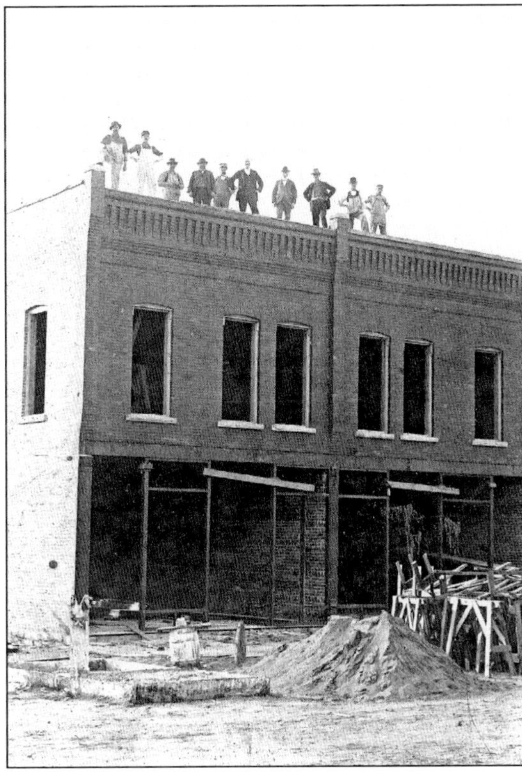

Livestock dealer, meat market operator, and real estate owner Rudolph Knapp began construction on this brick building in 1898. The building, on Main Street, in the middle of the block between Washington and Jackson Streets, housed the G. M. Croushorn Furniture Store and Undertaking Parlor, the Malcom Meat Market, and the Oswego Saloon when completed in the summer of 1898.

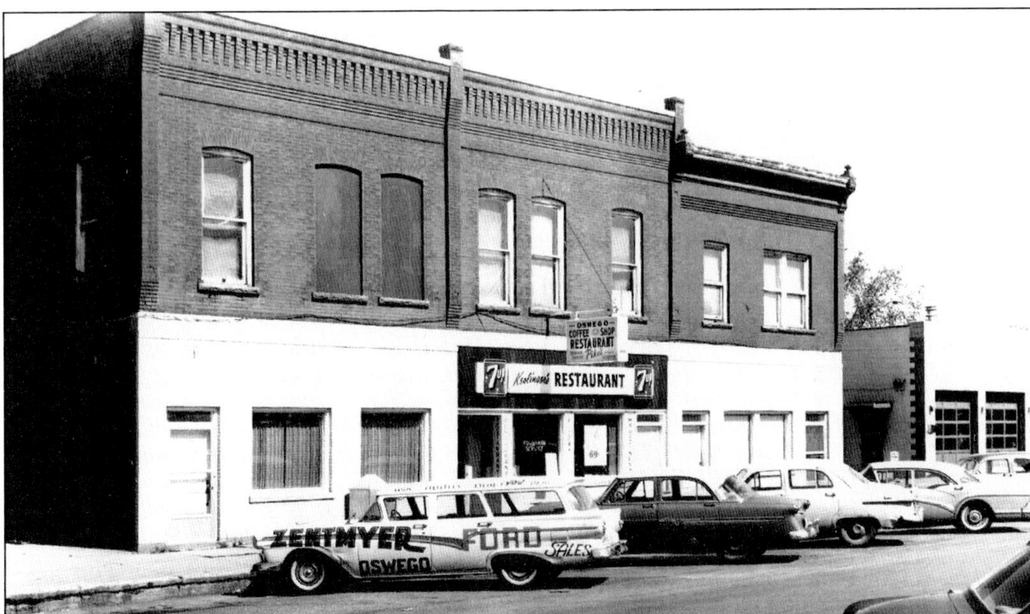

The Knapp Building is seen here in a photograph snapped in May 1958 by Homer Durand, when the building housed the Oswego Masonic Lodge in the left most portion and the Oswego Coffee Shop next door. Today the Masons still own the building and still hold their gatherings there. The restaurant's name has changed to the Oswego Family Restaurant, and Oswego Trophy and Awards occupies the old Oswego Saloon.

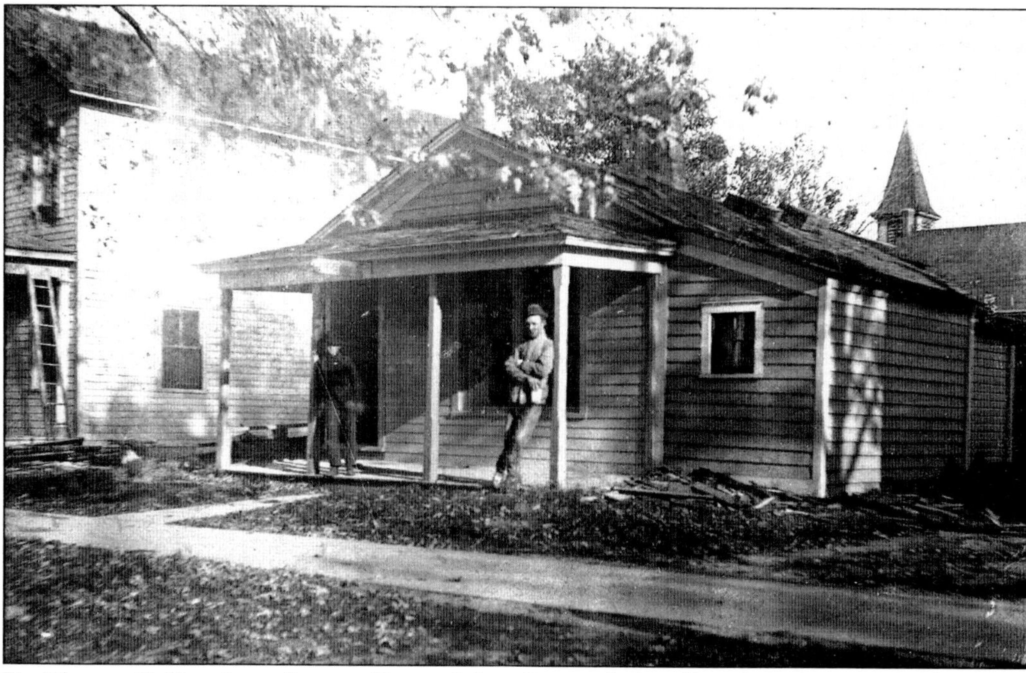

Dr. Thomas B. Drew's small new office on Main Street while still under construction about 1912 is an illustration of Oswego medicine's early days. Dr. Drew served as Kendall County Coroner from 1904 to 1912. Most doctors during the 19th and early 20th centuries ran their practices from their homes since house calls were still the order of the day.

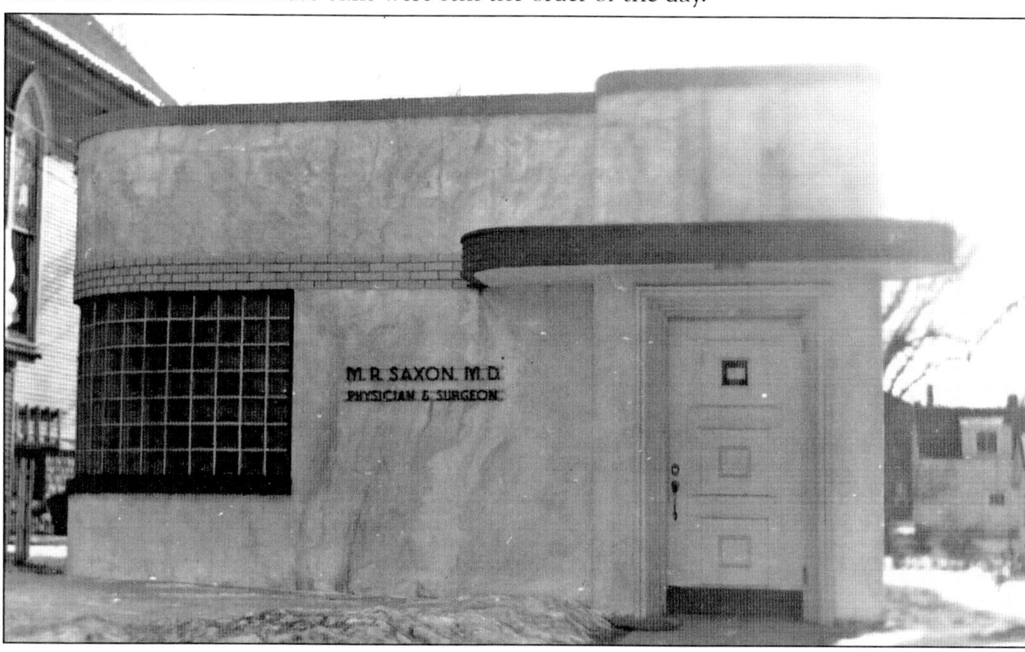

By the time his tiny—but stylish—art deco office was built in 1941 on Washington Street next to the present Church of the Good Shepherd United Methodist, Dr. Michael Saxon had practiced in Oswego for two years. He arrived in 1939 and took over the practice of Dr. A. H. Churchill, who had died that year.

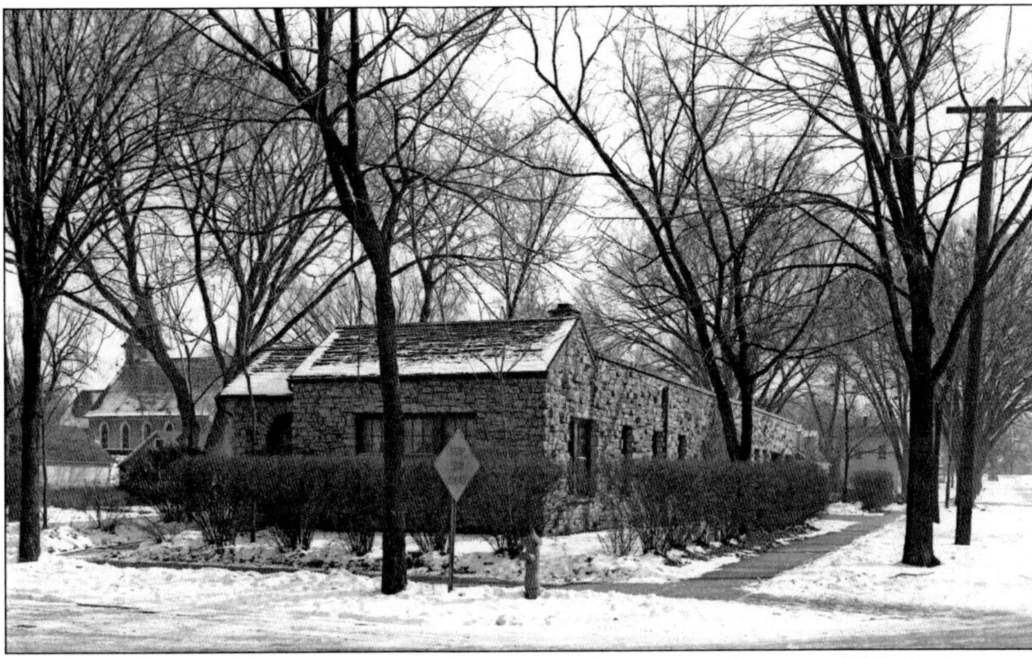

Dr. Lewis Weishew built his medical clinic at Main and Van Buren Streets in 1928. At that time, it was the most modern medical facility in Oswego. Weishew, who began his practice in Oswego in 1913, was drafted into the U.S. Army Medical Corps during World War I as a lieutenant. After the war, he returned to practice in Oswego.

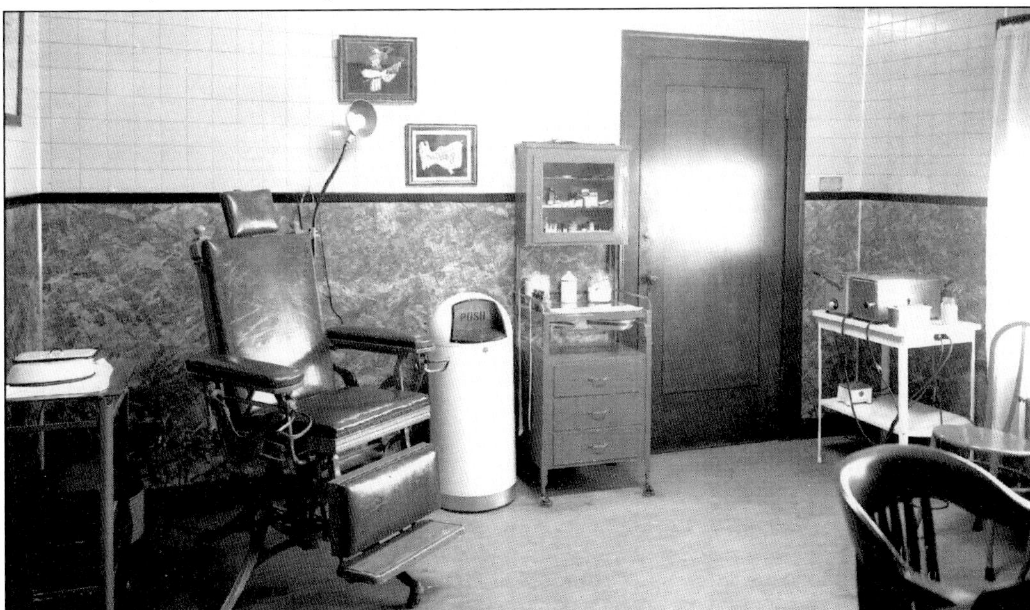

One of the treatment rooms in Weishew's new Oswego clinic is seen here. Weishew began practicing in a small office at the front of the current Oswego American Legion Post at 19 West Washington Street in Oswego. His clinic was later sold to Dr. Michael Saxon and then to Dr. Walter Brill before its purchase by the Dreyer Medical Group. Today the building houses offices including the Oswego Economic Development Corporation.

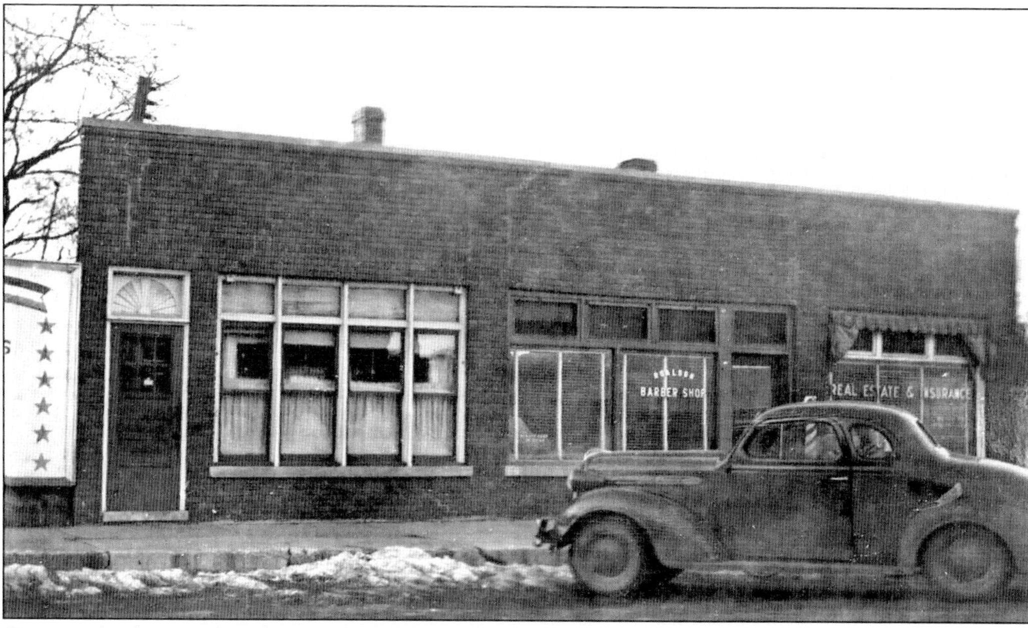

Oswego barber and politician Gus Voss built this brick barbershop in 1918. His brother, Dr. Lewis Voss, a dentist, added the storefront to the right, while at the same time, John Herren added the storefront to the left for his insurance business. By the time this photograph was taken in 1944, Roy Roalson was operating the barbershop.

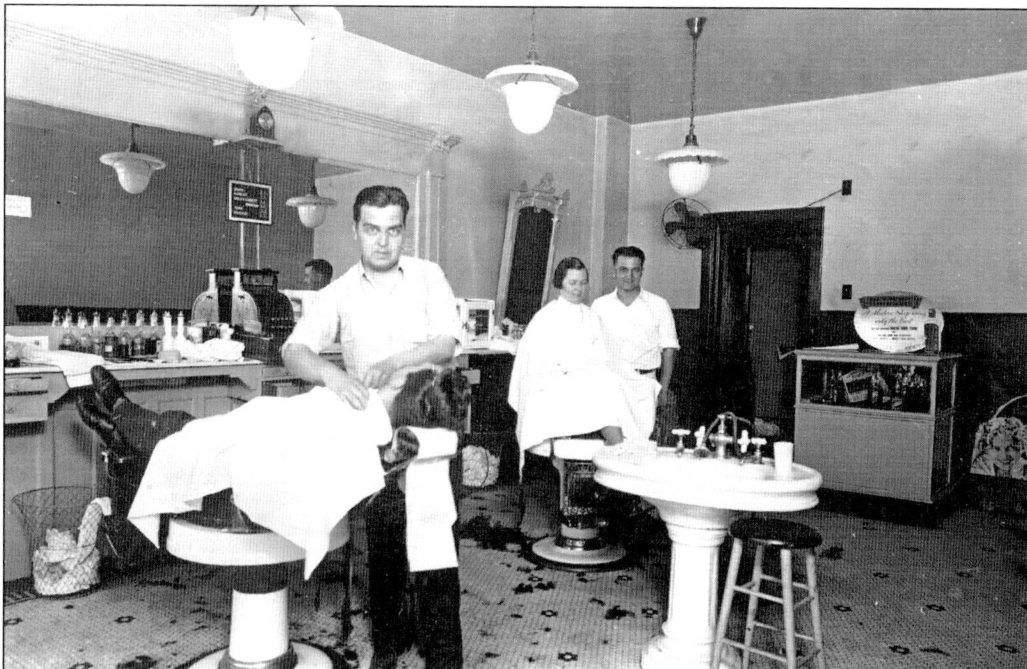

Unisex barbershops are nothing new. In this 1931 photograph, a young Roy Roalson readies Cole Smith for a shave in Roalson's Oswego barbershop, while his unnamed assistant gets Ella Apple ready for a trim. The shop was one of the only buildings in Oswego that was air conditioned, using a cooling exchanger that operated off the village water supply.

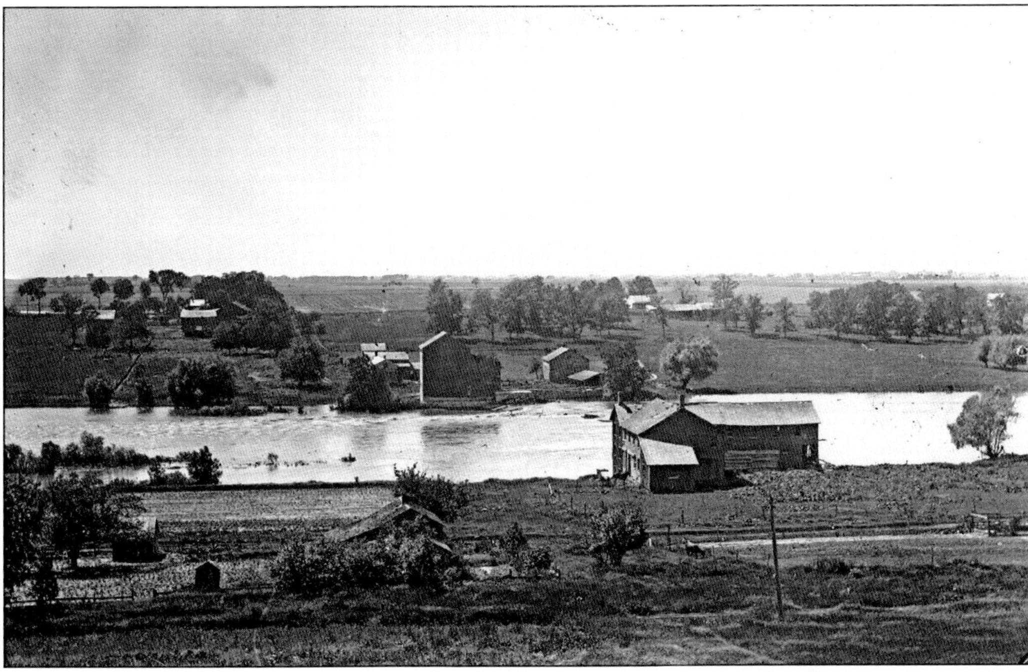

Just north of Oswego, the Fox River offered a fine spot for a dam and mills. Levi Gorton built the gristmill on the west bank at the far end of the dam in this photograph. Nathaniel Rising added a sawmill at the east end of the dam in 1848. Rising also laid out the village of Troy that included the sawmill and surrounding land on the east bank of the river.

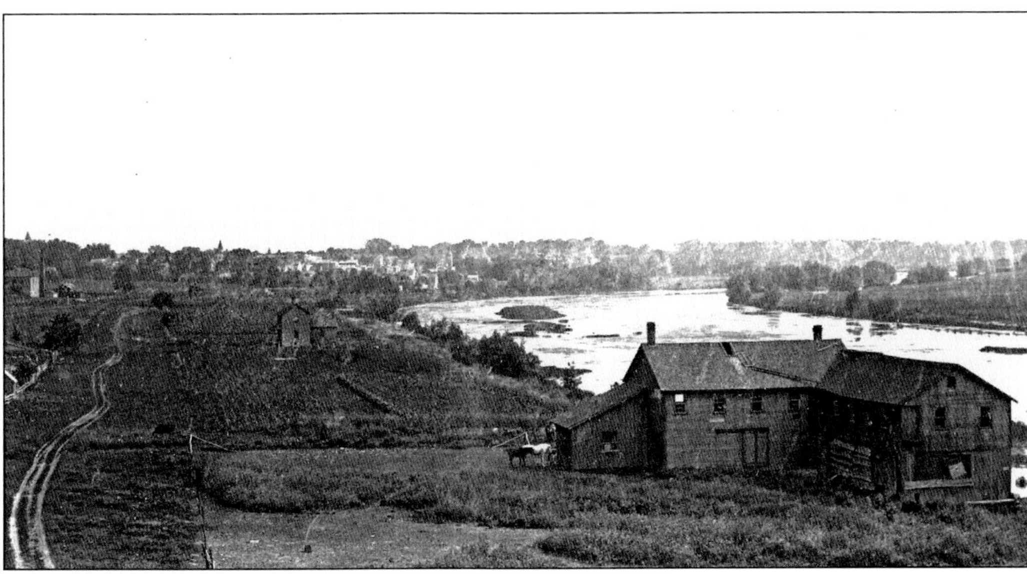

Rising's sawmill was built parallel to the river, with the millrace running beneath it to turn its turbine. William Parker bought the mill in 1852. After it was destroyed by the flood of 1857, Parker rebuilt it and added the furniture factory "L" addition. The Little White School Museum has some of the walnut furniture manufactured at the factory in its collection.

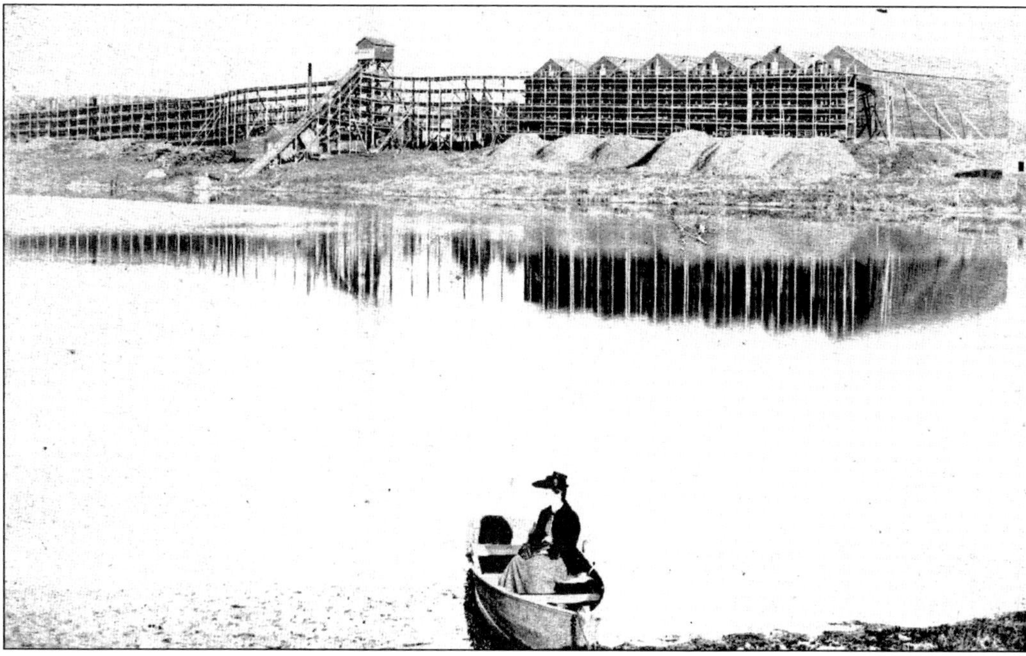

Ice became a salable commodity in the latter 19th century. The Esch Brothers and Rabe Ice Company built these huge icehouses above Parker's dam and mills. Each winter, ice was harvested by crews numbering up to 75 men and stored in the houses using sawdust from the Parker Sawmill as insulation.

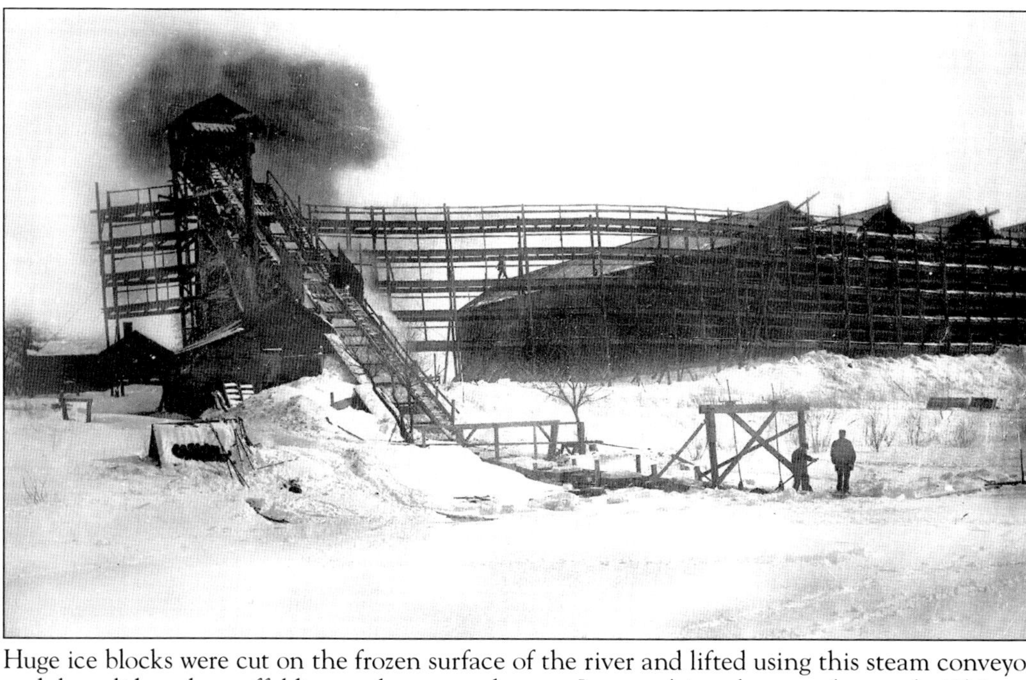

Huge ice blocks were cut on the frozen surface of the river and lifted using this steam conveyor and then slid on the scaffolding to the storage houses. Ice was shipped out on the nearby Chicago Burlington and Quincy Railroad. In September 1880, 124 railcar loads of ice were shipped from Oswego for use in home iceboxes and to keep railcar reefers full of meat from Chicago cool.

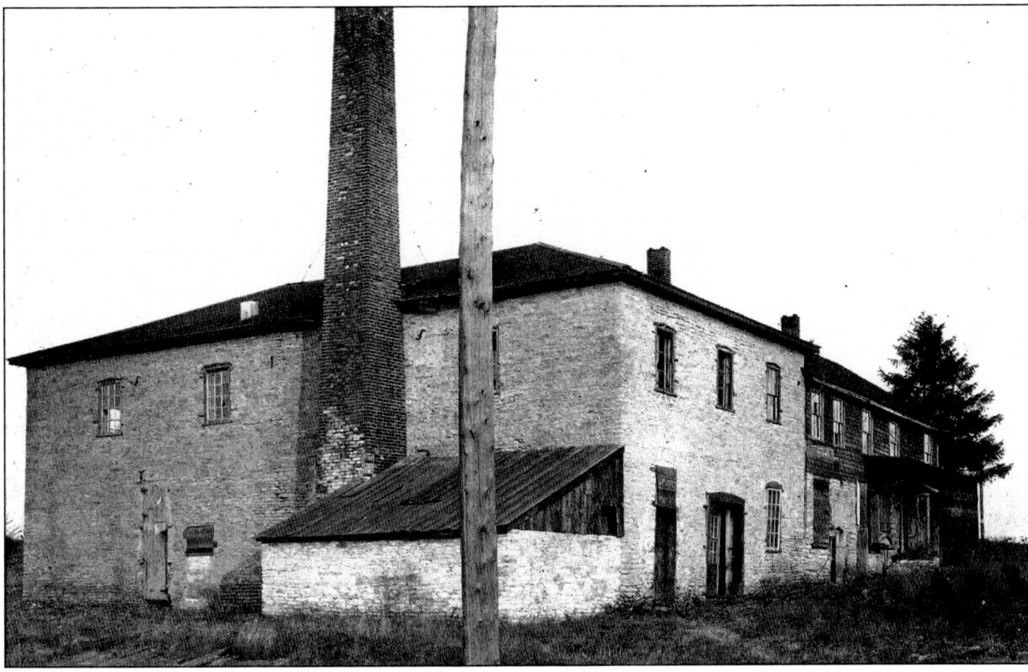

Originally built as a brewery, the Fox River Creamery took advantage of the natural spring that flowed under the building. As an indication of the amount of milk produced by local farmers, from May 1, 1878 to May 1, 1879, the creamery produced 177,000 pounds of butter and 354,000 pounds of cheese. This photograph, from the collections of the Aurora Historical Society, shows the building shortly before it was demolished.

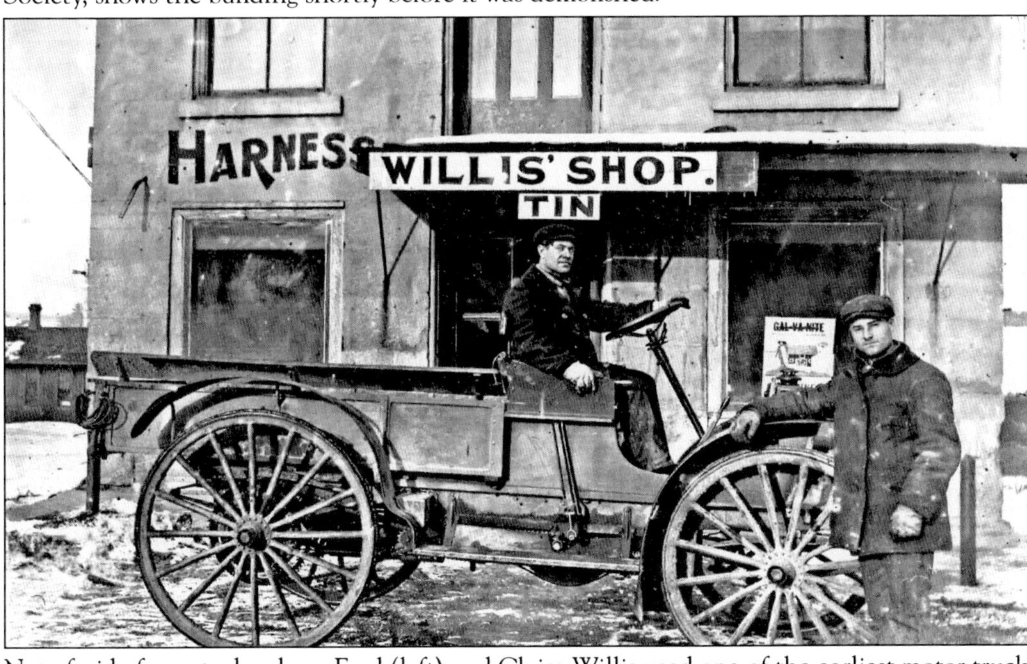

Not afraid of new technology, Fred (left) and Claire Willis used one of the earliest motor trucks to deliver the products they manufactured in their Oswego shop, which had displaced a harness shop in this photograph. Note the glimpse of the Oswego Depot at the far left.

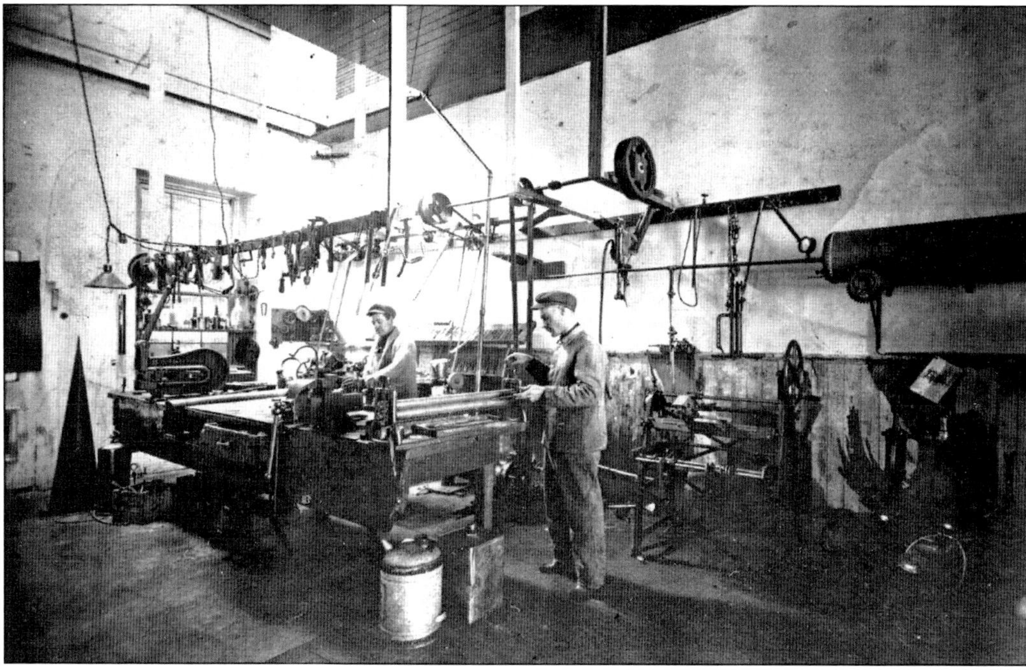

Fred and Claire Willis at work in their Oswego metal shop. The Willis business marketed some of the first central heating systems in Oswego, including new coal-fired furnaces by Caloric.

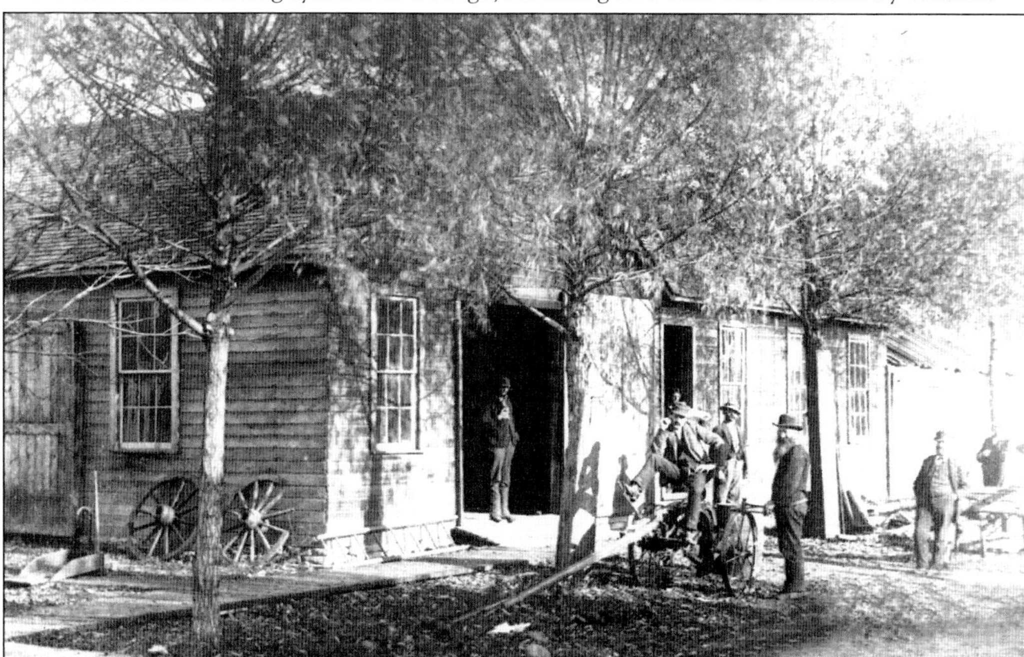

The John A. Young blacksmith and wagon shop stood at the corner of Madison and Tyler Streets. Blacksmiths of that era made and repaired wagons, as well as shoed horses. Young, in long beard, is standing holding his hammer, while at far right is Capt. Charles Mann, whose horse breeding barns were located across Tyler Street from the Young shop on the site of today's McKeown-Dunn Funeral Home.

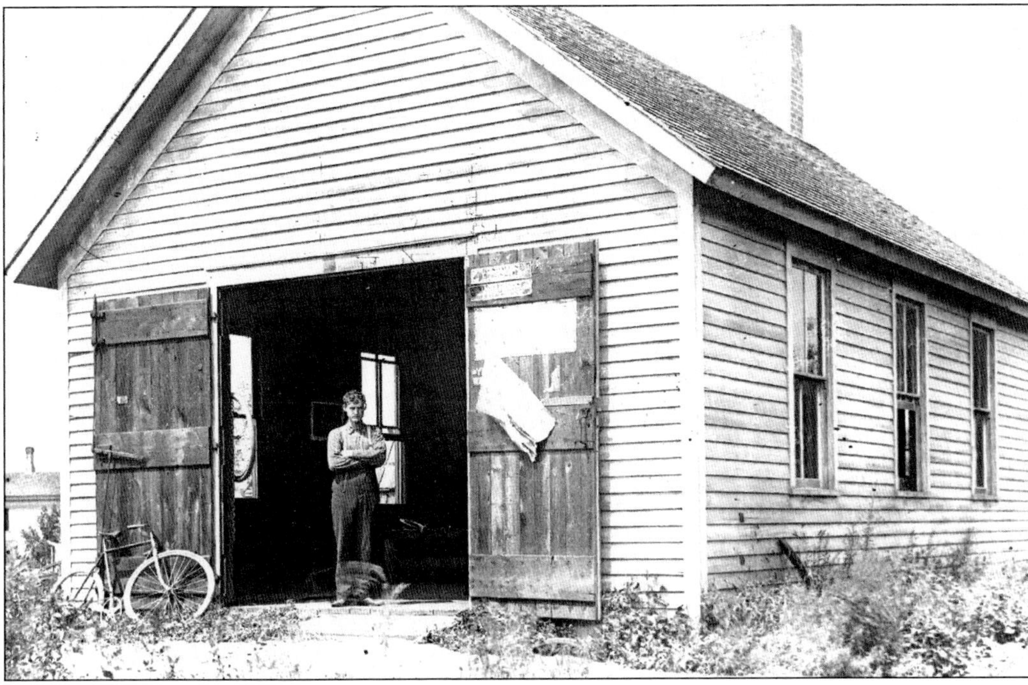

Charlie Reed stands in front of his blacksmith shop, located on Washington Street at Tyler Street around the beginning of the 20th century in this photograph by Irvin Haines. The shop is still standing at the same location.

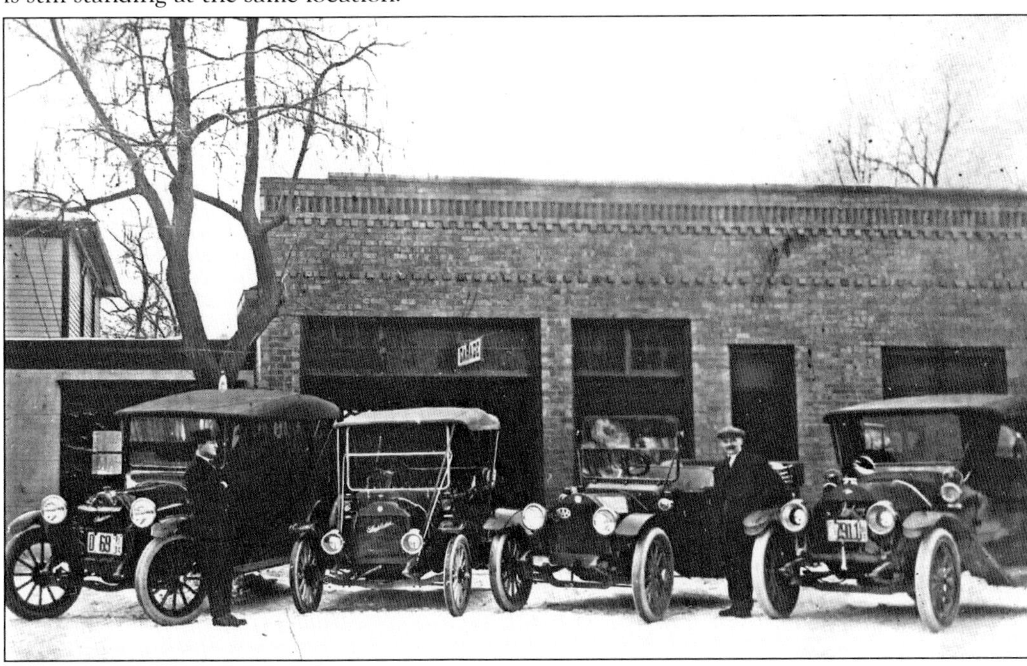

Oliver Burkhart (right) and Charles Shoger stand in front of their new automobile garage in 1914. As the automobile replaced the horse and buggy, blacksmith shops gradually disappeared. By 1931, every Oswego blacksmith shop shown on the 1895 Sanborn Fire Insurance Map of the village had turned into an automobile repair garage.

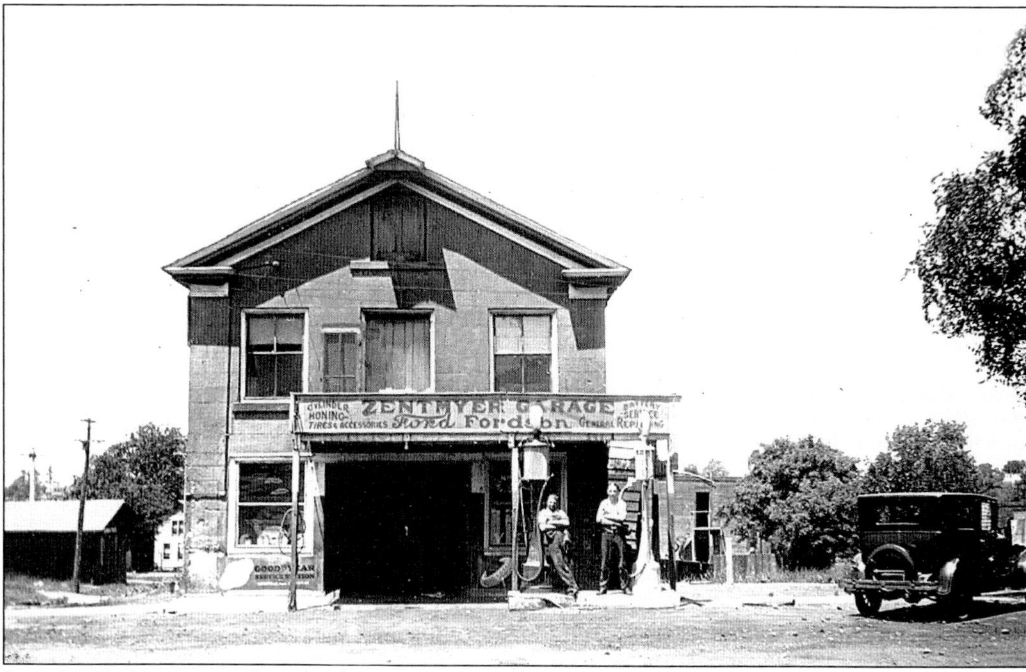

In 1922, Earl Zentmyer bought the Liberty Garage business from Ed Reed and, later, the building itself from Augustus Shoger. This photograph of the renamed Zentmyer Garage was taken about 1929, when the building featured gasoline pumps in front. Today, the building is the home of All-American Male and Company.

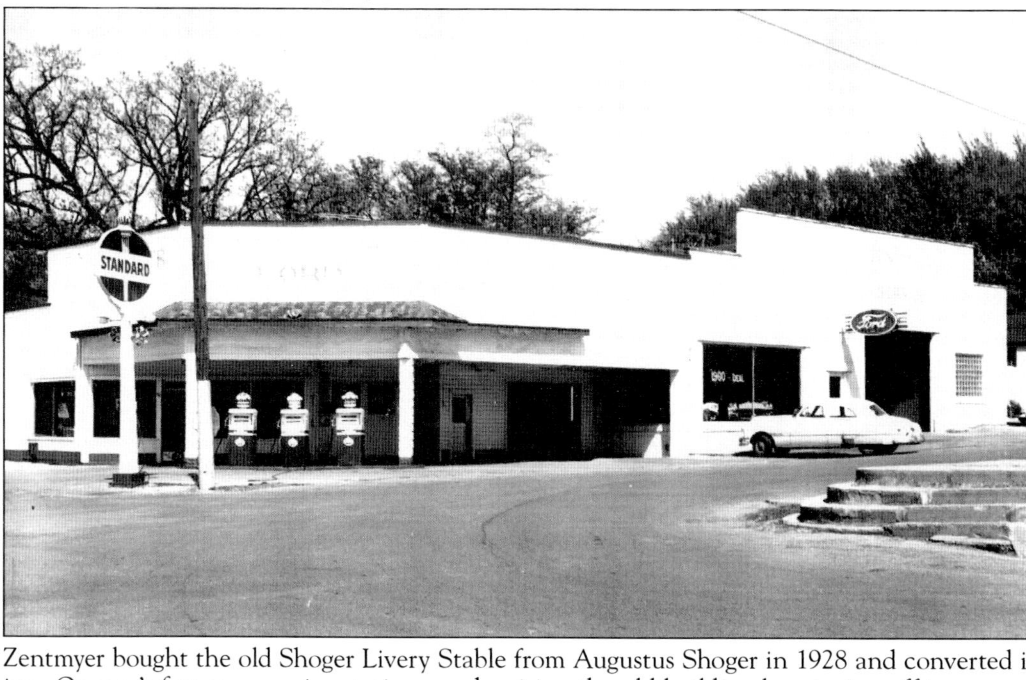

Zentmyer bought the old Shoger Livery Stable from Augustus Shoger in 1928 and converted it into Oswego's first true service station, modernizing the old building by nipping off its corner. The original gable roof had been replaced with a flat roof in 1917 after a second story fire. Later the service station became the sales office for Zentmyer Ford Sales.

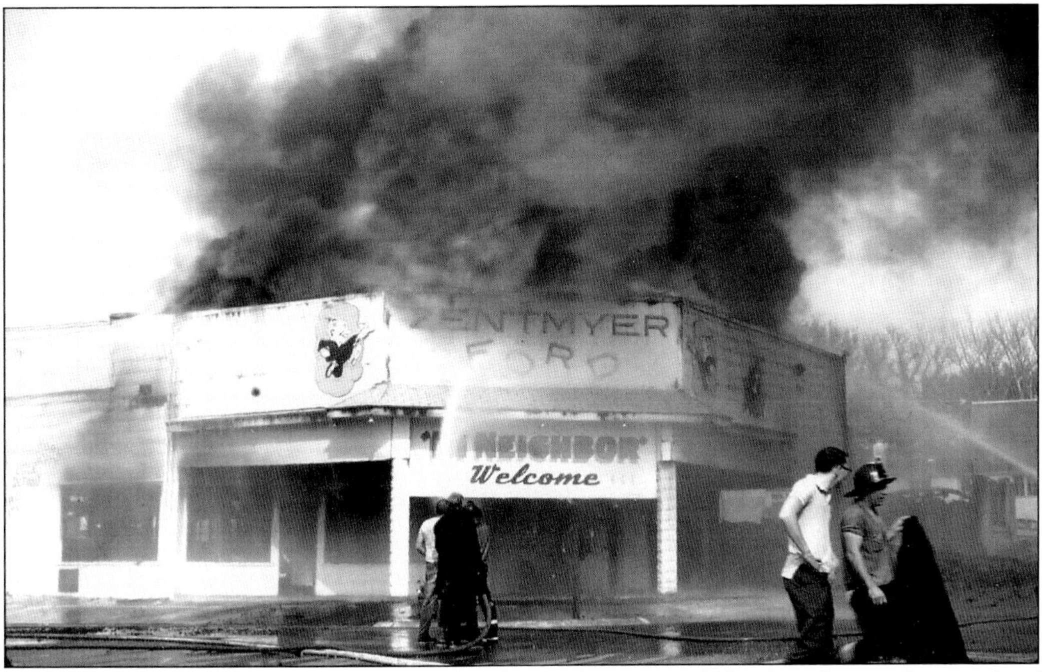

The Zentmyer dealership was destroyed by fire on June 10, 1965, after the gasoline tank of an automobile under repair caught fire. Fire departments from throughout the area were rushed to downtown Oswego to fight the blaze in the old converted livery stable, which was totally destroyed.

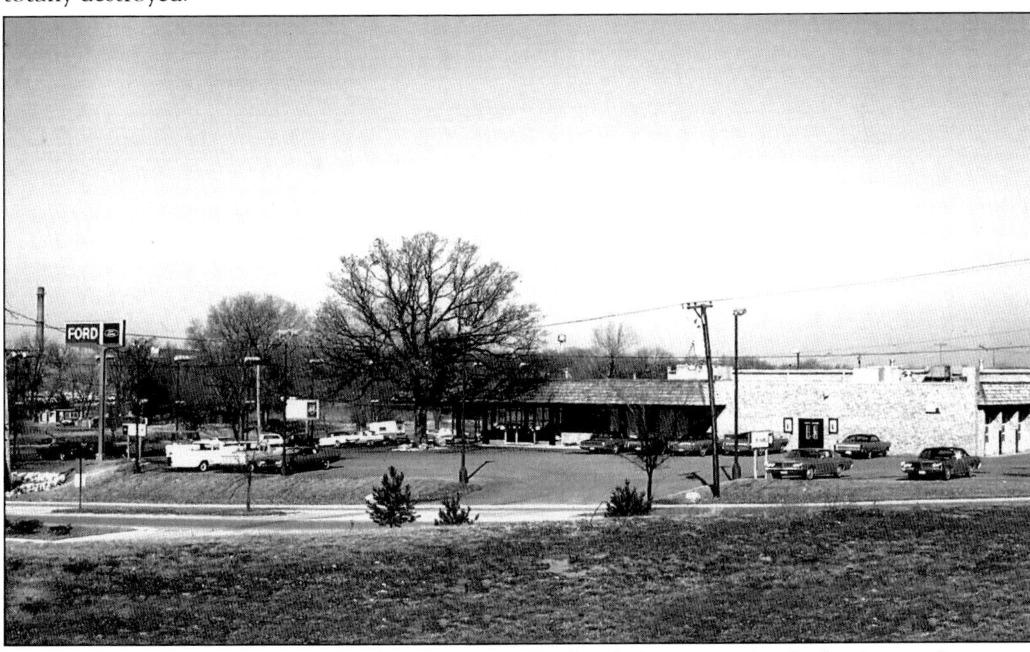

After the fire, James Zentmyer, Earl Zentmyer's son, decided to move the dealership to the corner of Illinois Route 25 and Boulder Hill Pass. Zentmyer's new dealership is shown here as it looked when it opened in 1966. The building, renamed Boulder Point Center, is now owned by the Oswegoland Park District.

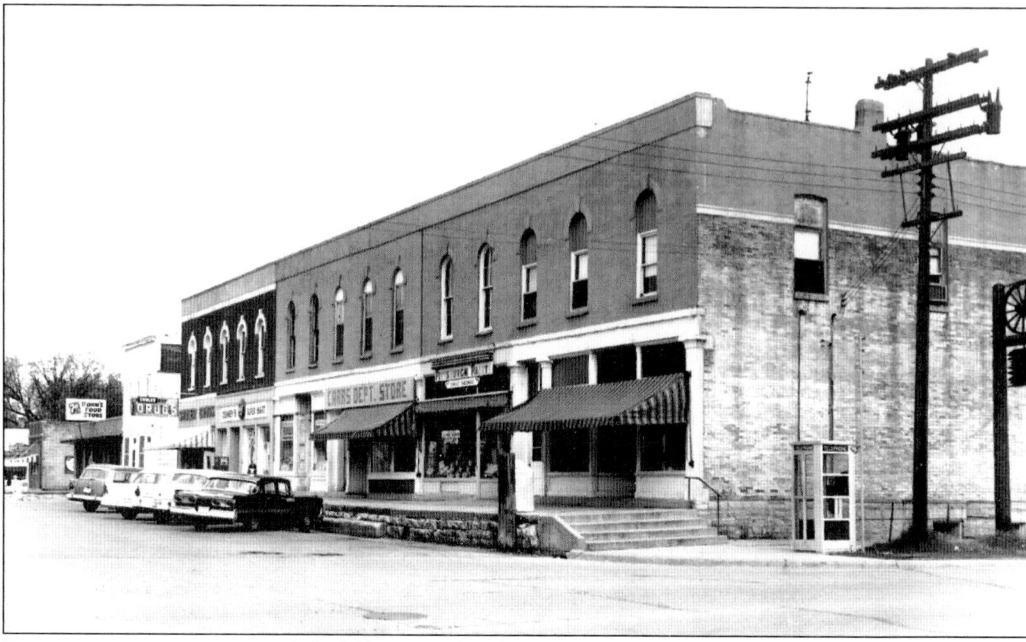

From its construction in 1867 following the destructive fire that February, downtown Oswego has continued to evolve. This Homer Durand photograph taken in 1958 shows the venerable Brick Block before many modern changes took place including replacing the old limestone based front walks.

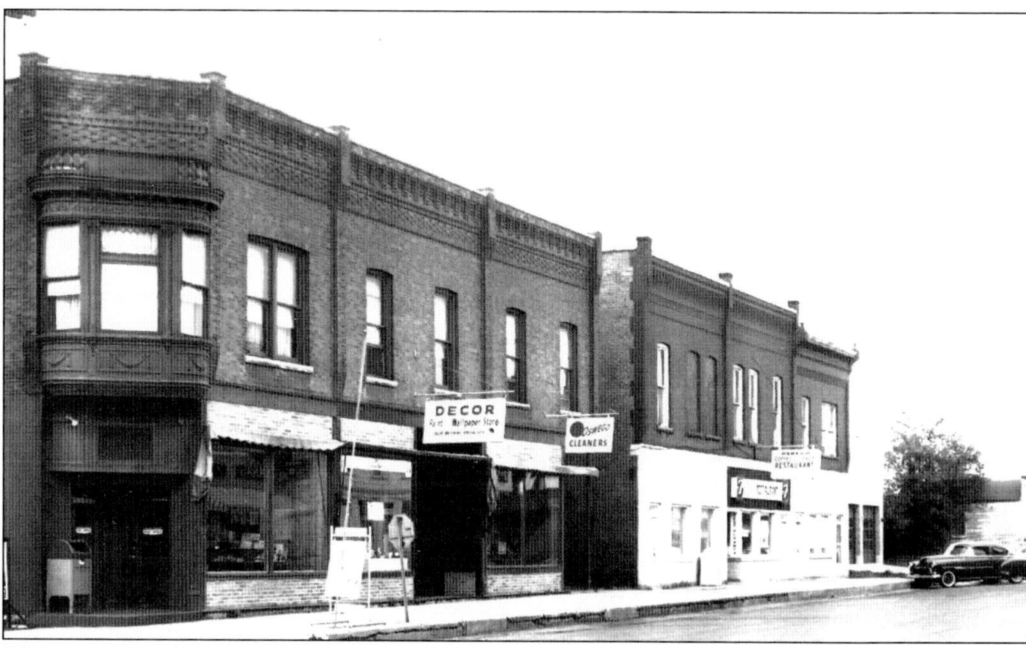

The west side of Main Street has changed little during the past several decades. In fact, it looks in this 1958 Homer Durand photograph much as it did after John Schickler built his block of brick stores at the corner of Main and Washington Streets in 1900.

Four

Trails, Trains and Trolleys

The first travelers to visit Oswego were just passing through, following the Ice Age big game on which they relied for food. Their distant descendants were still occupying the area when the first pioneers arrived in 1833.

Travel through the early 1850s was overland by foot, horseback, and horse-drawn wagon and carriage. Oswego had been established at an existing crossroads, where former Native American trails converged on a shallow ford across the Fox River. The earliest major road through Oswego linked Chicago with the head of navigation on the Illinois River at Ottawa. Shortly after, another trail connecting Ottawa with modern Geneva came up the west bank of the Fox River, crossed at Oswego and continued north up the east bank. The last early road through the area connected Joliet, via Oswego, with Dixon on the Rock River and then on northwest to the lead mining region at Galena.

In the late 1840s, rail lines had pushed west of Chicago and railroad companies were looking for a likely spot to cross the Fox River. They favored the narrows at Oswego, but local economic interests were hostile, deciding to back the Oswego and Indiana Plank Road Company, which had big plans to link Oswego, Joliet, and the Indiana state line. As a result, the railroad—later called the Chicago, Burlington and Quincy Railroad—crossed the river at Aurora in 1853, bypassing Oswego about two miles to the west. Not until 1870 did the village get its own rail link.

The interurban trolley craze that struck the nation in the late 19th century did not pass Oswego by. In 1900, the tracks of the Aurora, Yorkville and Morris Railway Company reached Oswego and the community had its first mass transit system.

The trolley's life was short, closing about 1927 due to affordable, dependable motor vehicles. The new automobiles and trucks required better roads, and Oswego once again found itself a crossroads where two state highways began, one U.S. highway passed through, and several local roads converged.

Today, most Oswego Township residents are likely unaware they still drive on many of the same roads pioneers used.

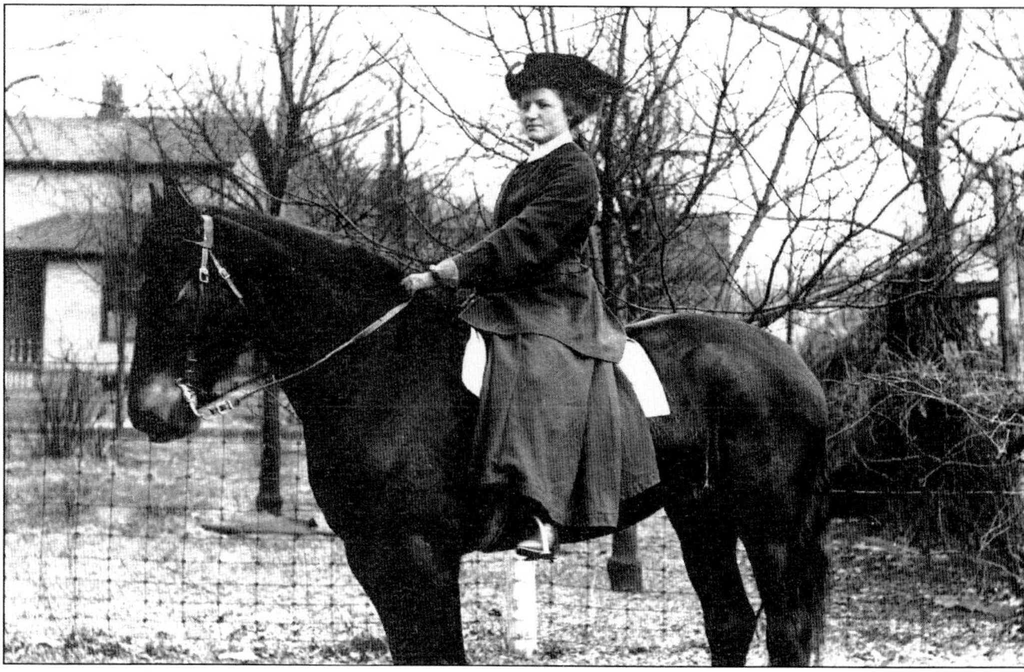

Oswego resident Floi Johnston sits astride her favorite horse, Tommy, in this photograph. Horseback travel was not uncommon in the Oswego area through the 1920s, with more than one rural schoolboy or girl riding their horse to school. Downtown Oswego boasted cast-iron hitching posts until the middle of the 20th century.

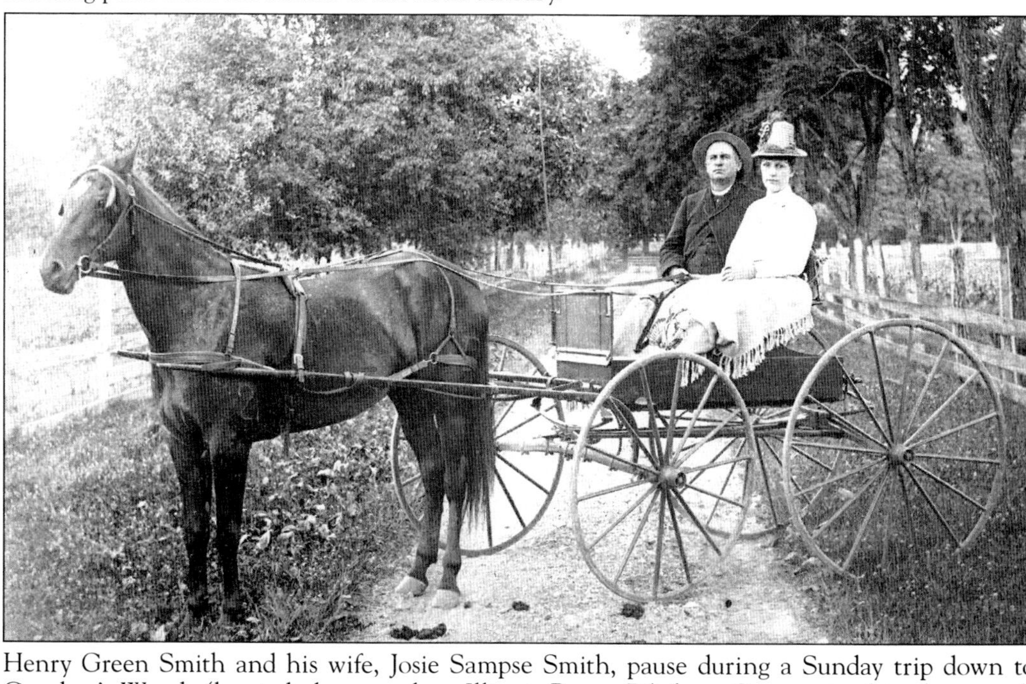

Henry Green Smith and his wife, Josie Sampse Smith, pause during a Sunday trip down to Cowdrey's Woods (located along modern Illinois Route 71) from Oswego in this photograph taken about 1880. Horse-and-buggy travel was the only way to travel the area's roads until the introduction of automobiles.

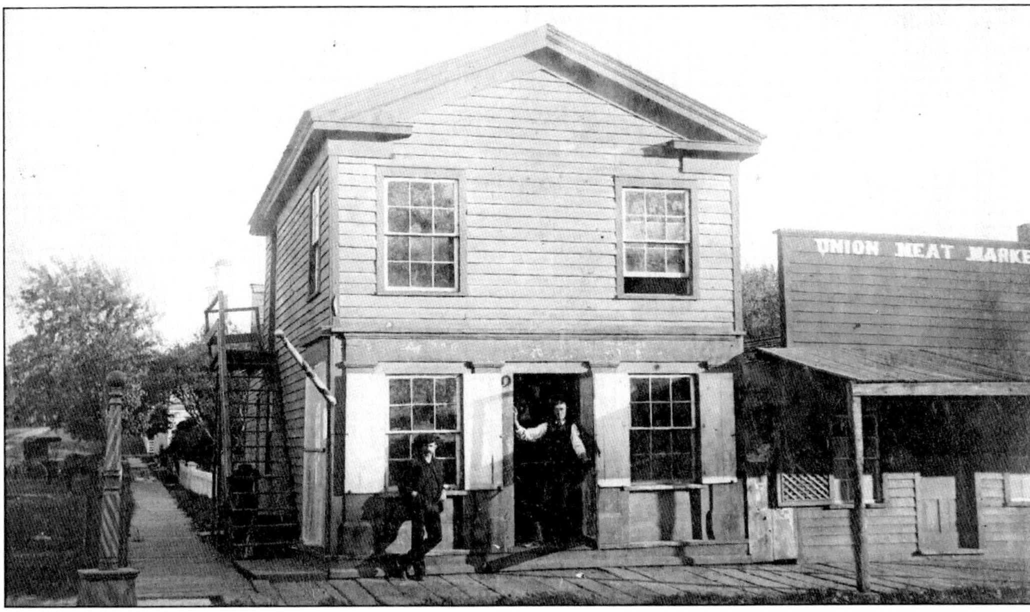

The huge numbers of horse-drawn vehicles required many local harness shops and harness makers. This frame building at the southeast corner of Main and Washington Streets in Oswego was a former harness shop owned by Moses Cherry.

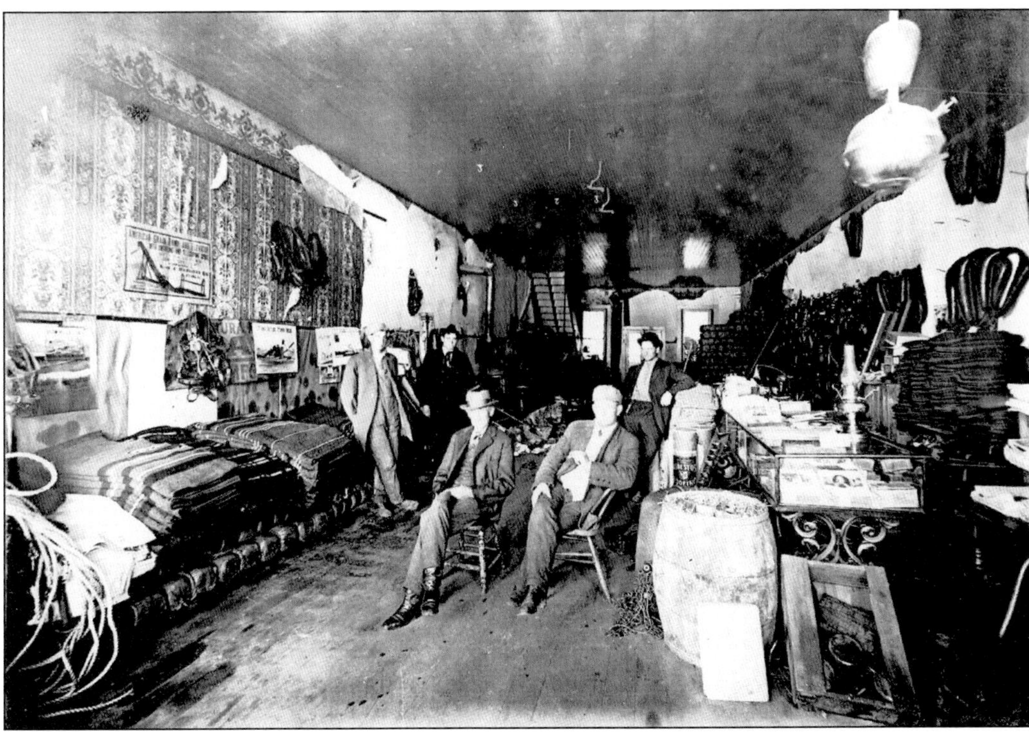

Bob Johnston's harness shop, on the east side of Main Street between Washington and Jackson Streets, boasted just about anything horse owners needed, from saddle blankets to harnesses for everything from light buggies to heavy farm wagons.

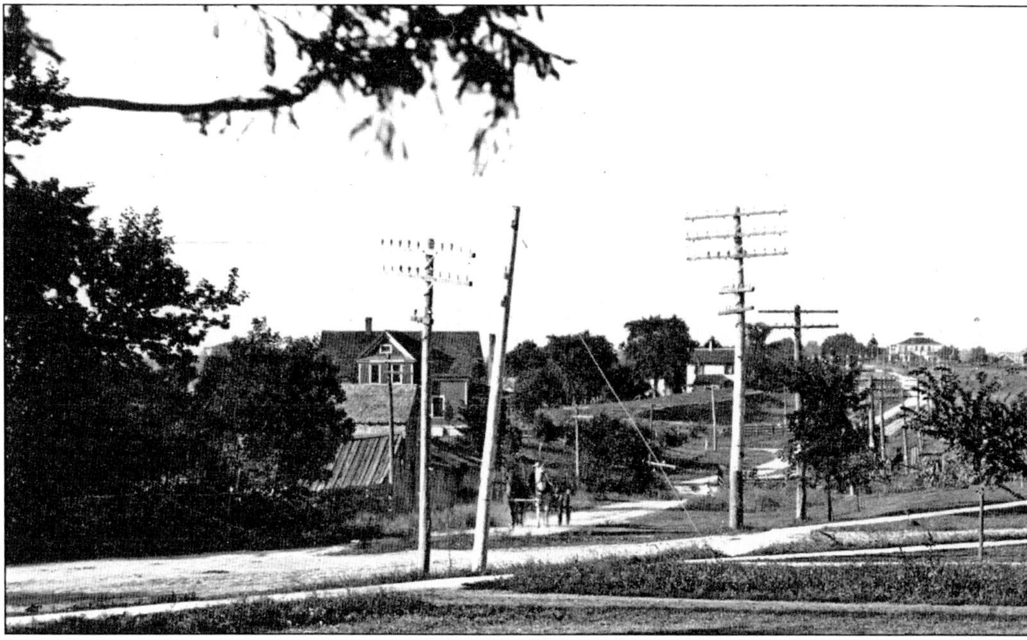

A team of horses pulling a wagon makes its way south to the Five Corners intersection in Oswego about 1905. At the time, Oswego was served by the Aurora, Yorkville and Morris interurban trolley line as well as passenger service on the Chicago, Burlington and Quincy Railroad line through town, but horse-drawn vehicles were still the norm.

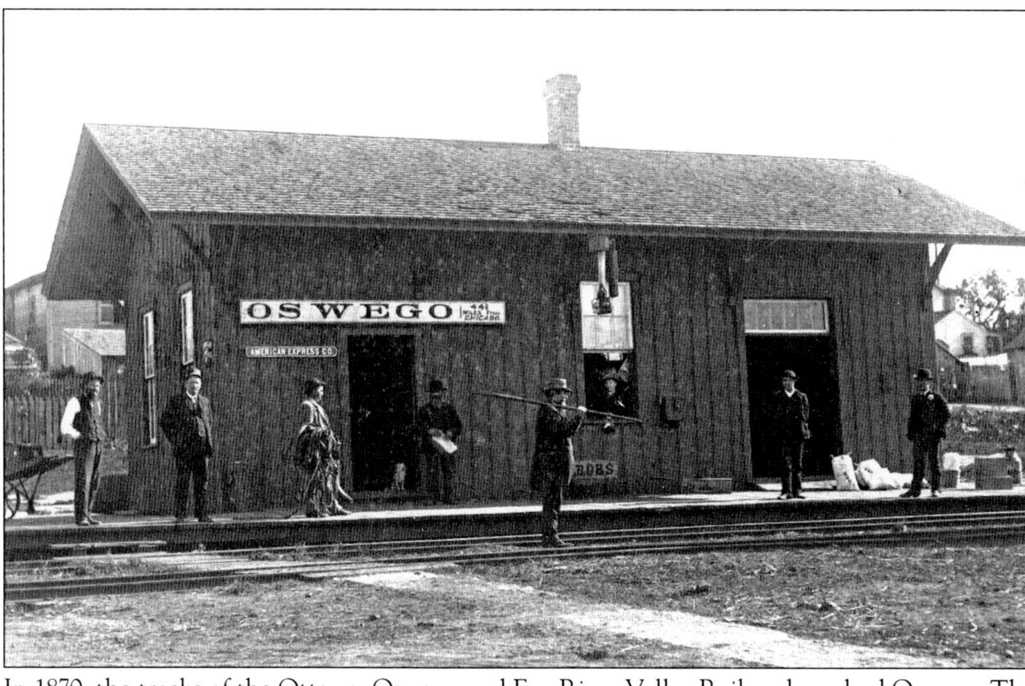

In 1870, the tracks of the Ottawa, Oswego and Fox River Valley Railroad reached Oswego. The rail line was almost immediately acquired by the Chicago, Burlington and Quincy Railroad, which built this station on Jackson Street near North Adams Street. In this 1880 photograph, station agent Henry Green Smith stands second from left.

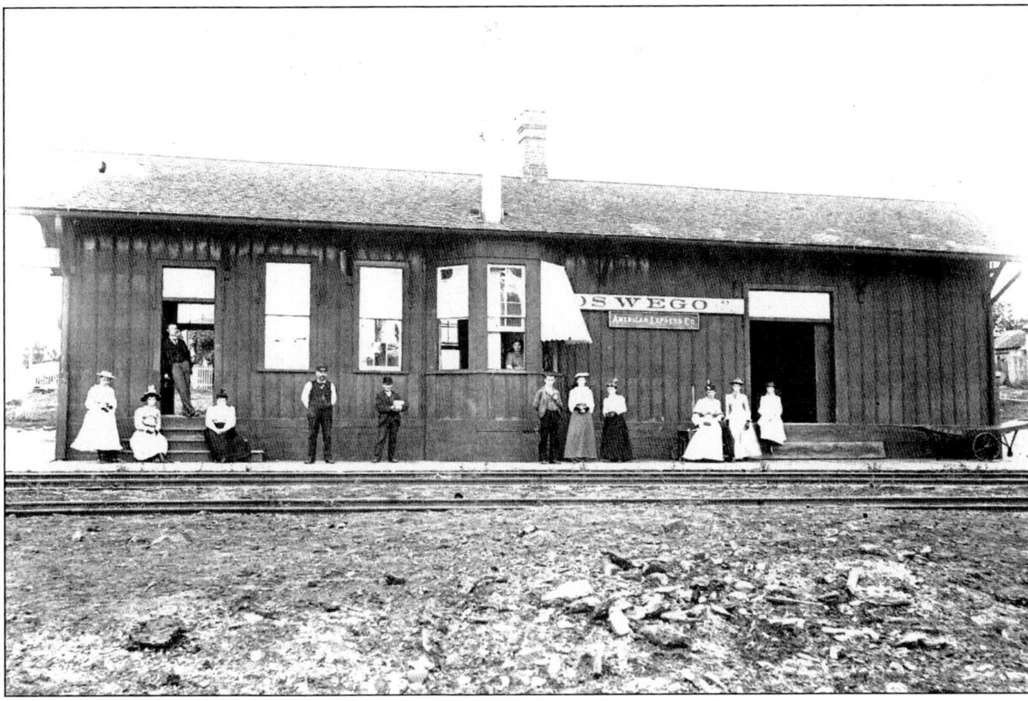

Between 1885 and 1892, the Chicago, Burlington and Quincy Railroad's Oswego station was enlarged with the addition of a new waiting room for passengers, as well as a new semaphore signal tower to warn passing trains if another train was traveling the opposition direction on the single-tracked line.

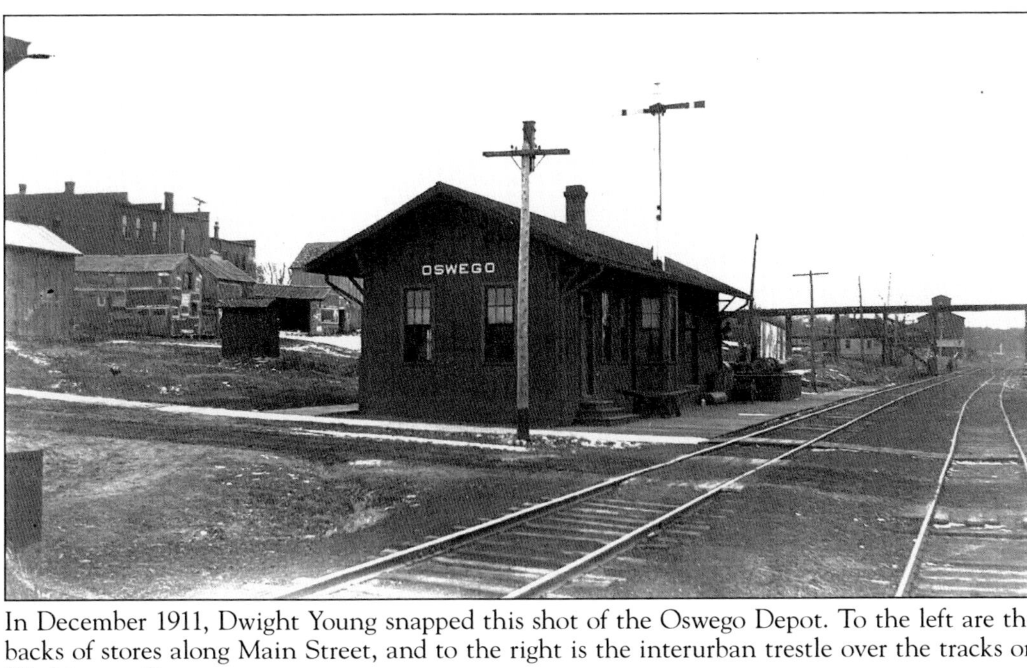

In December 1911, Dwight Young snapped this shot of the Oswego Depot. To the left are the backs of stores along Main Street, and to the right is the interurban trestle over the tracks on Washington Street.

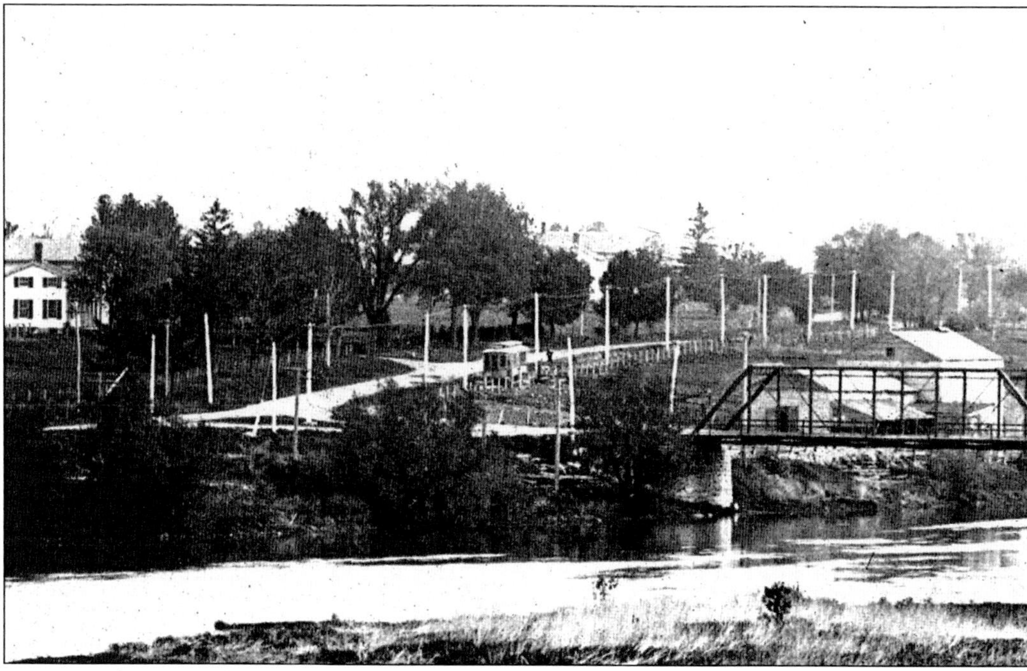

A car on the interurban trolley line at center nears the turn to cross the Oswego Bridge about 1905. The trolley route followed River Street from Aurora to Montgomery and then traveled alongside today's Illinois Route 31 to Oswego, where it crossed the Fox River.

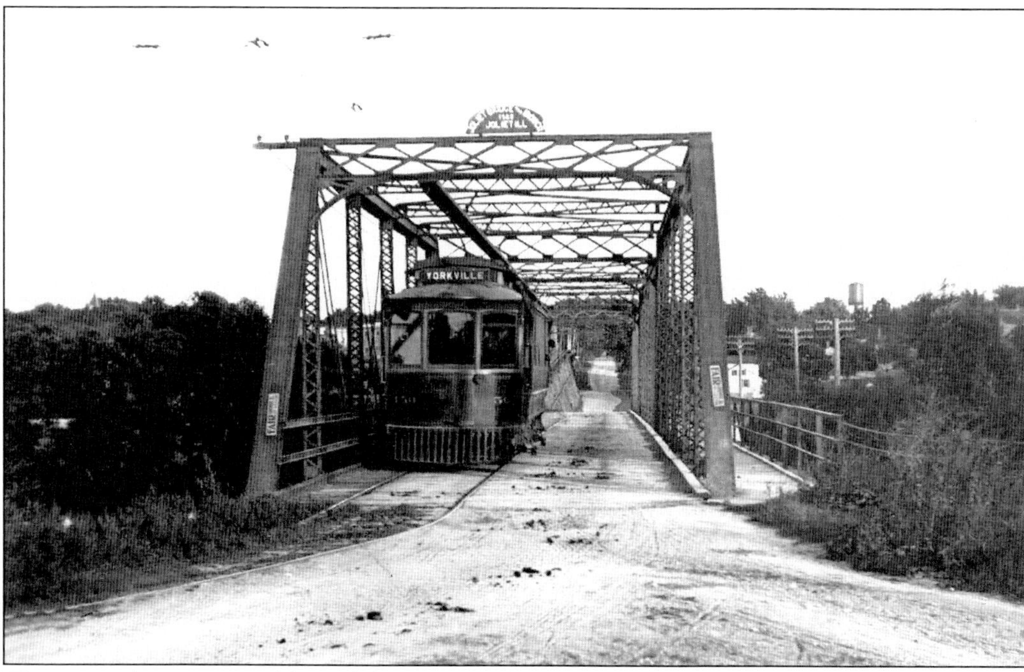

The interurban car northbound from Yorkville pauses for a portrait at the west end of the Oswego Bridge about 1910. The trolley used the same bridge as horse-drawn vehicles to cross the Fox River. Trolleys ran hourly from Yorkville to Aurora allowing residents living along the tracks to commute to work and school.

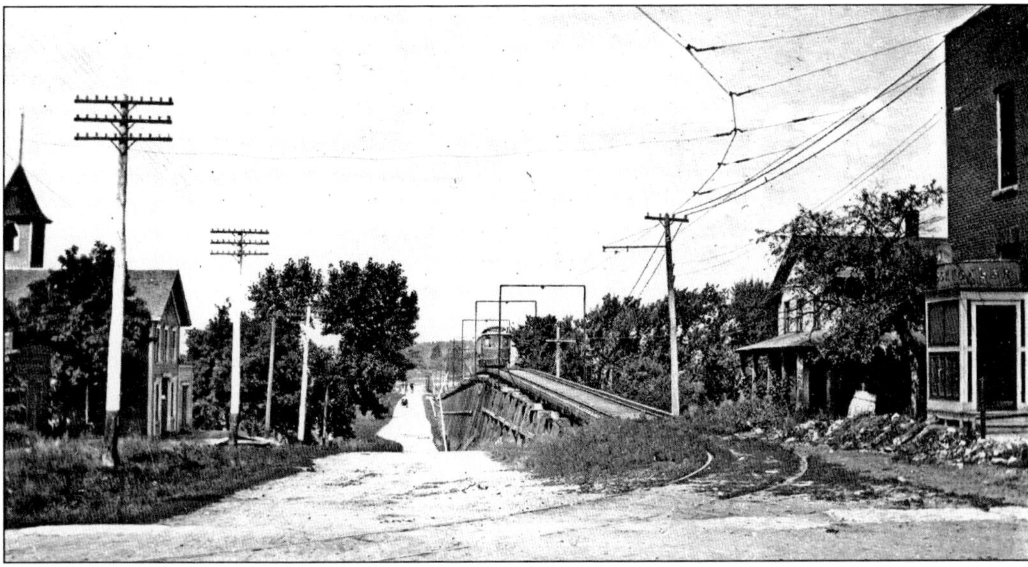

The trolley was photographed crossing the Washington Street trestle over the Chicago Burlington and Quincy Railroad tracks in this shot taken about 1910. At the top of the hill, the tracks curved south to travel along Main Street to modern Illinois Route 71, then down to Van Emmon Road, and on into downtown Yorkville.

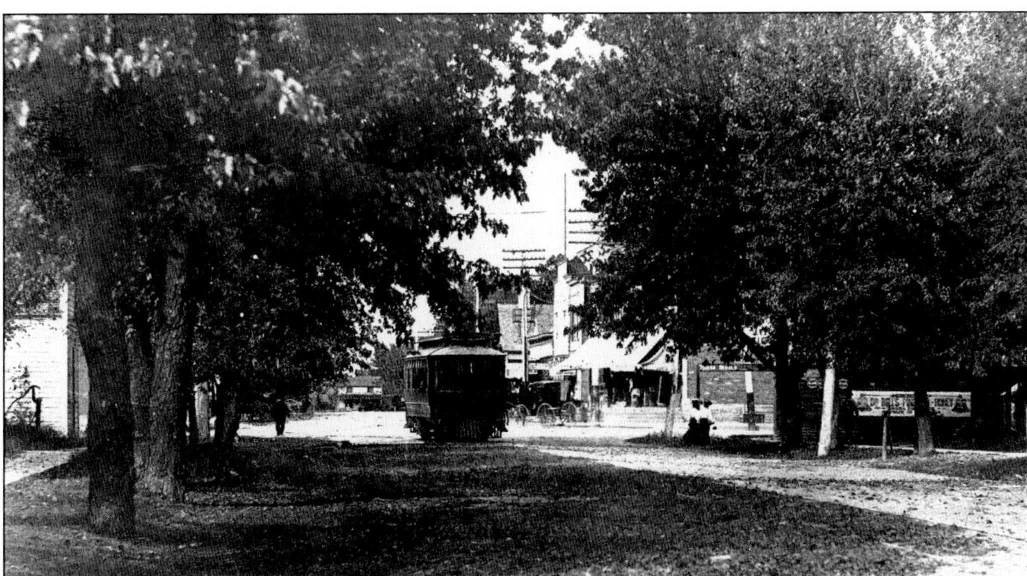

After stopping on June 9, 1909, to drop off Carrie Behr and Mary E. Young (walking away at right), the trolley heads down Main Street on its way to Yorkville in this Pearl Chase Shortman photograph. The trolley not only carried passengers, but also brought fresh bread and other baked goods daily, and delivered mail and freight hourly. Letters mailed and answered the same day were common during the trolley era.

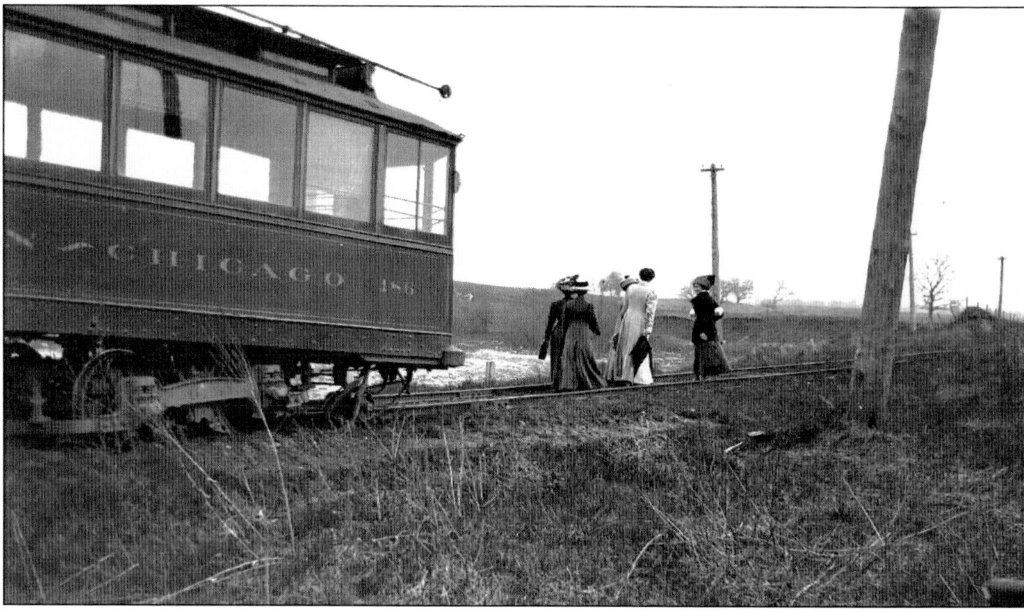

Although usually convenient, it was not that interurban trolleys did not have occasional problems, including the tendency of the lightweight cars to jump the tracks. Above, Dwight Young snapped this 1911 photograph of a derailed trolley between Yorkville and Oswego as the passengers decide to walk the rest of the way instead of waiting for repairs. By this time, the line was known as the Aurora, Elgin and Chicago Railway.

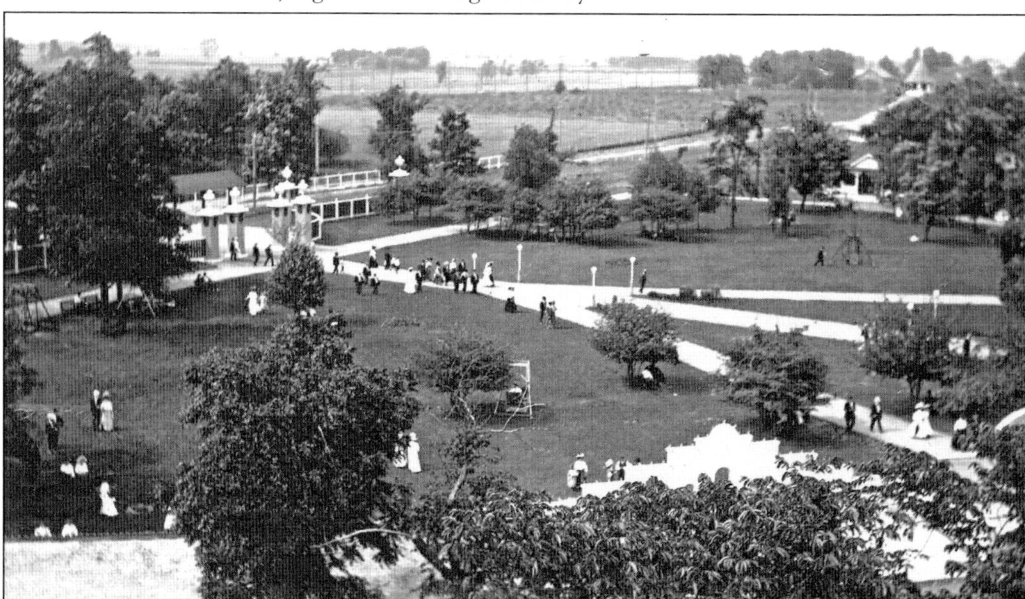

In order to encourage trolley passenger traffic on weekends, interurban companies established amusement parks. Riverview Park, later renamed Fox River Park, was located in Oswego Township just south of Montgomery. This bird's-eye view shows the trolley station and the main gates. The park drew thousands on weekends to enjoy picnicking, a roller coaster, lectures, and other entertainment. The park closed with the demise of the trolley and became the site of the Western Electric factory.

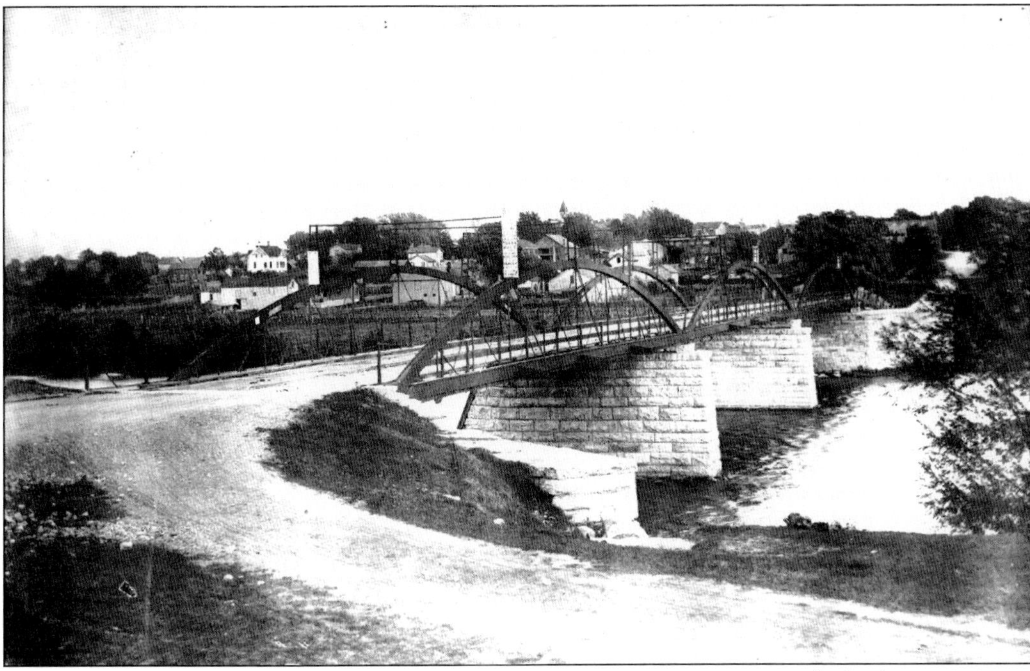

By 1867, the timber frame bridge across the Fox River at Oswego, originally built in 1848, and rebuilt after being demolished several times by floods, was badly deteriorated. Oswego Township paid the King Bridge Company of Canton, Ohio, $17,000 to build this iron-tied arch bridge on native limestone piers.

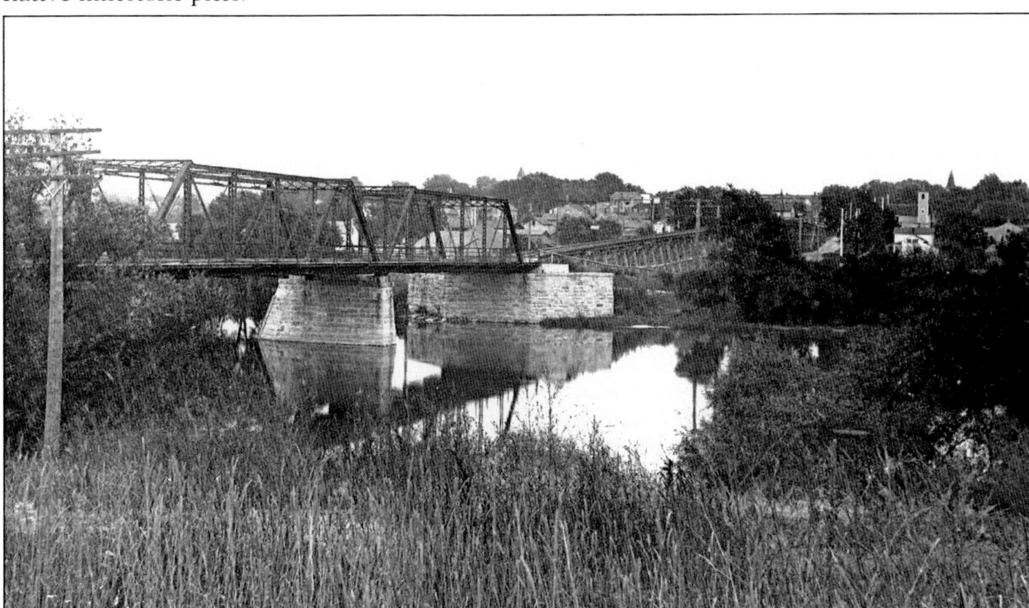

The old tied arch bridge was not sturdy enough to carry the new interurban line across the Fox River at Oswego, so this iron-box truss bridge replaced it in 1900 using the original limestone piers. The trolley trestle across the Chicago Burlington and Quincy Railroad line is visible at the east end of the bridge.

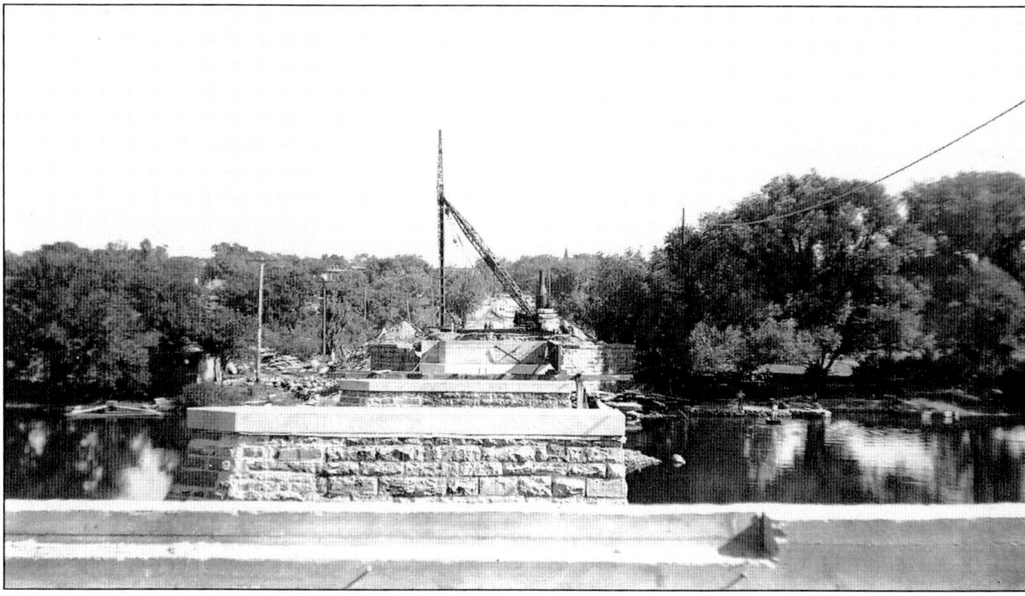

In 1937, the old box truss bridge had become obsolete due to more numerous, larger, and faster vehicles. The old bridge was dismantled by State of Illinois crews in the summer of 1937, and the old piers were enlarged to carry the wider span across the river. While the bridge was closed, residents used the old ford located just above the mouth of Waubonsie Creek.

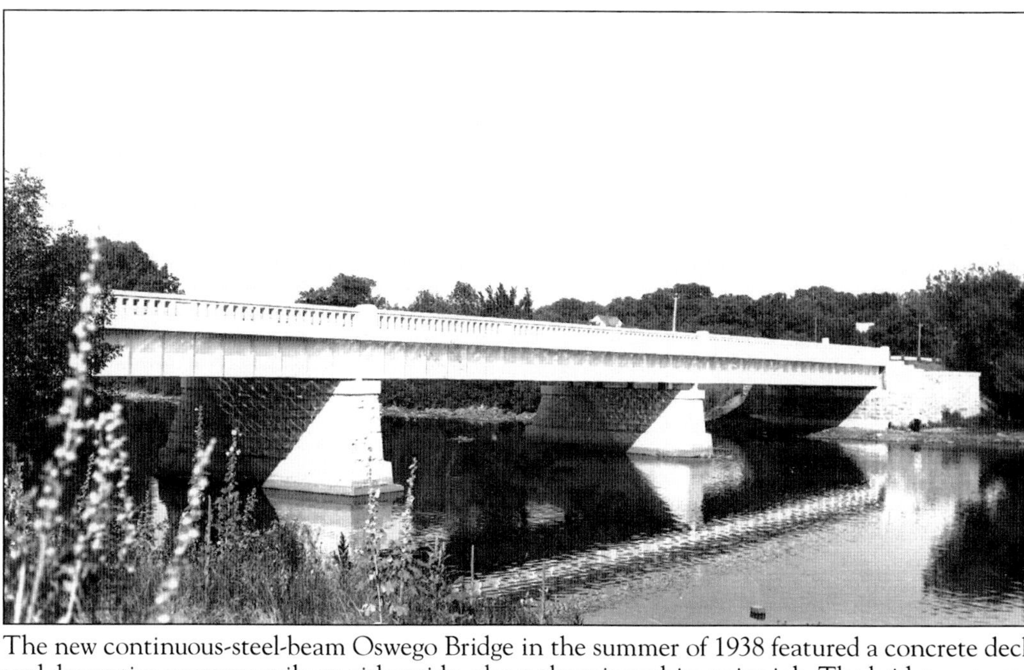

The new continuous-steel-beam Oswego Bridge in the summer of 1938 featured a concrete deck and decorative concrete rails on either side, plus a gleaming white paint job. The bridge was used for vehicle traffic until 1993, when it was replaced by a new four-lane bridge. The old bridge and its historic piers remain standing, however, renamed the Hudson Crossing Bridge Park.

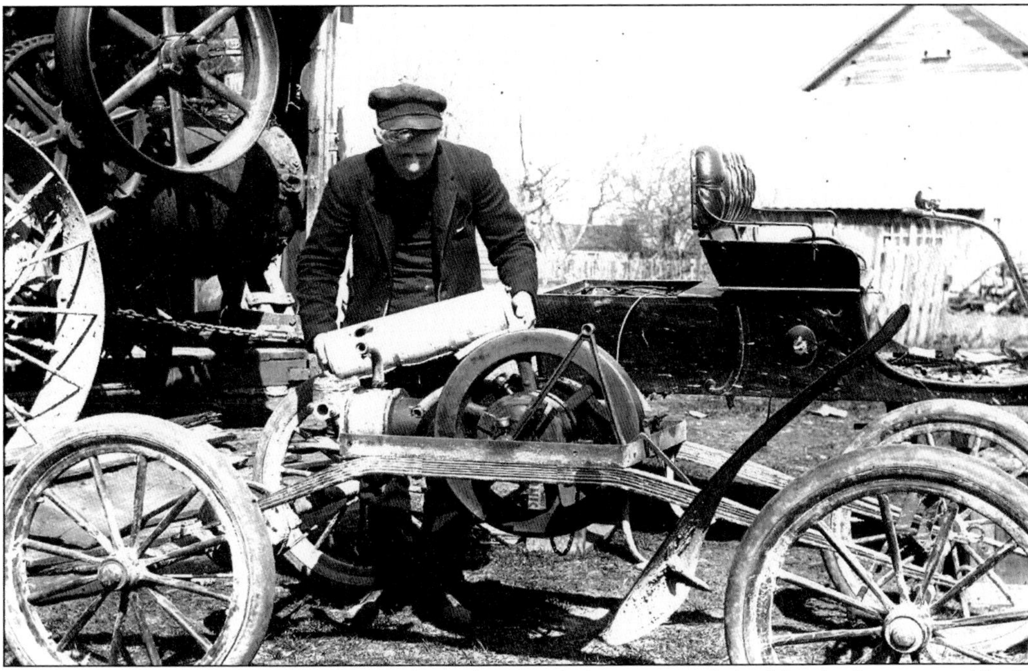

Automobile hobbyist Clarence Smith tinkers with his automobile (the body sits on blocks behind him) in this photograph taken by Irvin Haines about 1905. Oswego's first automobile was assembled from purchased and homemade parts by A. P. Werve in October 1903.

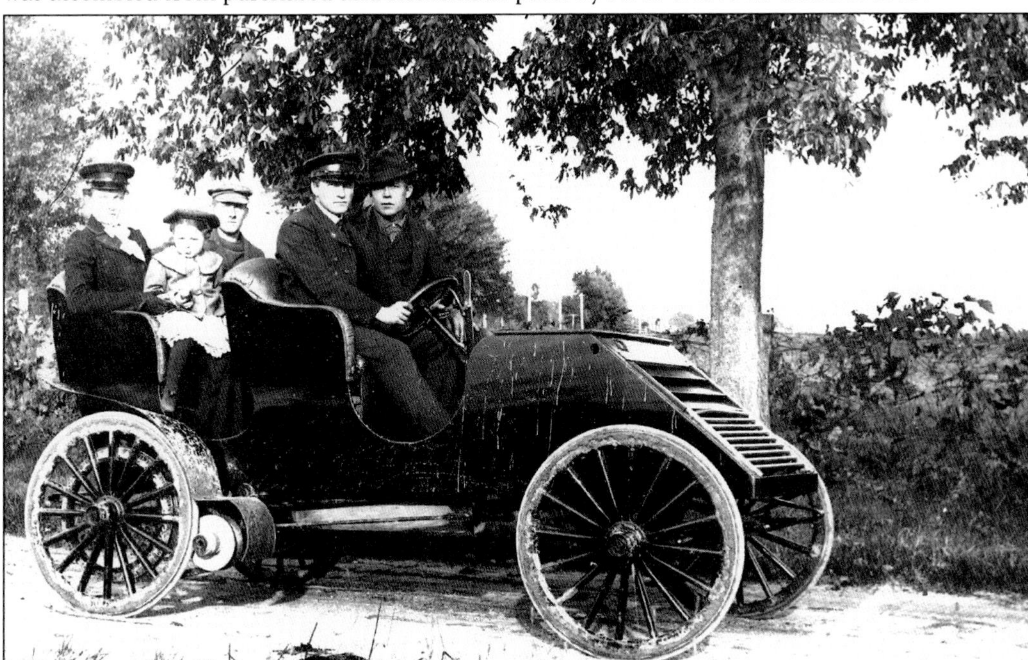

Oswego jeweler A. P. Werve sits proudly (and well uniformed) at the controls of his homemade automobile in 1906 near Oswego. In the backseat are his wife, Antionio Werve, plus their daughter and fellow auto hobbyist Clarence Smith. Next to Werve is John Varner. Werve used a gasoline boat engine to power his sturdy-looking automobile.

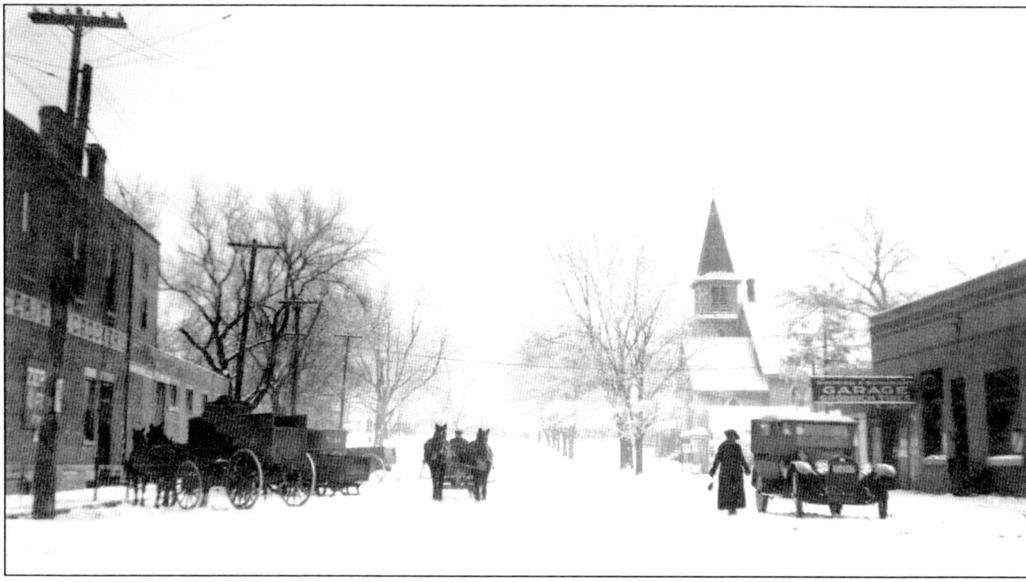

In the winter of 1914, Washington Street in Oswego was cloaked in snow. A horse-drawn bobsled proceeds west past the Burkhart garage in this image, and a women gets ready to enter an automobile as the transition from horse-and-buggy days to the era of the automobile got underway.

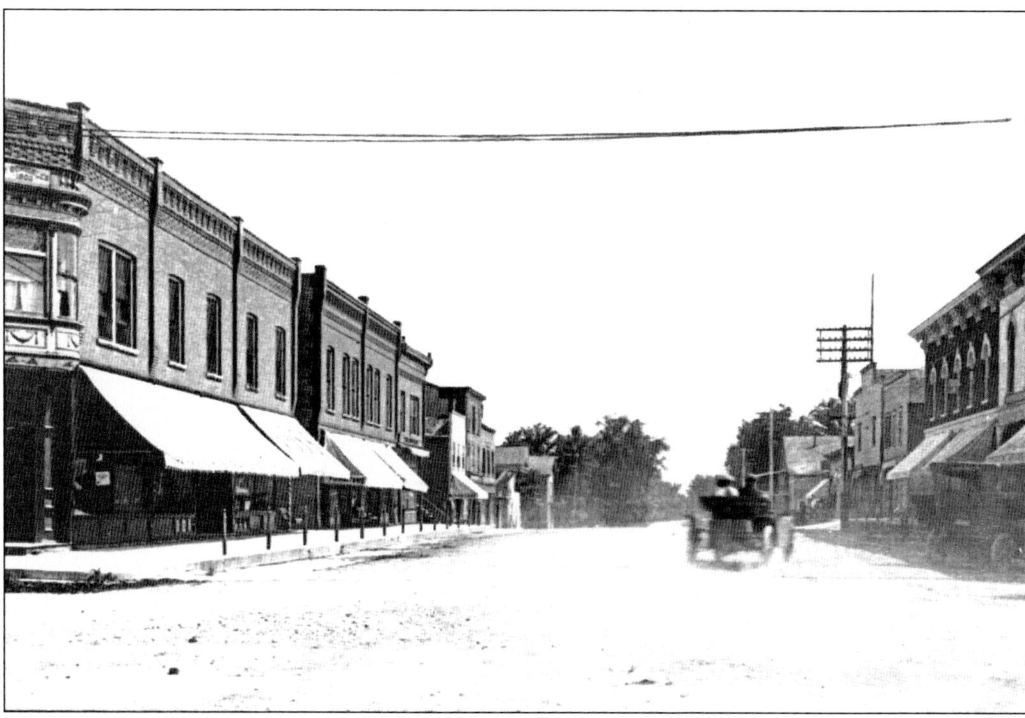

An automobile heads south on Main Street at speed about 1914, past empty hitching posts lining the curb. Main Street was not paved until about 1930. The dust was calmed by sprinkling the street periodically with oil during the summer months until it was finally paved.

Five

SCHOOL DAYS

The first school buildings in Oswego Township were built even before the first churches.

Education was considered vital by 19th century society so that citizens could participate knowledgeably in government at all levels.

The first school in Oswego Township was reportedly held in an old log cabin that stood near the former site of Chief Waubonsee's summer camp, along present-day Illinois Route 25, just north of Waubonsie Creek. The first teacher for that school in 1836 was reportedly George Washington Kellogg, whose descendants still live in the township.

During that era, funding public schools through property taxes had yet to be approved. As a result, schools were funded through subscriptions, with the parents of the students joining to support the buildings and teachers.

Then in 1850, the Illinois General Assembly approved the use of property taxes to finance public schools. The Old Stone School was built at Tyler and Monroe Streets in Oswego that same year and did duty for nearly 40 years.

Meanwhile, in the township's rural areas, farm families joined to establish local one-room school districts. More than 20 country school districts were established in the area now served by the Oswego School District. Ideally students had to walk no farther than about a mile and a half to attend class. Interestingly enough, that is the same radius from school Illinois students are still expected to walk to class.

Consolidation of the country schools into larger schools in town began in the 1940s and was finally completed with the closure of Church School just across the border in Wheatland Township after the 1957–1958 school year.

From the beginning of Oswego's educational history with one log school in 1836, the Oswego School District has grown, as of the start of the 2008–2009 school year, to 2 high schools, 5 junior highs, 14 elementary schools, and an enrollment of some 15,000 students.

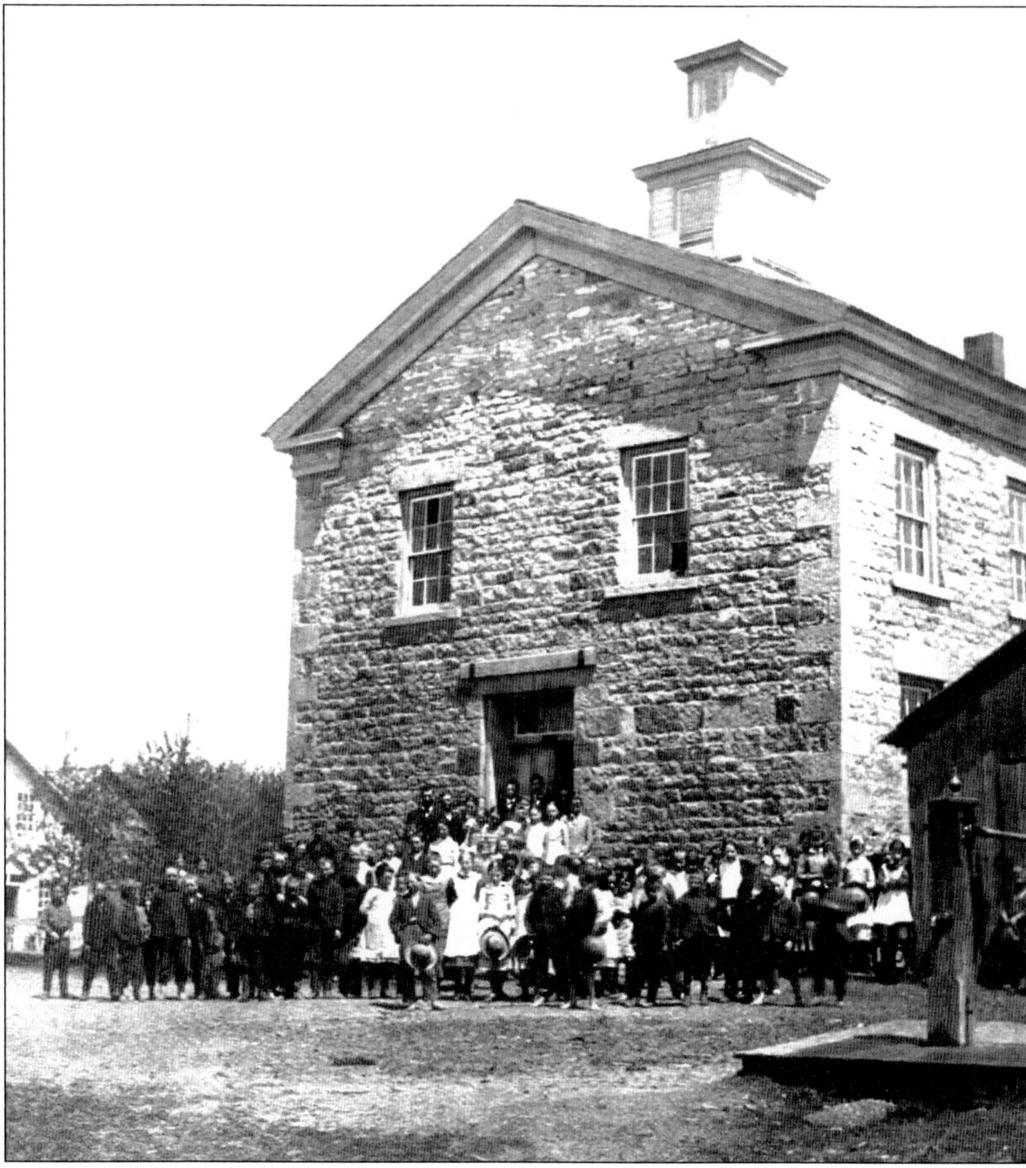

The Old Stone School and its entire student body are seen here in a stereo card probably produced about 1880. Although some high school classes were taught, there were no formal graduations. The building was gutted by fire in March 1885, and students finished out the year in the old Kendall County Courthouse, located on the block bounded by Madison, Jackson, Monroe, and Jefferson Streets.

The old courthouse was torn down during the spring and summer of 1885, and this two-story brick grade and high school completed for about $10,000 on the block now the site of the Oswego Community Bank and the Oswego Post Office. High school classes were held upstairs; elementary classes were held on the main floor.

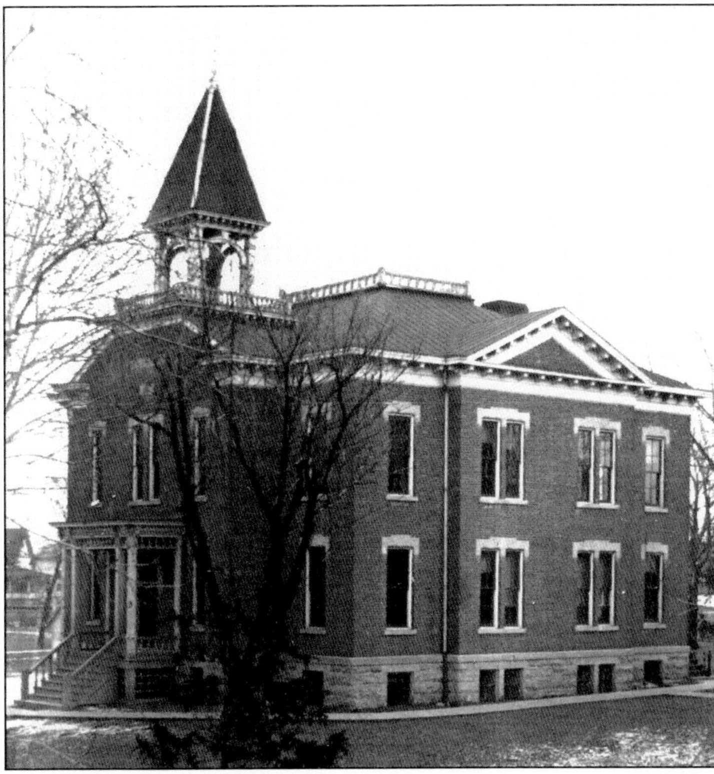

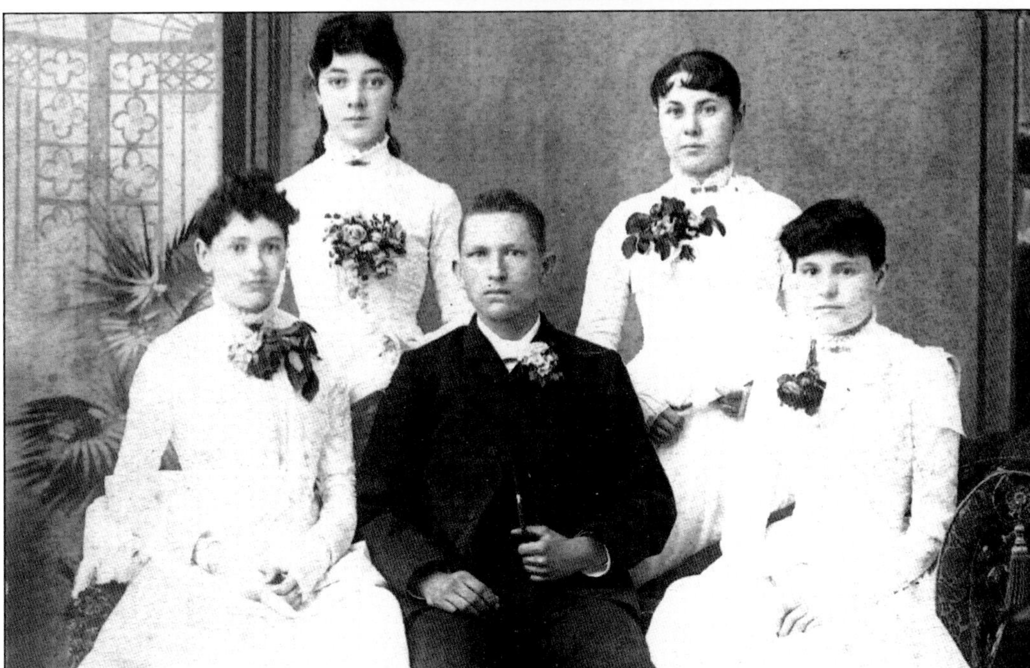

The new school, built of dark red brick, opened in February 1886, and the first graduating class of five students was honored on June 10, 1887. Oswego High School's first graduating class included Addie Kimball, Mamie Smith, Addie Wormley, Frank Lippold, and Bessie Armstrong.

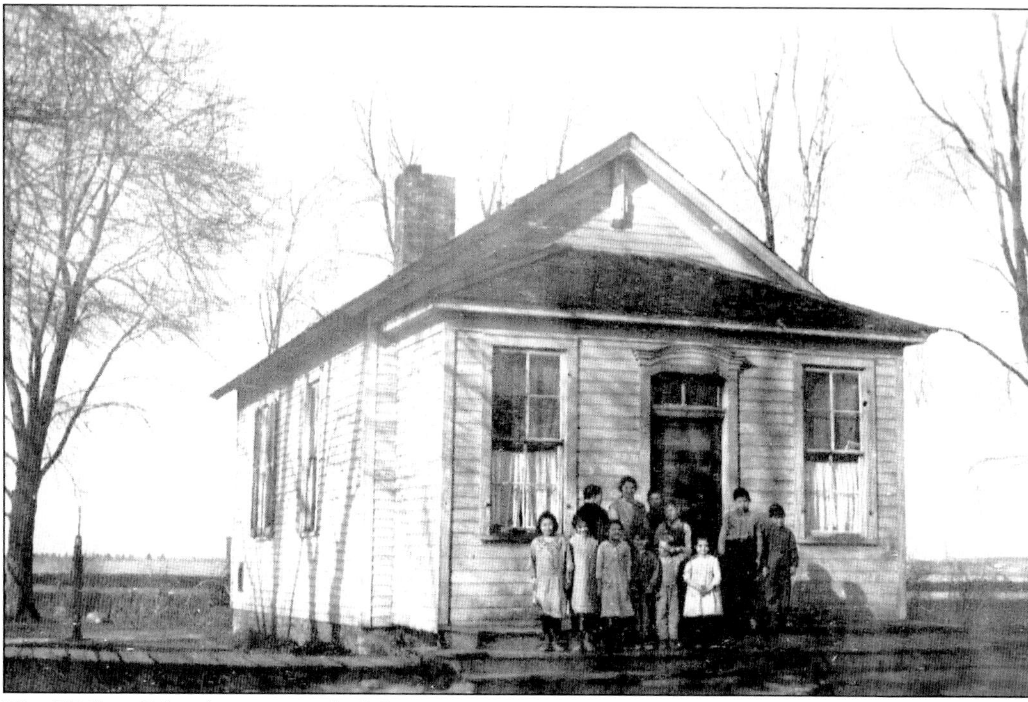

The Walker School was typical of the one-room country schools that dotted Oswego Township. It attracted students from a roughly two-mile radius from its location at the corner of Plainfield and Simons roads south of Oswego. The building, remodeled into a private home, still stands.

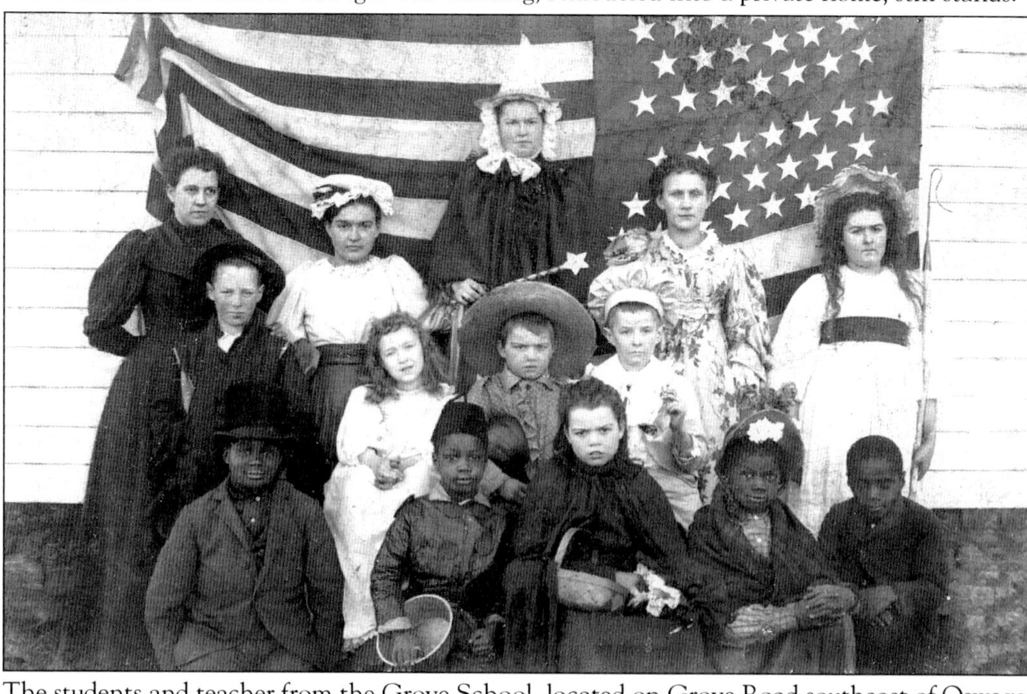

The students and teacher from the Grove School, located on Grove Road southeast of Oswego, are ready with their homemade costumes to enjoy a Mother Goose unit at school in this delightful photograph taken about 1885.

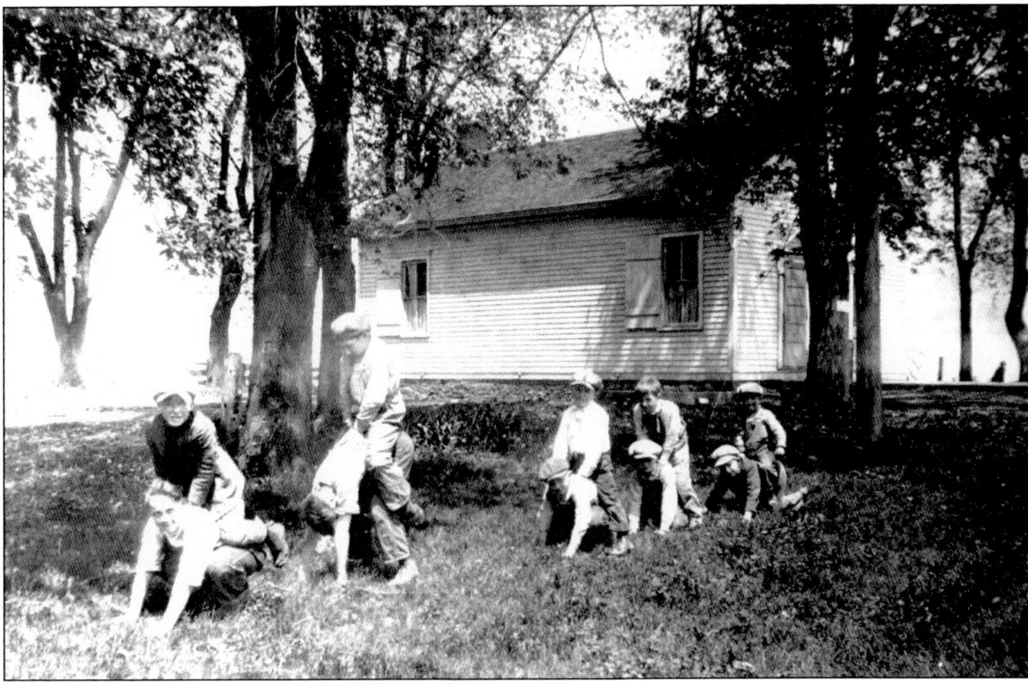

No fancy playground equipment was available at the Bronk School at the southernmost point of the modern Oswego School District. Instead students enjoyed games including leapfrog as they took a welcomed recess during a typical school day.

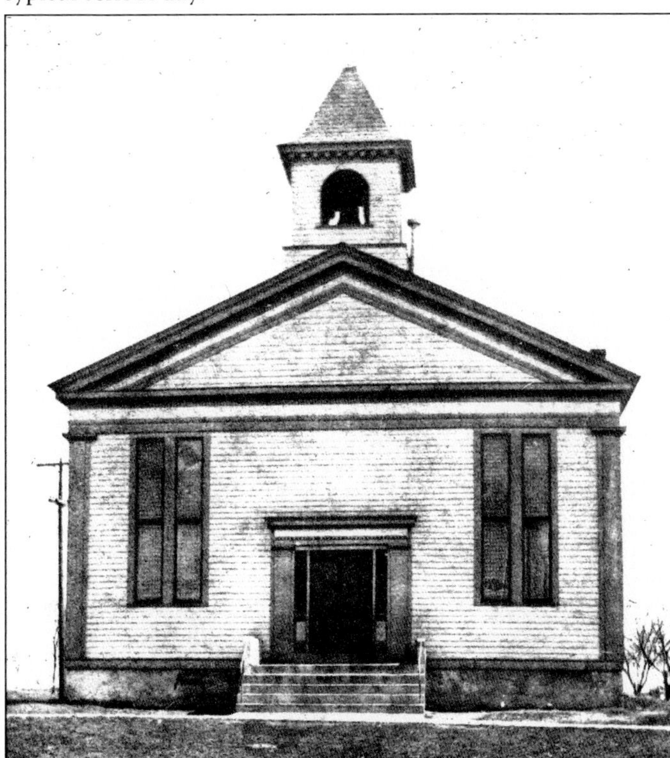

With the growth in students, another school was needed by Oswego in 1915. Fortunately, the old Methodist-Episcopal Church, dating to 1850, was available for sale. The school district purchased the building and modified it into a one-room school for students living in and nearby Oswego. Fred Holzhueter took this snapshot of the building in 1919.

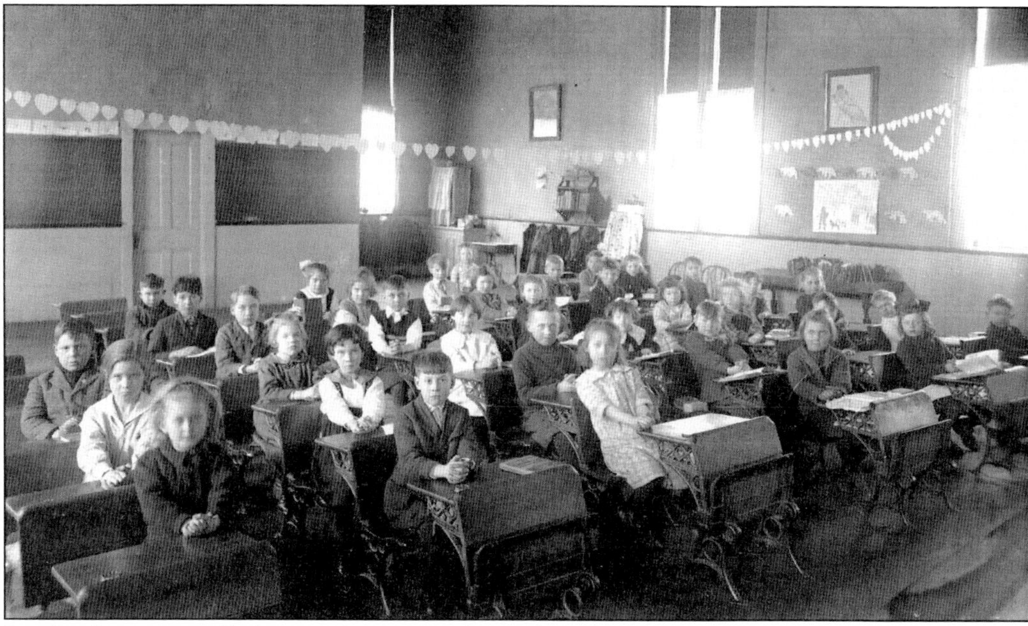

Inside what eventually became known as the Little White School in February 1919, students in first through third grades sat patiently for their photograph. The students have decorated the room in preparation for Valentines Day. Coats are hung in the back of the room near the sink.

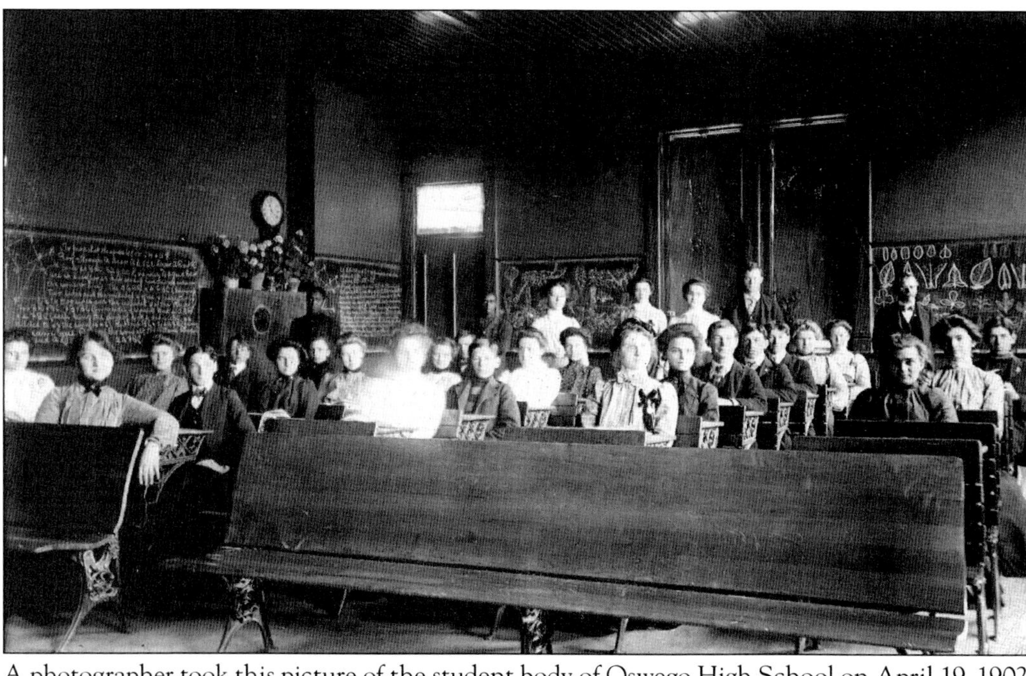

A photographer took this picture of the student body of Oswego High School on April 19, 1902. Among those standing around the back of the room are Ferdinand Smith, who became Oswego High's first African American graduate in 1903, and his sister Frances, who was the first African American female graduate in 1906.

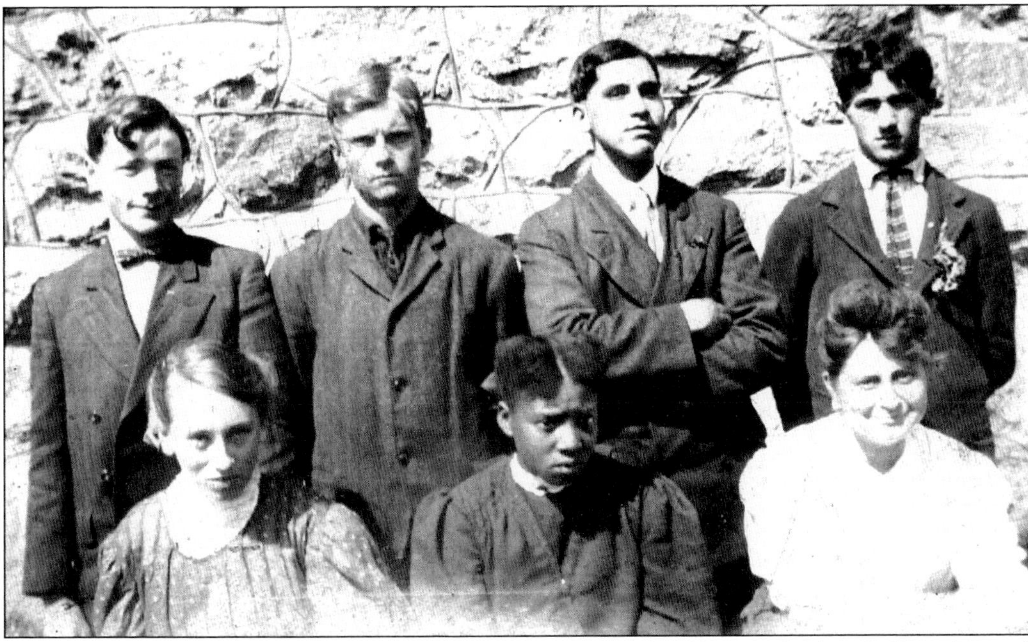

The Oswego High class of 1906, including, from left to right, (first row) Elsie Collins (Young), Frances Smith, and Allie Wold; (second row) John Condon, Louis Young, Cass Figge, and Oscar Shoger, seems satisfied that their high school careers are nearly over.

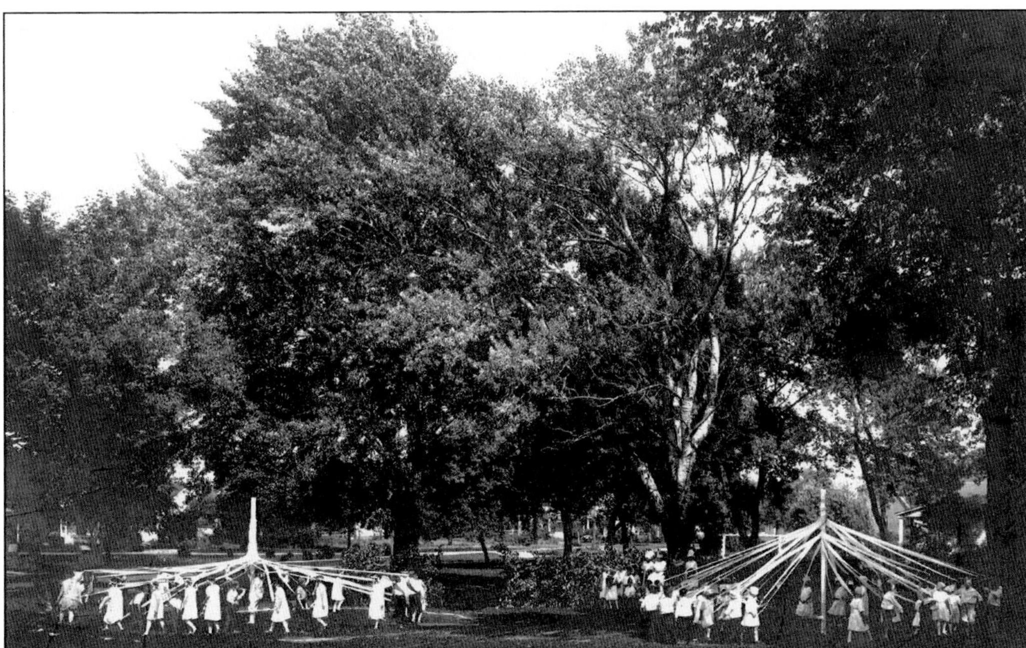

Elementary students at Oswego's Red Brick School celebrate May Day by marching around maypoles set up on the school grounds in this photograph taken sometime during the 1920s. The Oswego High School football field was on the same site as the school, located along the Jefferson Street side of the block.

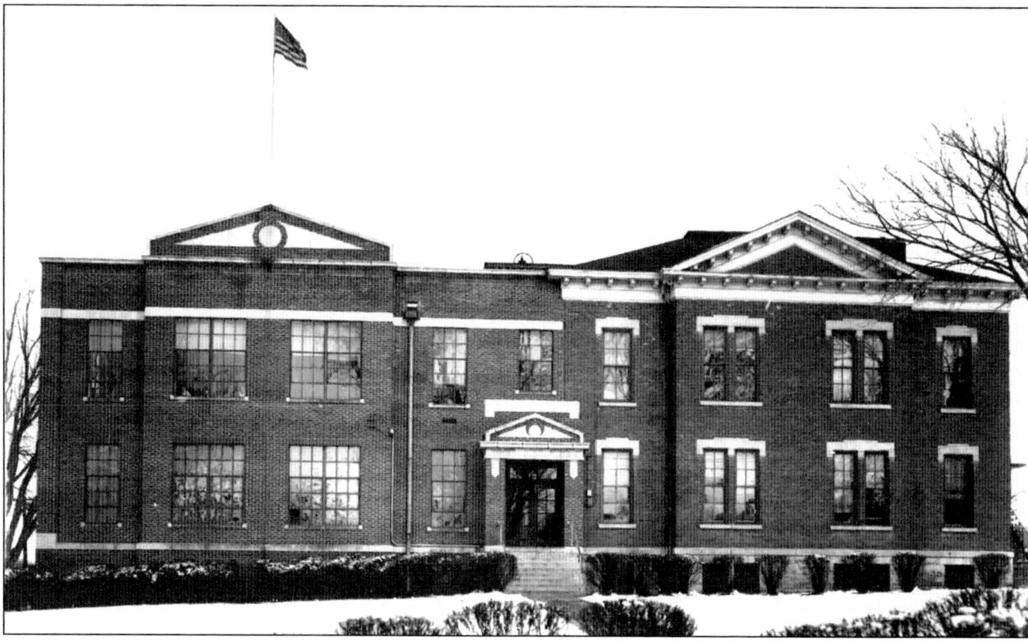

Here is Oswego High School, also known as the Red Brick School, as it looked in 1939 with the gymnasium and classroom addition (left) to the original building. The gym occupied the ground floor of the new addition, along with locker rooms. The wing was added following a successful referendum in 1926 at a cost of $22,000.

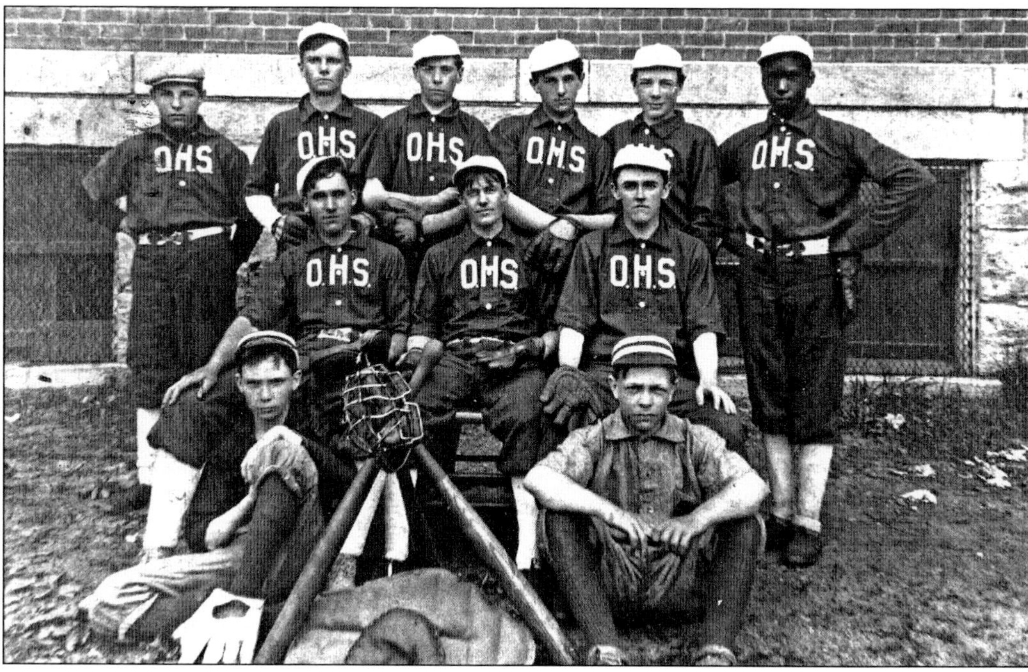

Sports have been a part of high school life in Oswego for decades. The 1907 Oswego High School baseball team included, from left to right, (first row) Adelbert Richards and David Young; (second row) Cass Figge, Fred Willis, and Harold Russell; (third row) Maurice Leigh, Louie Young, Milton Hem, Oscar Shoger, John Condon, and Robert Smith.

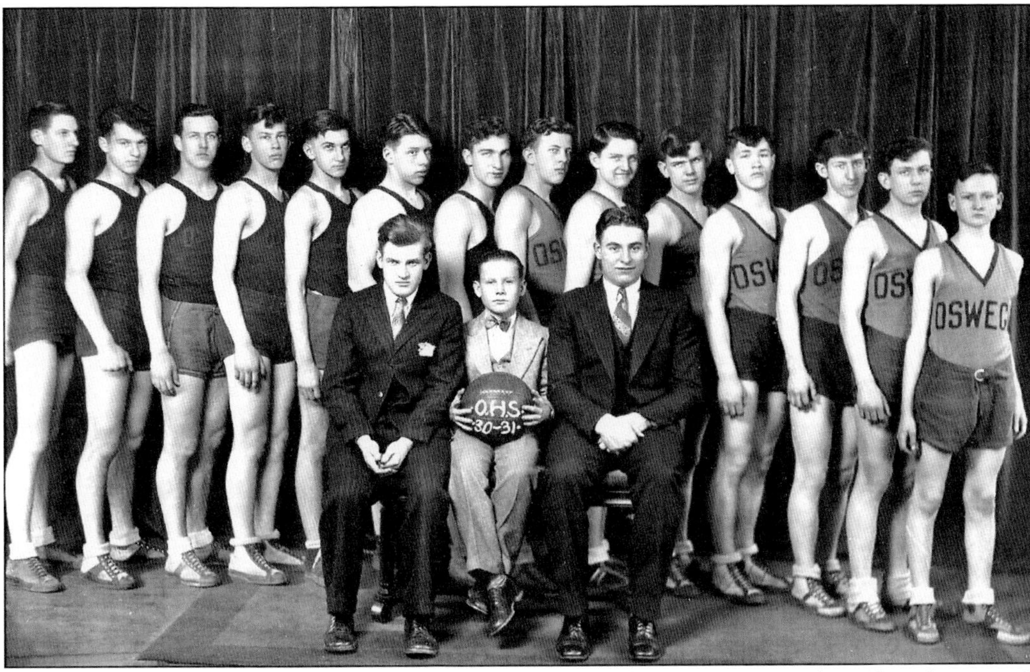

Oswego High School's 1930–1931 cage squad was ready for competition when this photograph was taken in the Red Brick School gym. Members included Robert Schmidt, Franklin Pearce, Leonard Hafenrichter, Ford Lippold, Clyde Johnson, James Vinson, Harlan Peshia, Roland Jensen, Gerald Seaton, Marion Osborne, Paul Shoger, Donald Lippold, Earl Henley, and Harland Collins. Sitting in front are mangers Roy Jennings (left) and Burman Etsinger (center) and coach Marvin Marquardt.

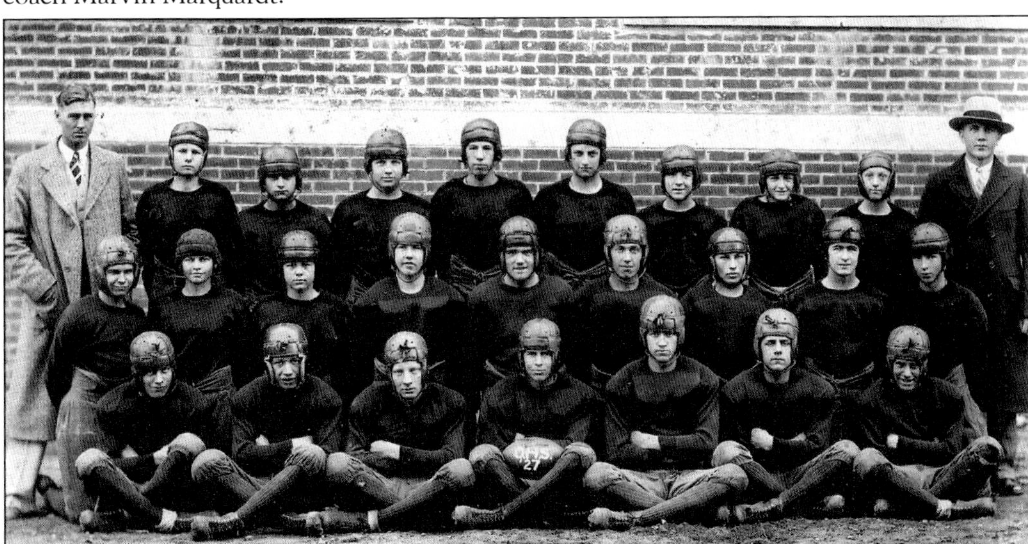

The members of the 1927 Oswego High School football team and their coaches look eager in this photograph, as well they might. The team finished their 1927 season with an undefeated record. Team starters included Carl Hafenrichter, Melvin Parkhurst, Merrill Wolf, Arnold Bower, Orville Skeen, Warren Norris, John Minich, Franklin Pierce, Frank Clauser, Roswell Howard, Barney Brown, Alec Harvey, and Alan Schlapp.

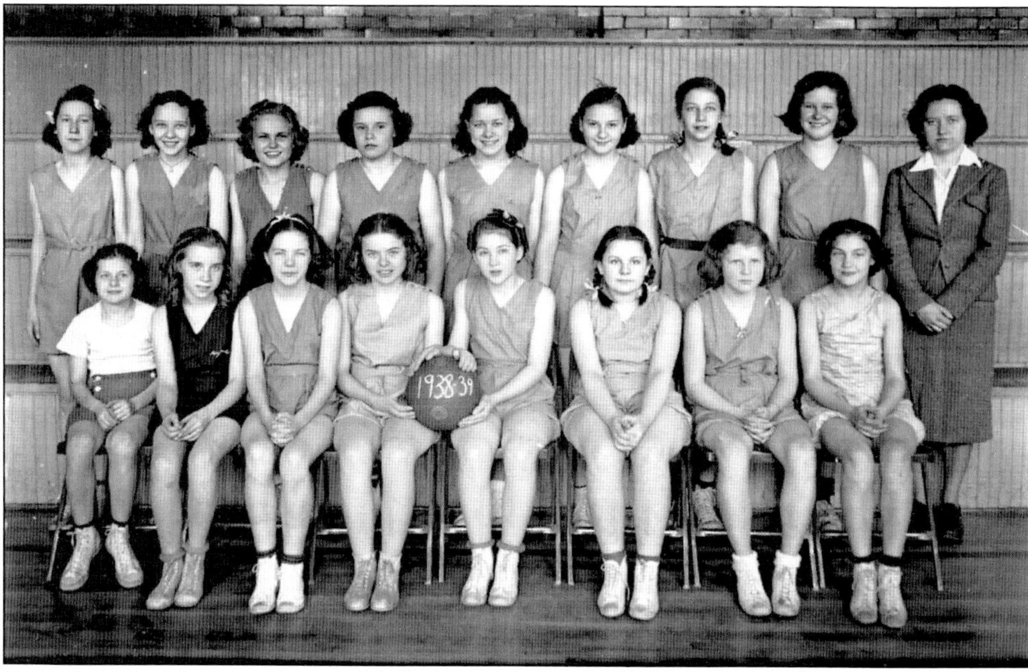

Formal girls' athletics at Oswego High School did not really start until the 1970s. But the 1939 Oswego girls' basketball team played a number of games with other towns. Here they are ready for a game in the gym at the Red Brick School.

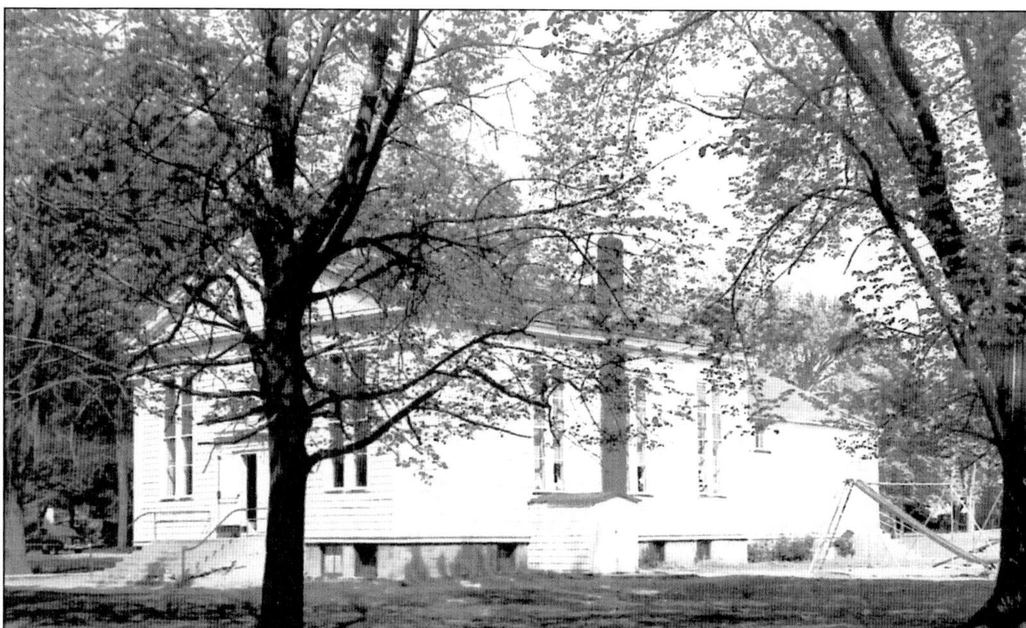

By the 1940s, the Little White School had gotten its coat of white paint. In 1930, the main room had been divided into two classrooms and in 1934, the building was raised, and a basement dug beneath it. In 1936, a larger entry hallway and third classroom were added to the back of the building. The building, now restored as a community museum, was last used as classroom space in 1964.

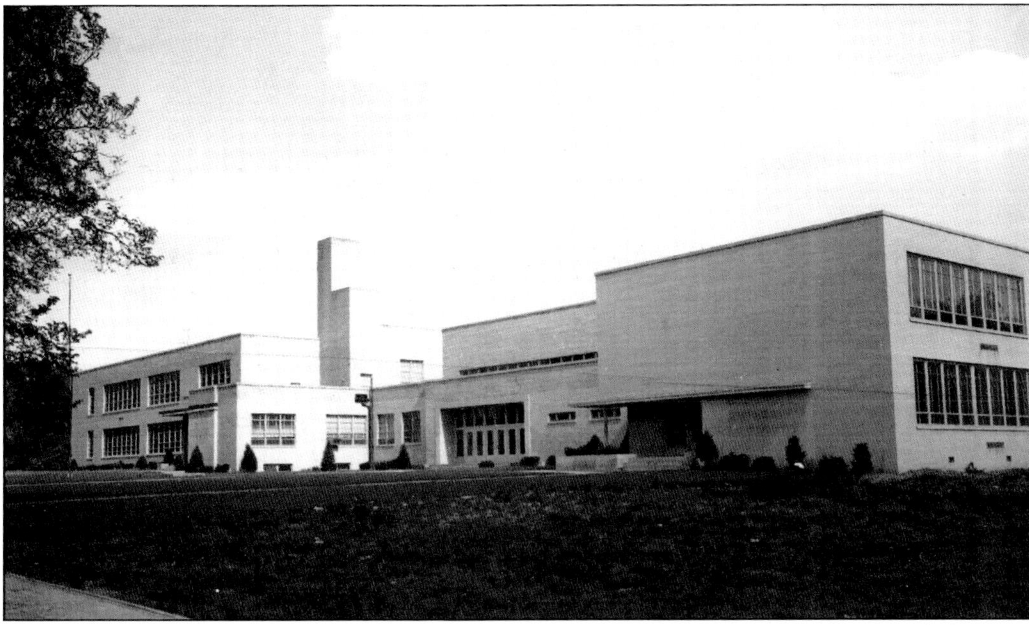

With growth beginning in the area after World War II, more classroom space was needed. A new high school was begun on property on Franklin Street at Washington Street and finished in the spring of 1951. The junior high addition in the right foreground was added in 1955. It served as a junior high school from 1964 to 2008, when it was converted into administration offices and special classroom space.

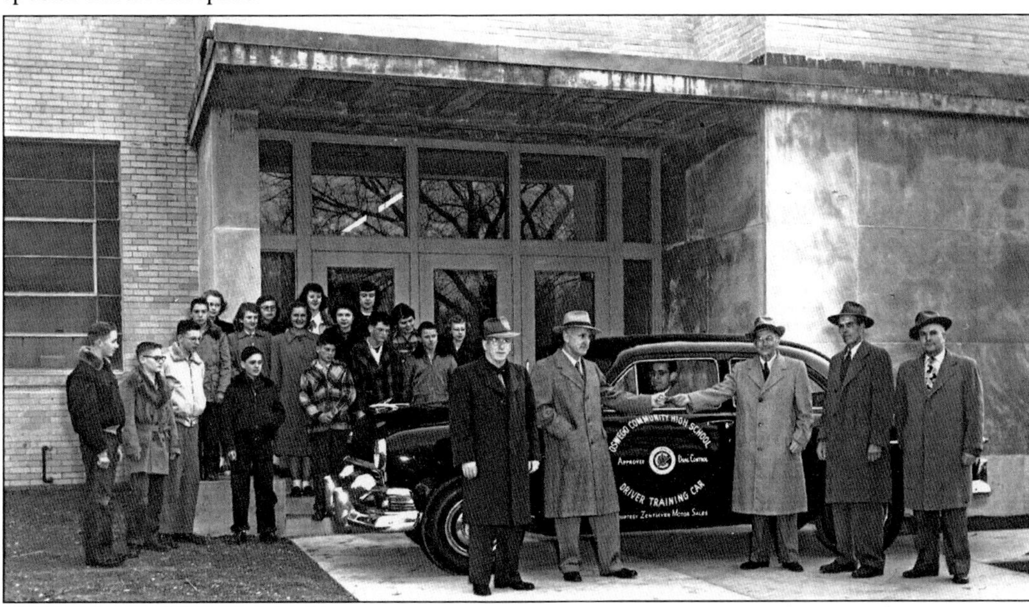

After moving into the new high school in 1951, new programs, like driver's education, were possible. Here Earl Zentmyer of Oswego's Zentmyer Ford (fourth from right) hands the keys for a new Ford driver's training car to school board secretary Charles Schultz as school board member Jack Cherry (second from right) and school superintendent T. Lloyd Traughber (right) look on. Driver's education teacher and Oswego High School coach Herb Hasenyager sits at the wheel of the new Ford.

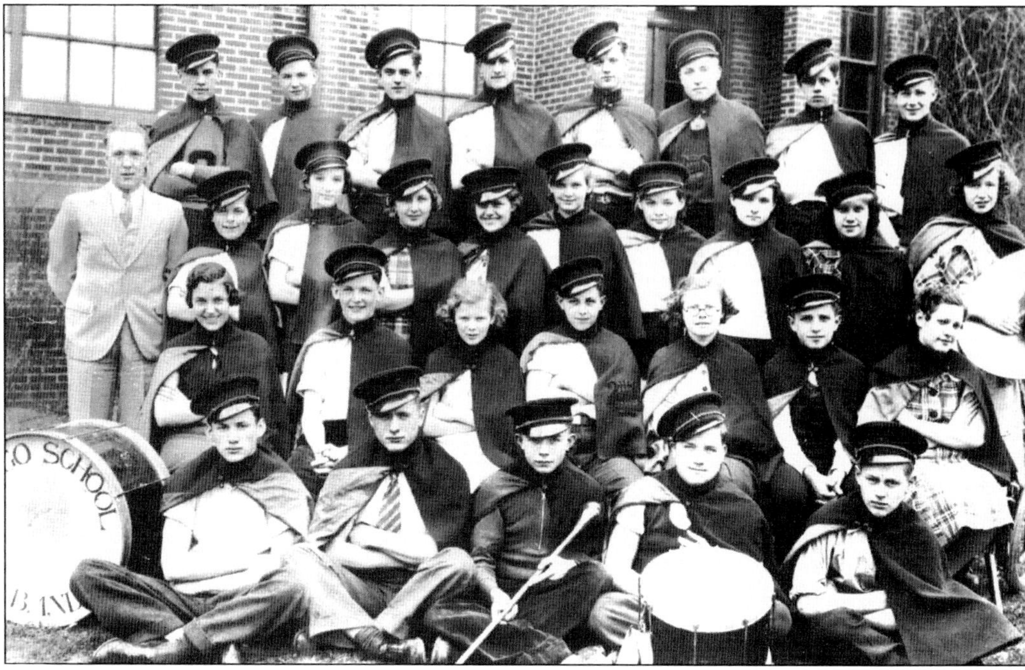

Reeve R. Thompson (at left in suit) established the Oswego School District's band and choral programs after he arrived in the district in the late 1920s. He was responsible for creating the marching band program and is seen here pictured with the high school marching band in 1936. The bass drum in this photograph is now on exhibit at the Little White School Museum.

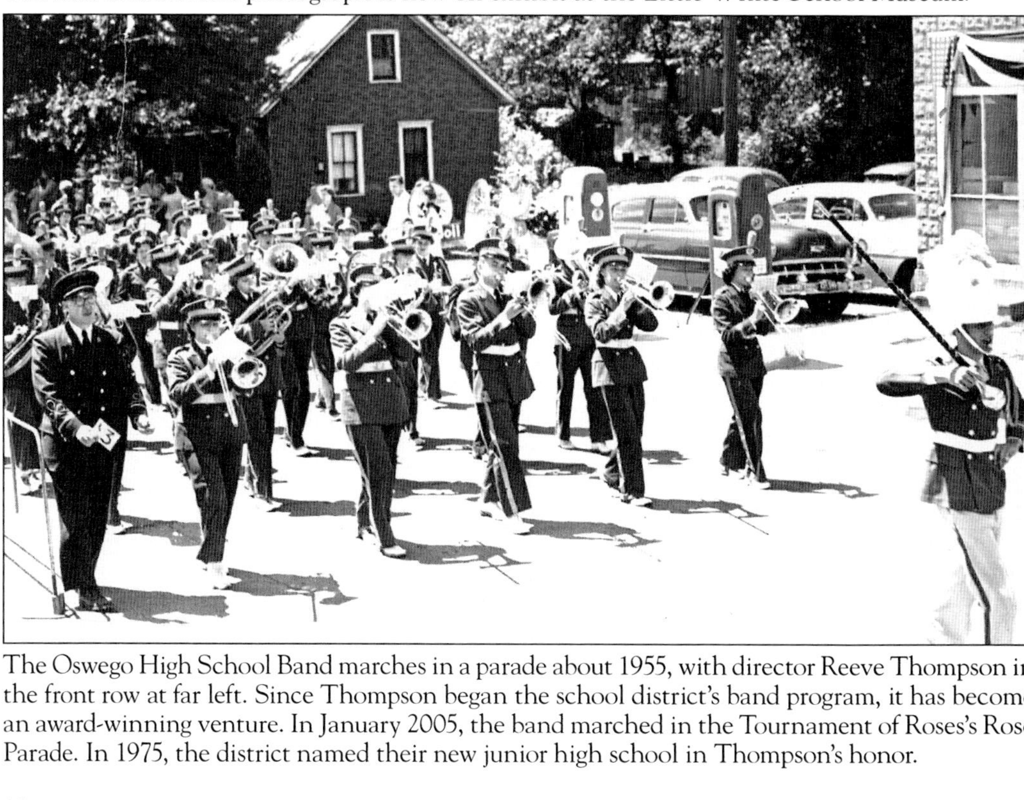

The Oswego High School Band marches in a parade about 1955, with director Reeve Thompson in the front row at far left. Since Thompson began the school district's band program, it has become an award-winning venture. In January 2005, the band marched in the Tournament of Roses's Rose Parade. In 1975, the district named their new junior high school in Thompson's honor.

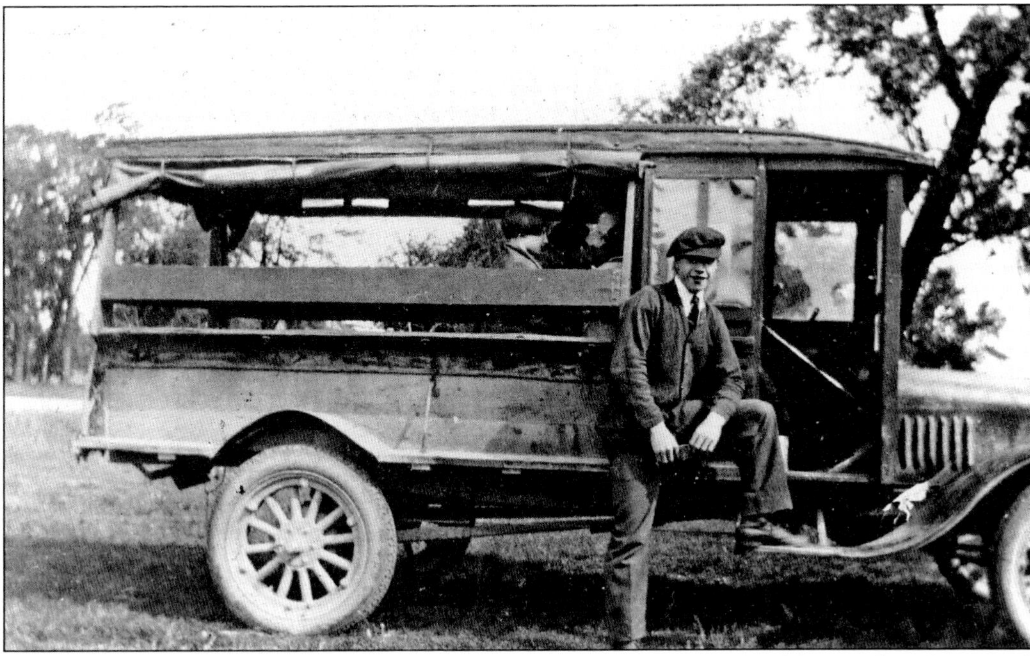

Alex Harvey stands beside the Oswego School District's first ever school bus in this photograph taken about 1929. The bus was used to bring high school students into town. Sitting in the bus ready to head for school is Harvey's sister Virginia.

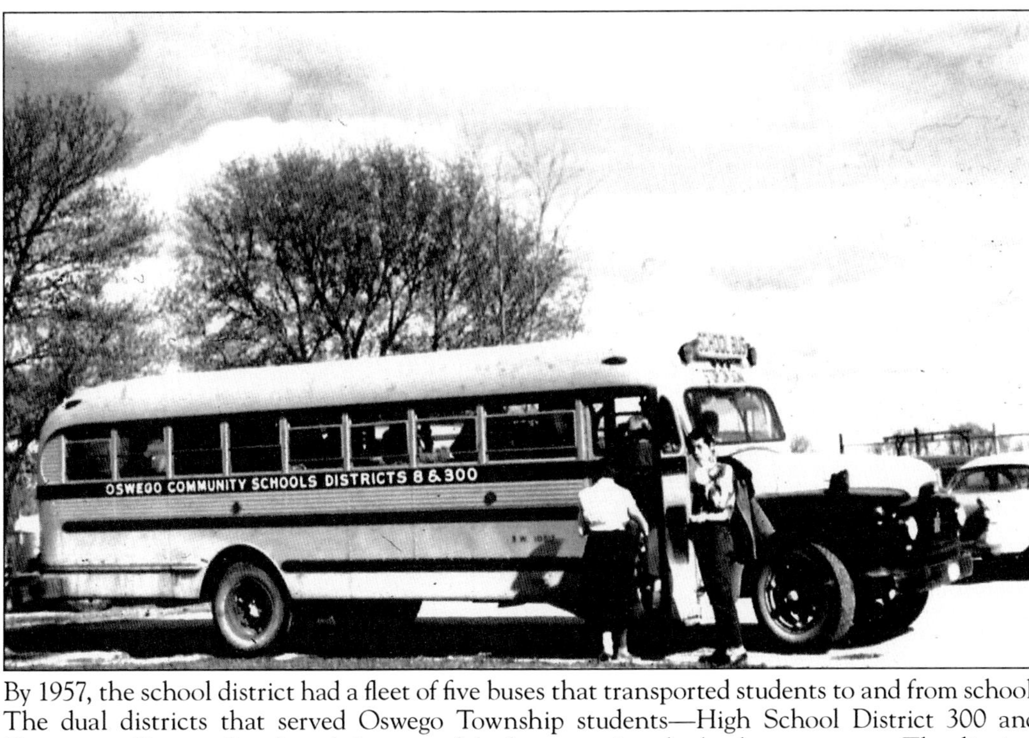

By 1957, the school district had a fleet of five buses that transported students to and from school. The dual districts that served Oswego Township students—High School District 300 and Elementary District 8—shared the cost of the buses, easing the load on taxpayers. The districts consolidated into Oswego Community Consolidated School District 308 in 1961.

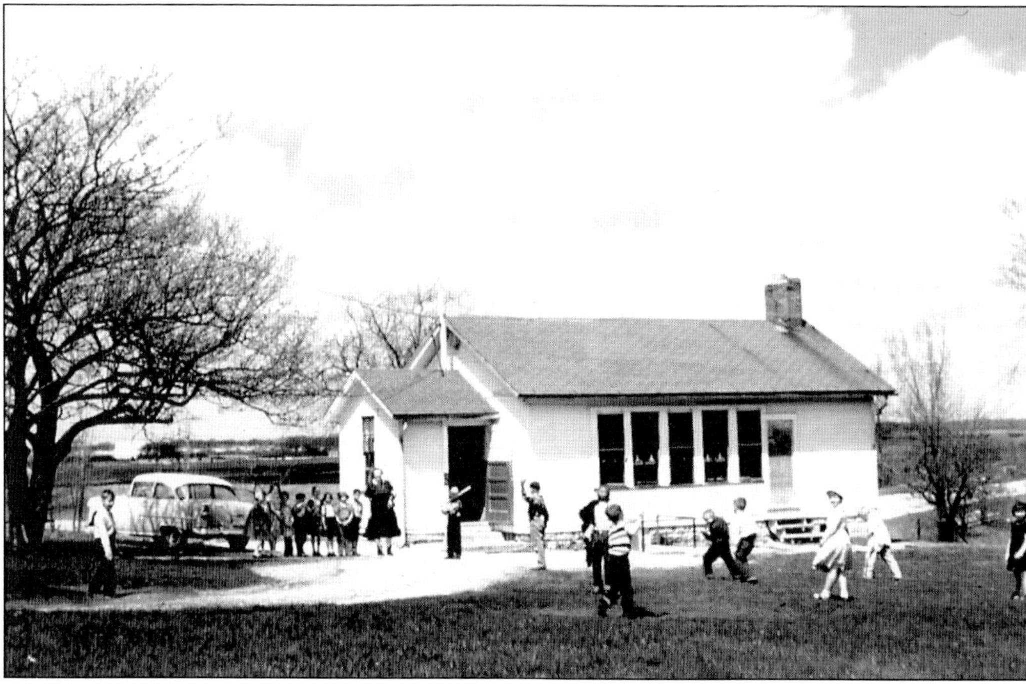

Willow Hill School at the intersection of U.S. Route 34 and U.S. Route 30 was one of the last one-room schools in the Oswego School District to close. Here students enjoy a recess softball game under the watchful eye of teacher Gertrude Wormley Hefflefinger in the spring of 1958.

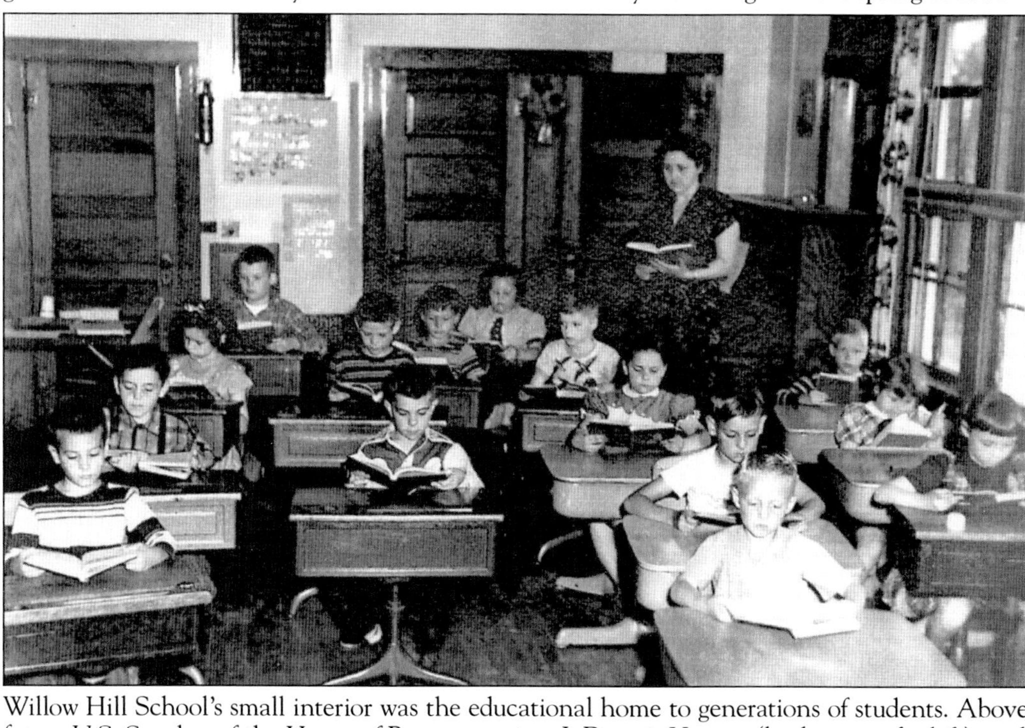

Willow Hill School's small interior was the educational home to generations of students. Above, future U.S. Speaker of the House of Representatives J. Dennis Hastert (back row at far left) reads with the rest of the students at the school about 1951 in this photograph by Everett Hafenrichter.

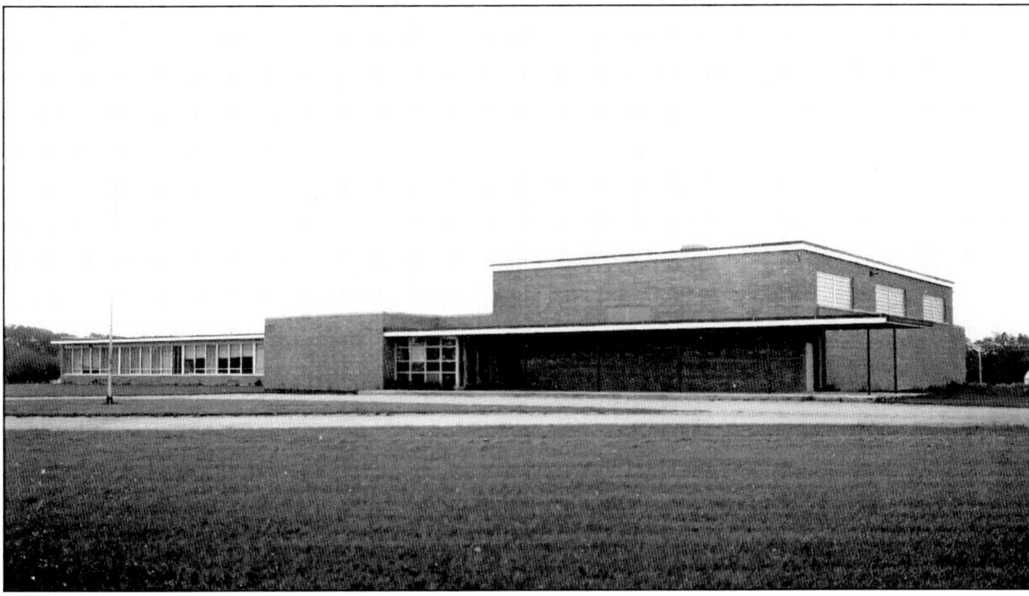

When it finally opened in the fall of 1958, East View School, located on Illinois Route 71 in Oswego, was the first new elementary school built in the village since the Red Brick School opened in 1886. Sixth grade student Diane Paydon submitted the winning name for the school.

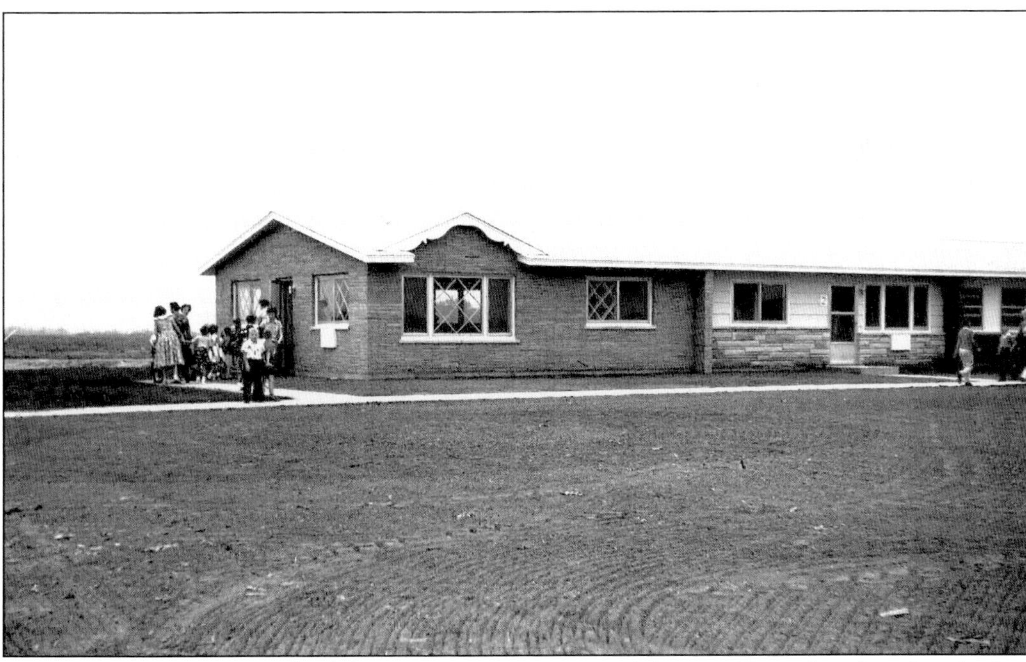

The sprawling Boulder Hill subdivision in unincorporated Oswego Township drew hundreds of new families starting in 1955. Classroom crowding in Oswego's schools was eased in 1960 when developer Don L. Dise offered space in the new Boulder Hill Apartments for classrooms. Here is the temporary school on opening day, September 2, 1959.

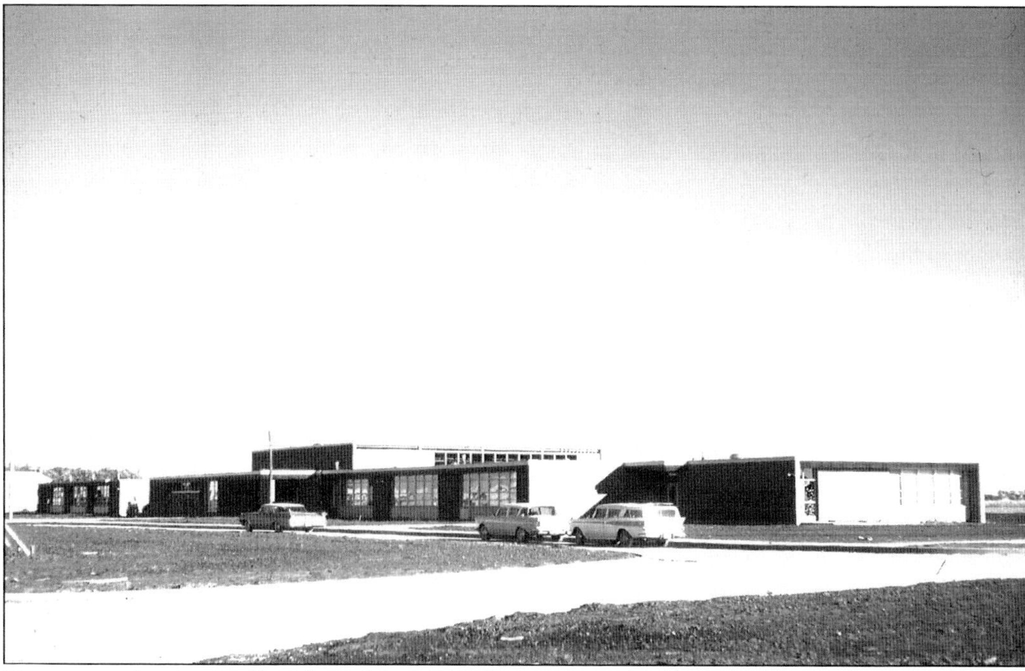

Using a combination of bonds authorized by the voters and cash contributions from Boulder Hill developer Don L. Dise, Boulder Hill School was built on a site Dise also donated on Boulder Hill Pass. The school was photographed on the first day of classes when it opened in September 1961, the district's second new elementary school in less than five years. As of 2008, the district has 14 elementary schools.

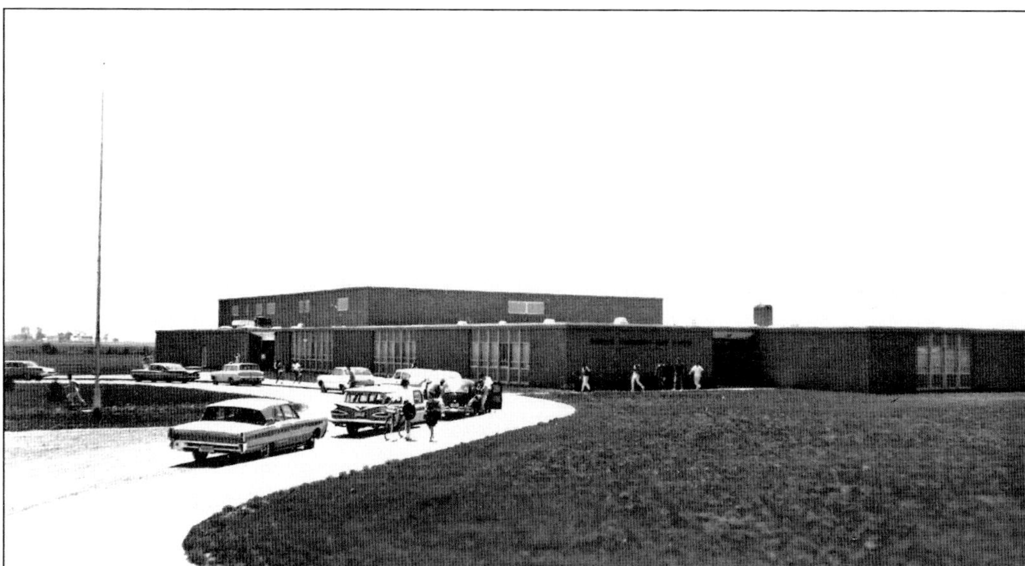

Although many community residents thought the high school finished in 1951 was too large and would never be filled with students, it was already overcrowded by 1960. A new Oswego High School, shown above shortly after it opened, was finished in the fall of 1964 and, with many additions, served the school district as its only high school until Oswego East High opened in the fall of 2004.

Six

Oswego Goes to War

Since it was settled in 1833, Oswego Township has sent soldiers to every war the United States has fought, starting with the Seminole War of 1836 in the swamps of Florida and extending to the current wars in Iraq and Afghanistan.

In 1846, at the outbreak of the Mexican War, torchlight parades were held in Oswego and meetings were held at the old frame schoolhouse located on Madison Street just south of the intersection with Van Buren Street. According to the Reverend E. W. Hicks's 1877 history of Kendall County, "A. R. Dodge and A. B. Smith spoke, but not many enlisted at first. During the following days, however, some fifty volunteers were obtained, and were known as 'Capt. Dodge's Company.'"

According to Hicks's account, the company was transported to Peoria with the help of local residents and then on to Alton, where they were mustered in. Members of the company reportedly fought at the Battle of Buena Vista before being mustered out.

When the Civil War burst upon the nation, torchlight parades were once again held in Oswego to drum up support for the war. About 10 percent of Kendall County's total population served in the Civil War, most in local companies recruited for the 36th and 127th Illinois Volunteer Infantry and the 4th Illinois Volunteer Cavalry. Civil War heroics netted Oswego Township its only Medal of Honor winner—and to this day, Robinson B. Murphy remains Kendall County's lone recipient of the nation's highest award for valor.

Area men fought in the Spanish-American War, and many Oswego area men and women volunteered or were drafted during World War I. After the war, the local Red Cross unit in Oswego continued to make items that were sent to war refugees instead of service personnel.

World War II was also heavily supported by Kendall County men and women. Capt. Slade Cutter was one of the most successful submarine commanders of the war, earning several Navy Crosses for his efforts.

After the conclusion of the last world war, Oswego Township residents have continued to serve in Korea, Vietnam, and the new conflicts of the 21st century.

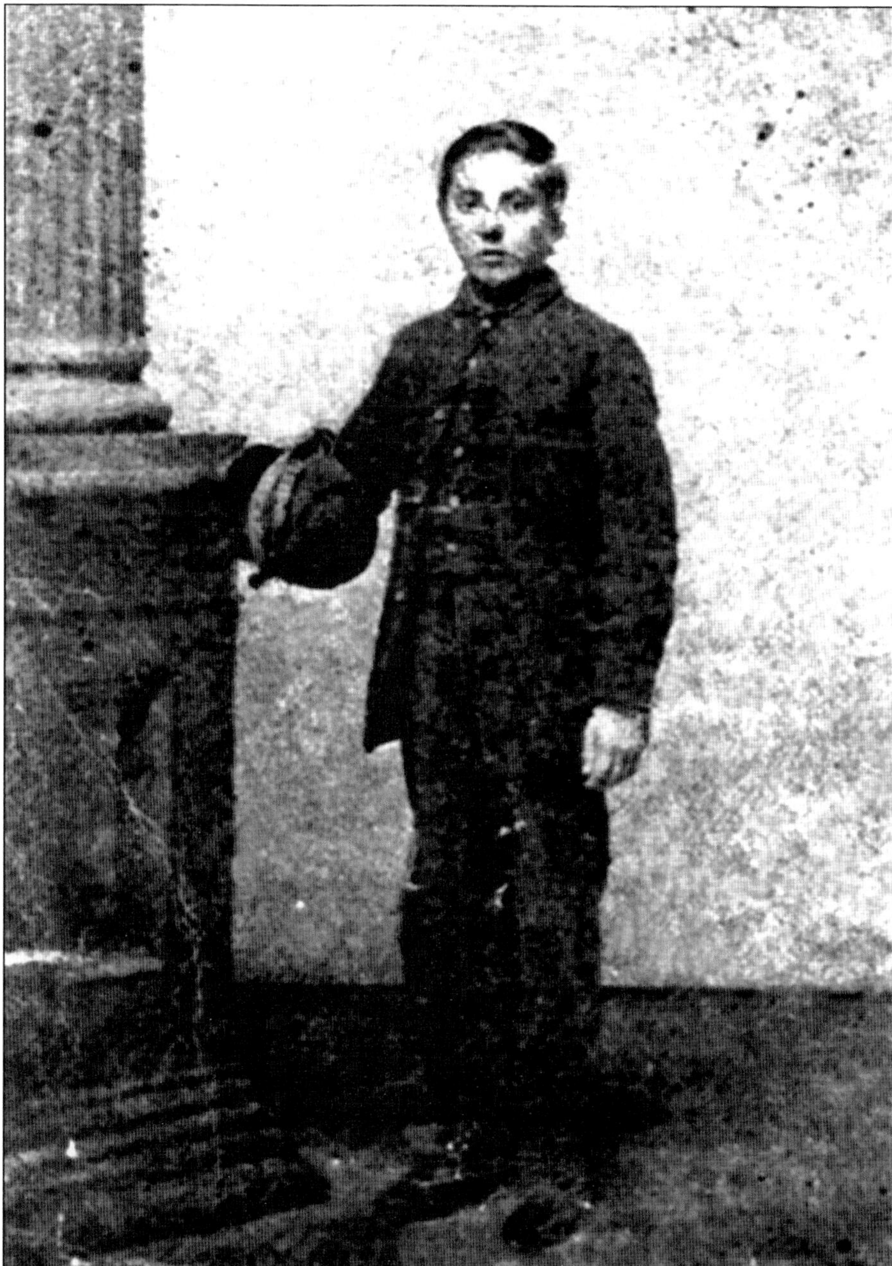

Robinson B. Murphy, then just 15, earned the Medal of Honor for his heroic actions during the Battle of Ezra Church near Atlanta on August 28, 1864. At just 13 years old, Murphy enlisted in the 127th Illinois Volunteer Infantry as a drummer boy with his father, local lawyer and politician Wright Murphy. By the time of the Battle of Ezra Church, Murphy was serving as an orderly on the staff of Gen. J. A. J. Lightburn. When Confederate Gen. John Bell Hood's army nearly broke the Union flank held by Murphy's old regiment, the 127th Illinois Volunteer Infantry, General Lightburn ordered the youngster to guide reserve troops to the trouble spot. And that he did, getting one horse shot from beneath him during the action. Besides a recommendation for the Medal of Honor, General Lightburn also gave Murphy a battlefield promotion to lieutenant.

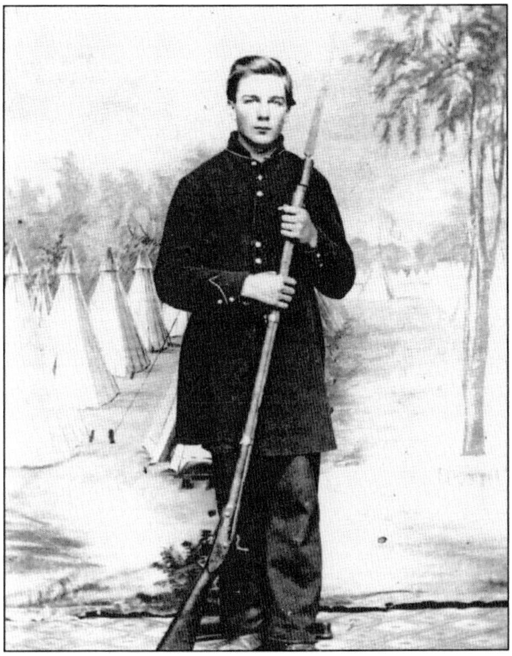

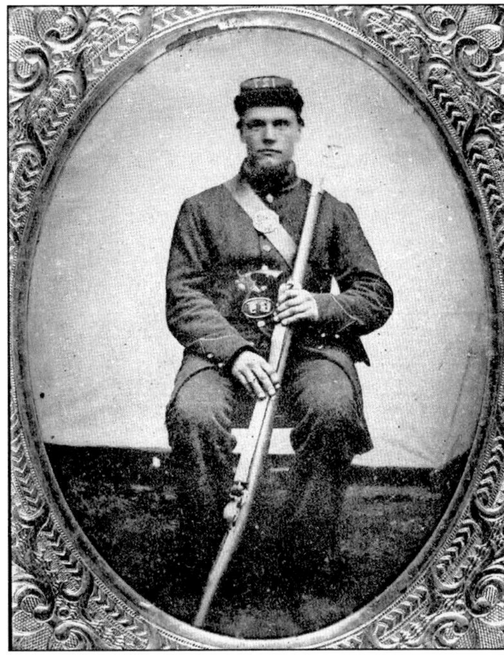

While young Murphy was winning the Medal of Honor, two other young Oswegoans were giving their lives during the Battle of Ezra Church. Alfred X. Murdock (left) and William Pooley both fell in battle on that terrible August day. While both are buried on the battlefield in Georgia, Murdock's sacrifice is recounted on a tall memorial in the Oswego Township Cemetery.

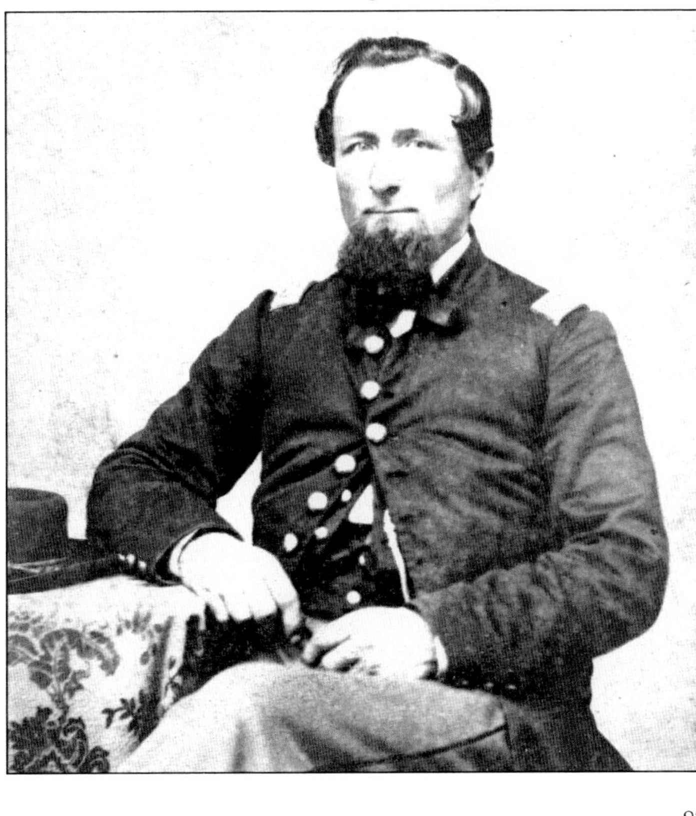

Capt. William S. Bunn commanded Company A of the 127th Illinois Volunteer Infantry, which included many Oswegoans, during the Battle of Ezra Church. It was his sad duty to inform the parents of both Murdock and Pooley that their sons had died in battle. In a letter to Murdock's parents, Bunn noted that after the furious Battle of Ezra Church, Company A had only five men fit for duty.

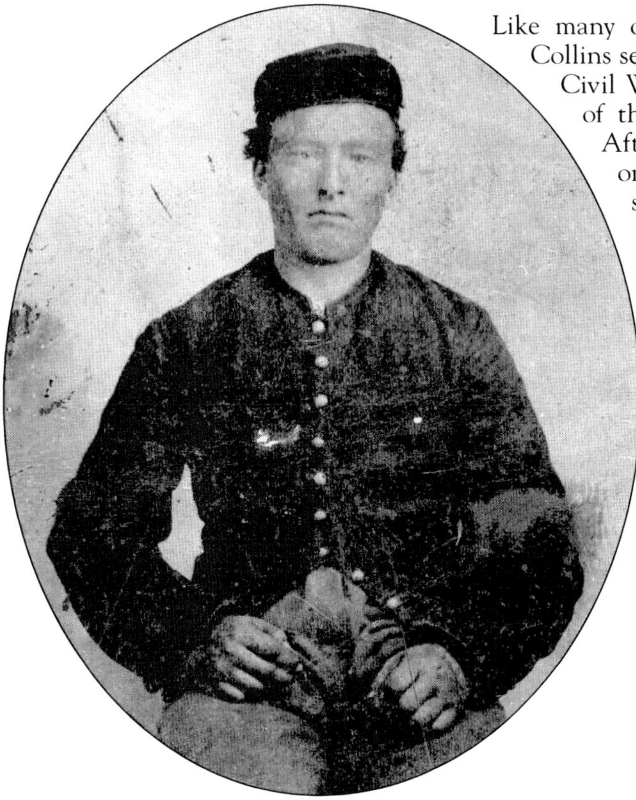

Like many of his neighbors, farm boy George Collins served in the Union Army during the Civil War. Collins enlisted in Company F of the 18th Illinois Volunteer Infantry. After the war, he returned to become one of Oswego Township's most successful farmers.

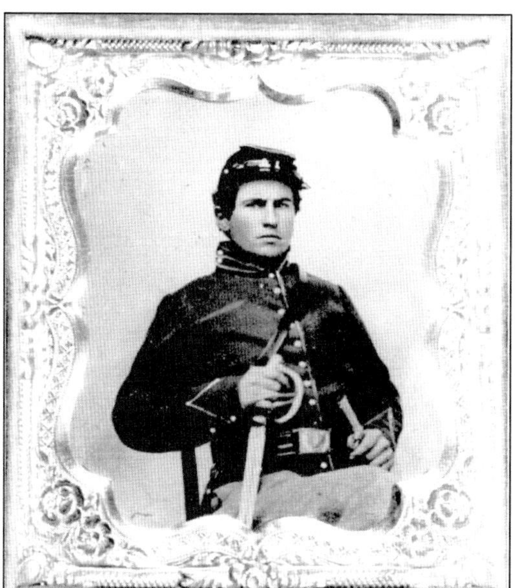

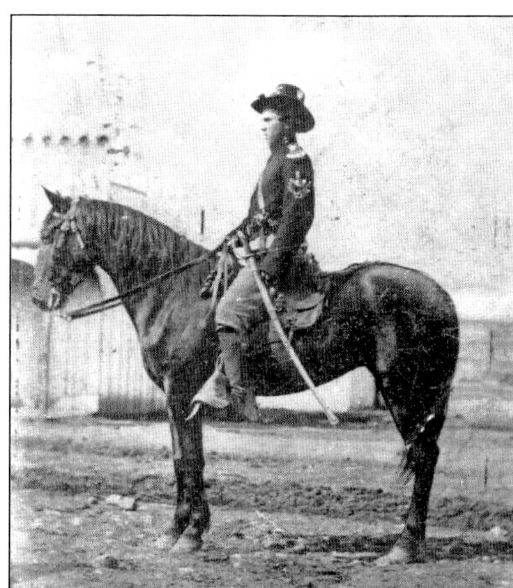

Young Oswego resident Henry Green Smith wanted to serve as a horse soldier and ended up in the 1st Wisconsin Cavalry. In the tintype at left, Smith holds his cavalry saber. At right, he's seated on his mount. Smith came back to Oswego after the war to become the town's station agent for the Chicago, Burlington and Quincy Railroad.

Orville Beebe was one of the few local men to serve in the U.S. Navy in the Civil War. Beebe served aboard the USS *Moose*, a river gunboat. The *Moose* was involved in an unusual battle between Confederate general John Hunt Morgan's cavalry and units of the U.S. Navy on the Ohio River. Artillery fire from the *Moose* disrupted the Southerners' attempt to cross the river and led to Morgan's capture.

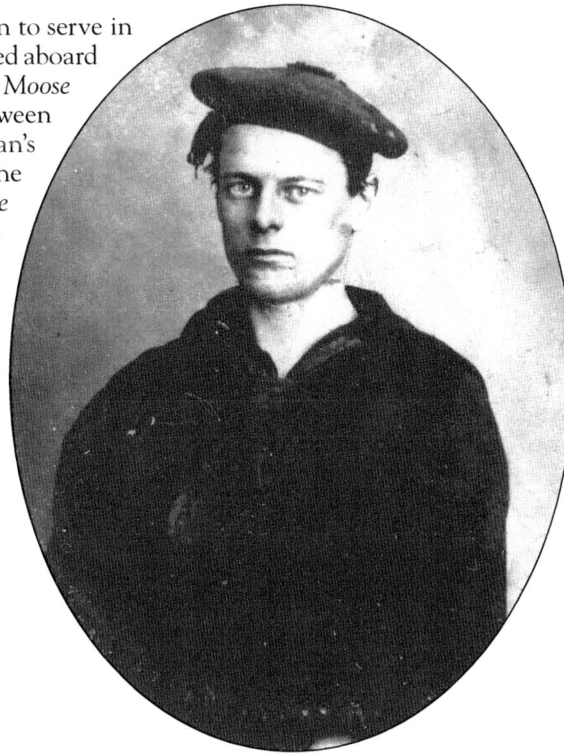

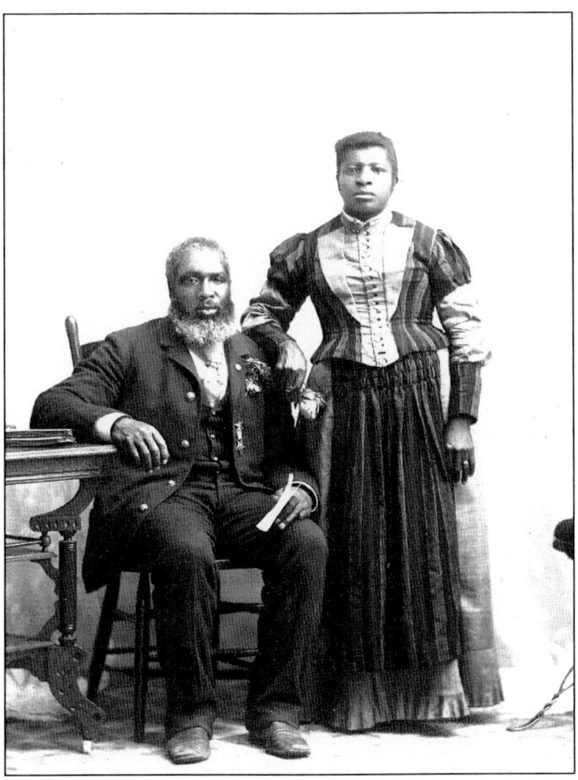

Five African American veterans of the Civil War, including Nathan Hughes, are buried in the Oswego Township Cemetery. Hughes, an escaped slave, enlisted in the 29th U.S. Colored Infantry Regiment, and fought at the infamous Battle of the Crater, made famous in the 2003 film *Cold Mountain*. After the war, Hughes returned to Oswego Township where he farmed along Minkler Road. Here, he is proudly wearing his Grand Army of the Republic pin.

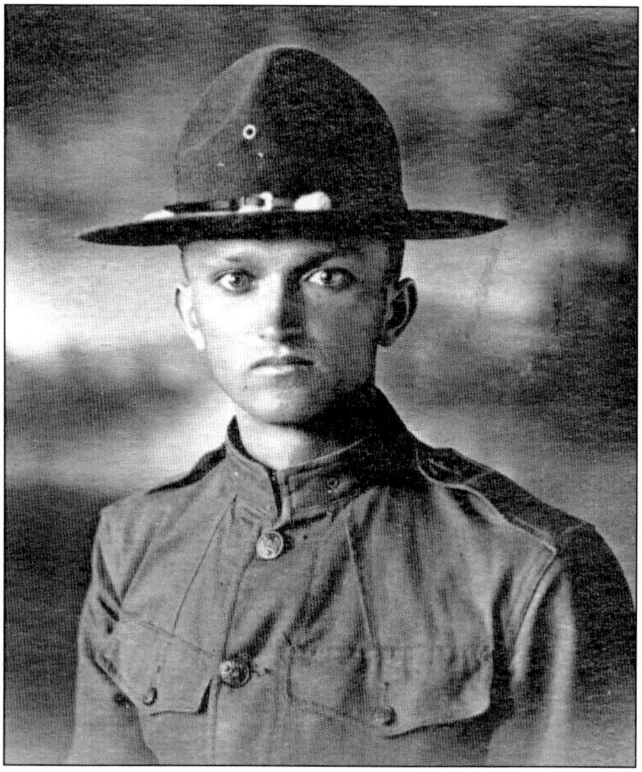

Oswego Township native Clayton Roth was typical of the farm boys who went off to fight in World War I after the United States entered the war in 1917.

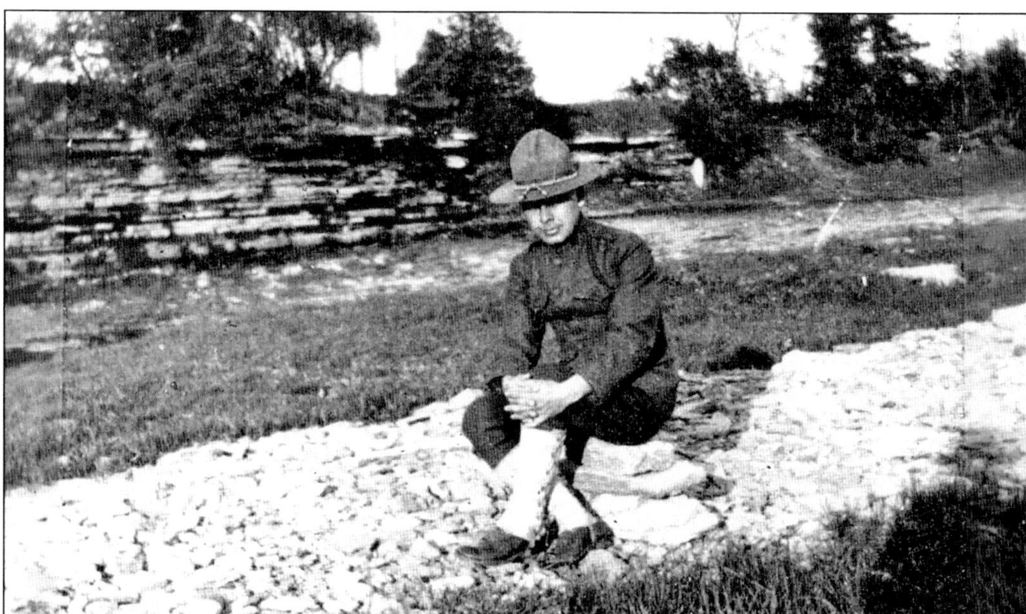

Dwight S. Young was one of several Oswego residents who served in what would one day become the U.S. Air Force during World War I. When the United States entered the conflict in 1917, it had few aircraft or pilots. Initially part of the U.S. Army Signal Corps, the U.S. Army Air Service was established in May 1918. Young was among those in training as cadets when the war ended in November 1918.

Robert Herren enlisted in the U.S. Army's officer training corps and had just begun training at the University of Illinois when the end of World War I also ended his military career. Herren returned to Oswego to operate a successful real estate and insurance company until his death.

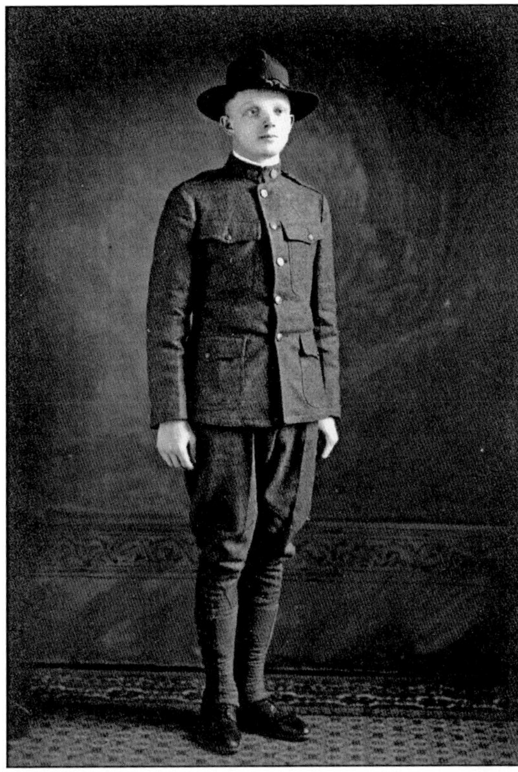

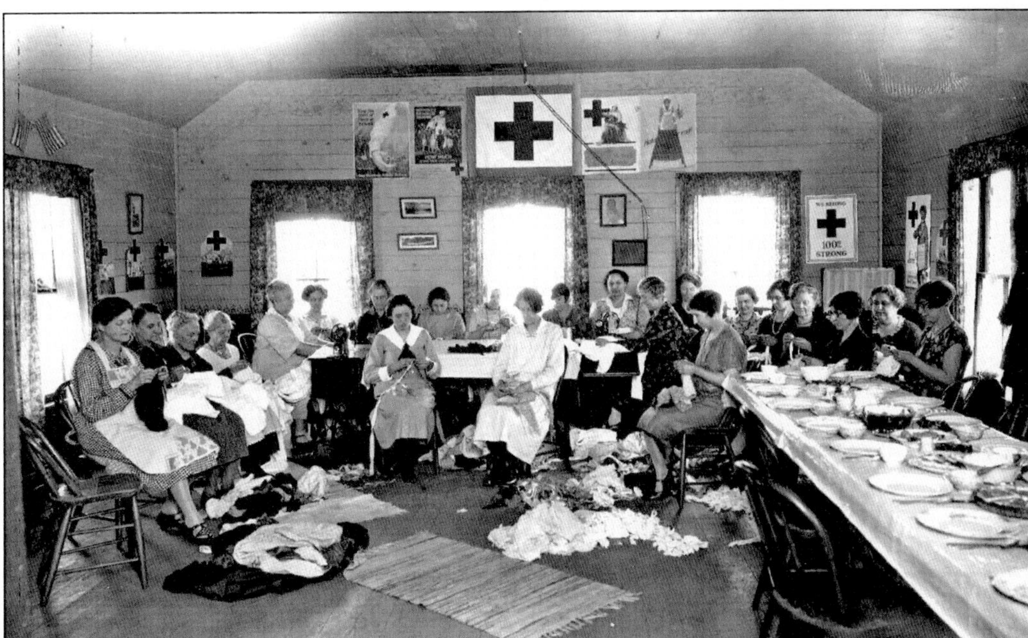

The Oswego Chapter of the Red Cross met regularly in the hall on the second floor of the Oswego Township Hall on Washington Street in Oswego. Above, Red Cross members work on their current project before sitting down to a potluck meal. During the war, the organization made and sent items to those serving. After the war, items were sent to European war refugees.

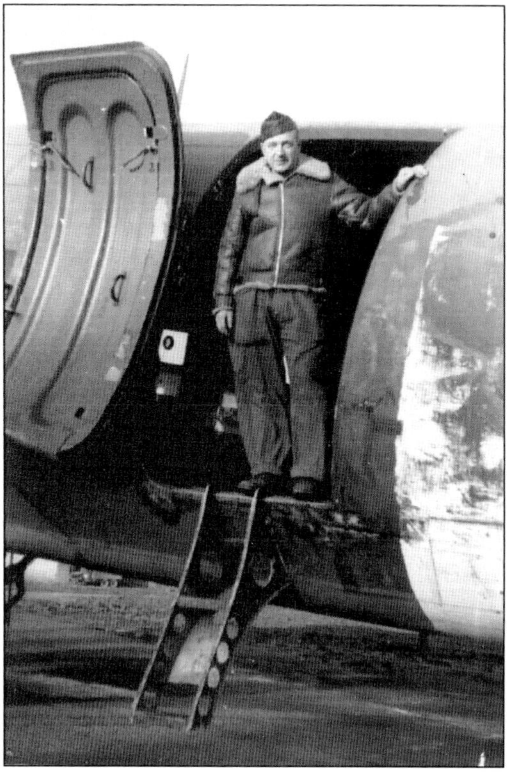

When World War II broke out, Kendall County men and women wasted no time in enlisting to fight against the Axis powers. Here, Oswegoan Jack Weis poses in his flight jacket aboard his transport aircraft.

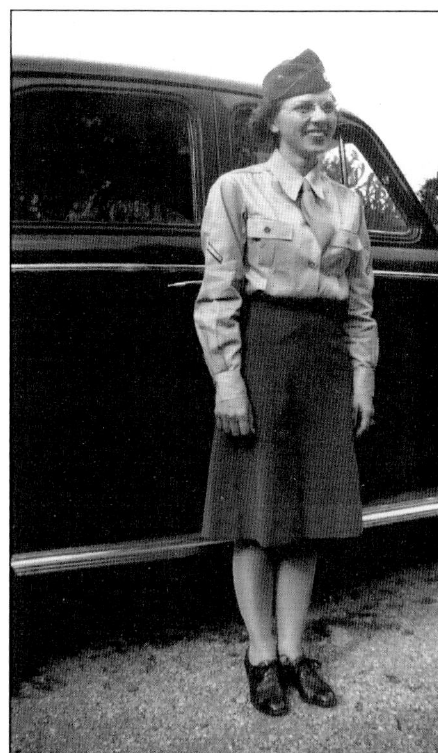

Jewel Patton, a young Oswego girl, enlisted in the Women's Army Corps (WAC). The WACs provided a variety of support services to free up male service members for combat duty.

At the age of 18, Oswegoan Paul Miller found himself in a U.S. Army uniform serving in Italy piloting an amphibious truck the U.S. Army called the DUKW (popularly called a "duck"). In August 1944, he participated in the invasion of Southern France. Then in 1945 he was transferred to the Pacific Theater. Fortunately the war ended before he was set to participate in the invasion of Japan.

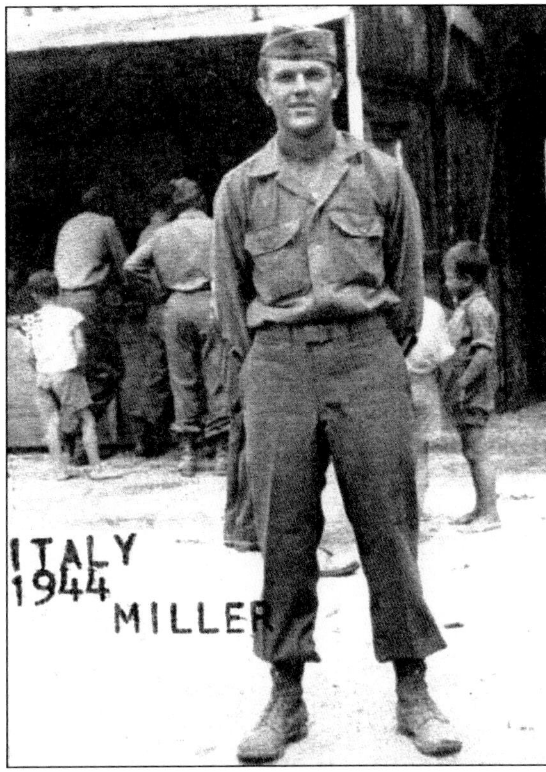

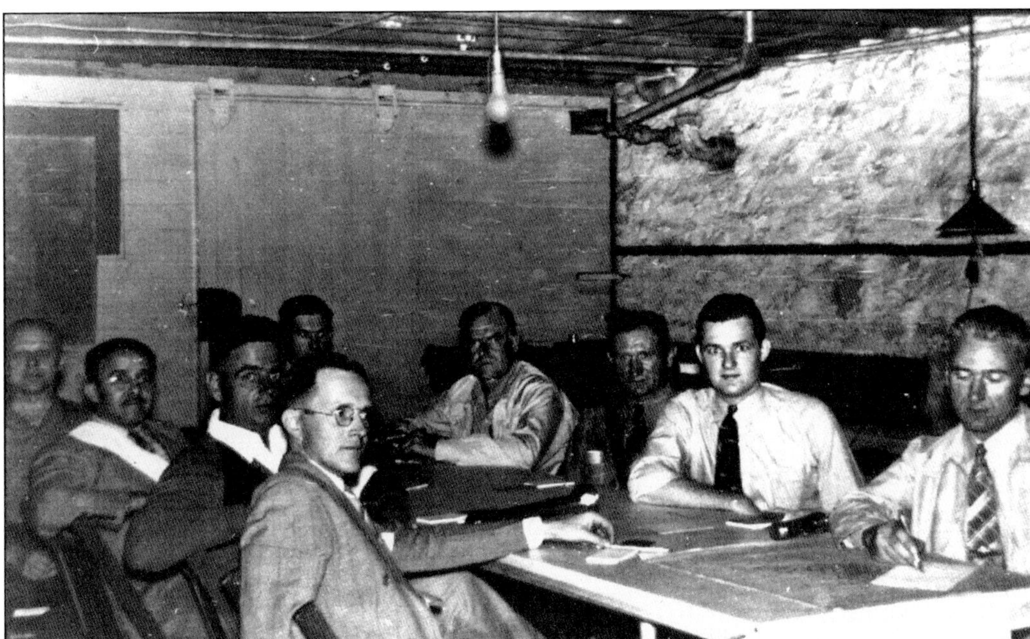

During the World War II years, the home front was responsible for keeping the civil defense system to guard against sneak enemy attack. Here, about 1943, Oswego Civil Defense officials meet in the basement of the Masonic hall, including grocery store owner Carl Bohn, fire chief Kenneth Tripp, Oswego village employee Lyle Shoger, and village president Earl Zentmyer.

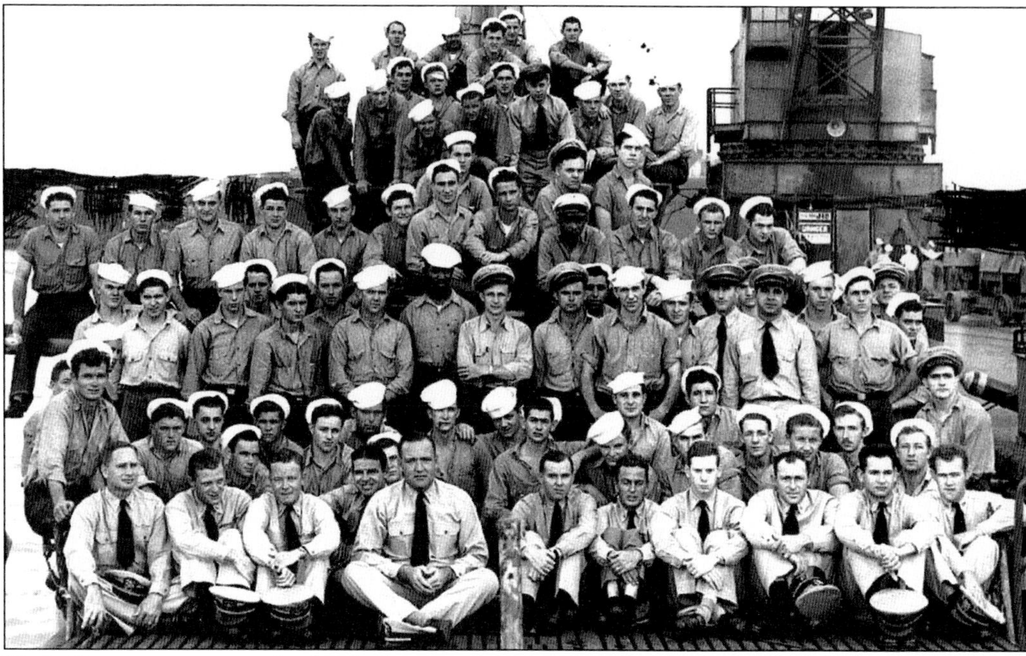

Slade Cutter grew up on the family farm in Oswego Township and attended the one-room Cutter School. A talented musician as a youngster, he attended the U.S. Naval Academy at Annapolis where he discovered athletics. He was both a football and boxing All-American. Sitting in the first row, fourth from left, Captain Cutter poses with his crew on the deck of the submarine he commanded so successfully, the USS *Seahorse*.

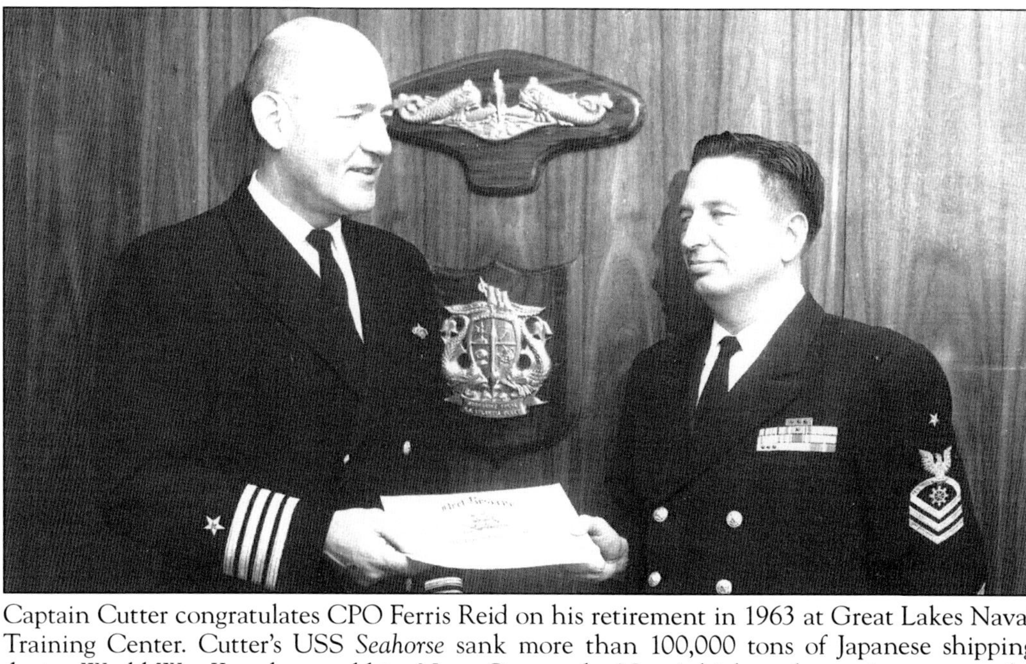

Captain Cutter congratulates CPO Ferris Reid on his retirement in 1963 at Great Lakes Naval Training Center. Cutter's USS *Seahorse* sank more than 100,000 tons of Japanese shipping during World War II and earned him Navy Cross—the Navy's highest decoration next to the Medal of Honor—with three stars in lieu of additional Navy Crosses. He served the rest of his career in the U.S. Navy before dying June 9, 2005.

Seven

Serving the People

In 1840, the effects of the financial panic of 1837 were still serious enough that the counties in northern Illinois found themselves in fiscal trouble. That problem, along with the long travel times to get to county seats in either Ottawa or Geneva, led residents of the nine townships that eventually became Kendall County to petition the legislature to establish a new county. In February 1841, Illinois officials established Kendall County by taking three townships—including Oswego Township—from Kane County and six townships from LaSalle County.

Yorkville was the original county seat, but after a successful vote in 1845, the county seat was moved to Oswego, where it remained until 1864 when voters decided to move it back to more centrally-located Yorkville.

Although settled in 1833 and laid out in 1835, Oswego was not incorporated until the spring of 1855. Until later in the 19th century, many police and municipal functions were handled by either Kendall County or Oswego Township. Gradually Oswego established its own local government responsible for the services residents of even small towns take for granted.

Starting in the 1950s, a variety of special taxing districts were established to provide more services. The Oswegoland Park District was established in April 1950, while the Oswego Public Library District is the end product of more than a century of volunteer efforts by the Nineteenth Century Club's members. Their efforts led to the construction of the first township-supported library in 1964.

The Oswego Fire Protection District was established in 1936 after some disastrous rural fires graphically illustrated the need for an adequate firefighting force.

As the community has continued to grow, services provided by local governmental agencies have increased proportionally. In 1980, Oswego's municipal population stood at 3,018. As of late 2007, the village's population was estimated at nearly 30,000 people.

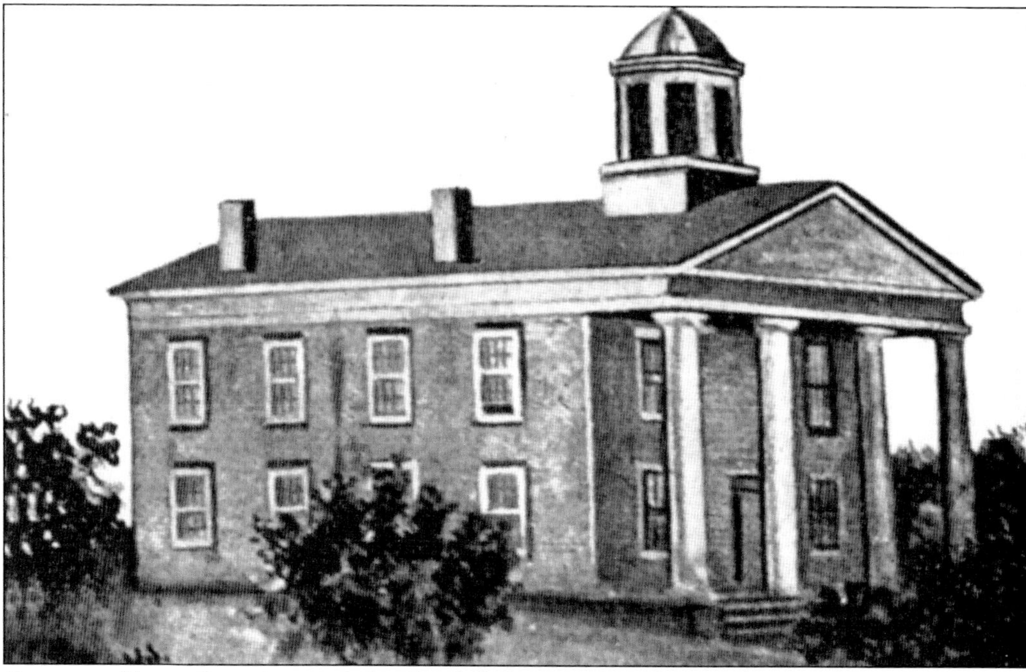

Oswegoan Festus Burr designed the Kendall County Courthouse that was built on the block bounded by Madison, Jackson, Monroe, and Jefferson Streets after the county seat was moved to Oswego in 1845. After the county seat was moved back to Yorkville, the building was used as a school and for other municipal purposes, until it was demolished in 1885 to make way for the Red Brick School.

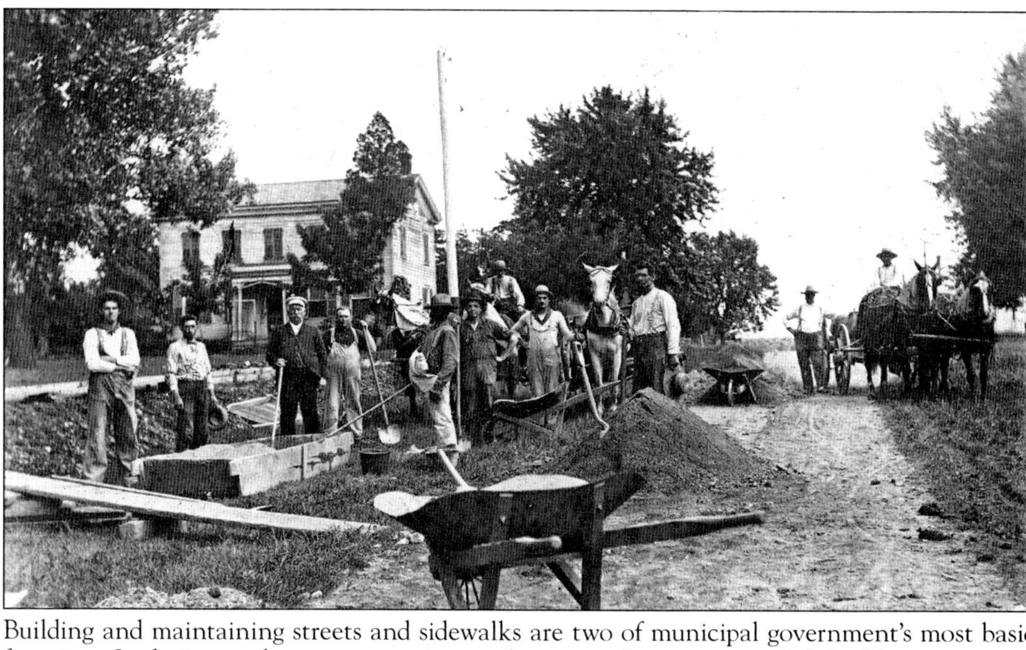

Building and maintaining streets and sidewalks are two of municipal government's most basic functions. In the image above, construction workers pause for a moment while building a concrete sidewalk along Jackson Street beside the Red Brick School in 1902. The Oswego Community Bank and Oswego Post Office occupy the old school site in 2008.

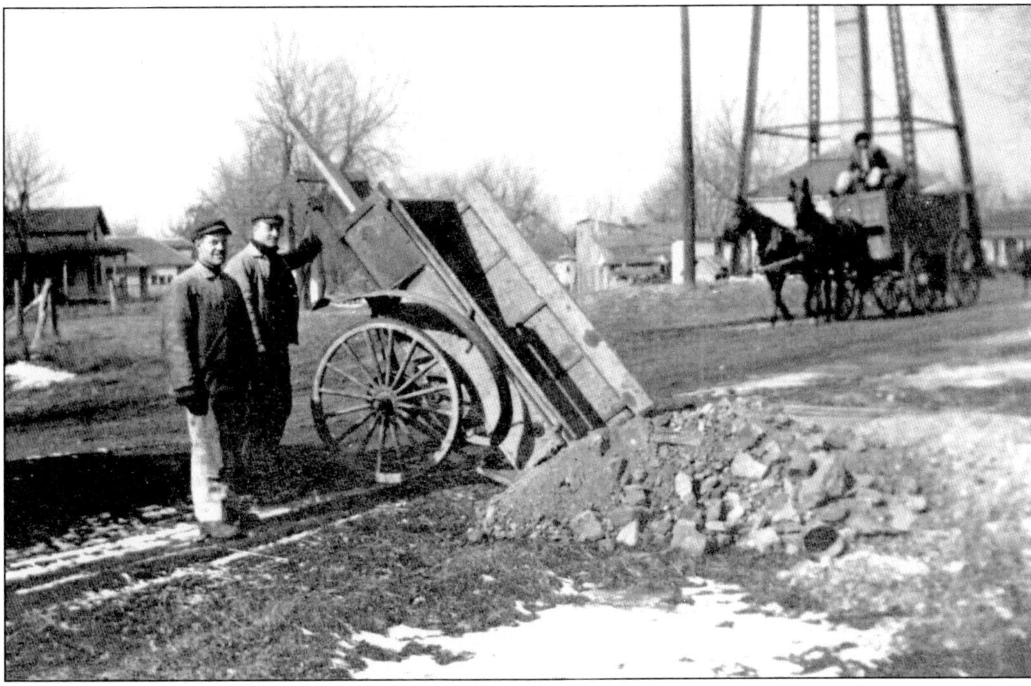

Street maintenance used to be a lot more labor-intensive in the early years of the 20th century—no dump trucks or other machinery. Seen above, Fred (left) and Claire Willis take a time-out while filling holes on Washington near Van Buren Street. The old Oswego Water Tower is visible at right rear.

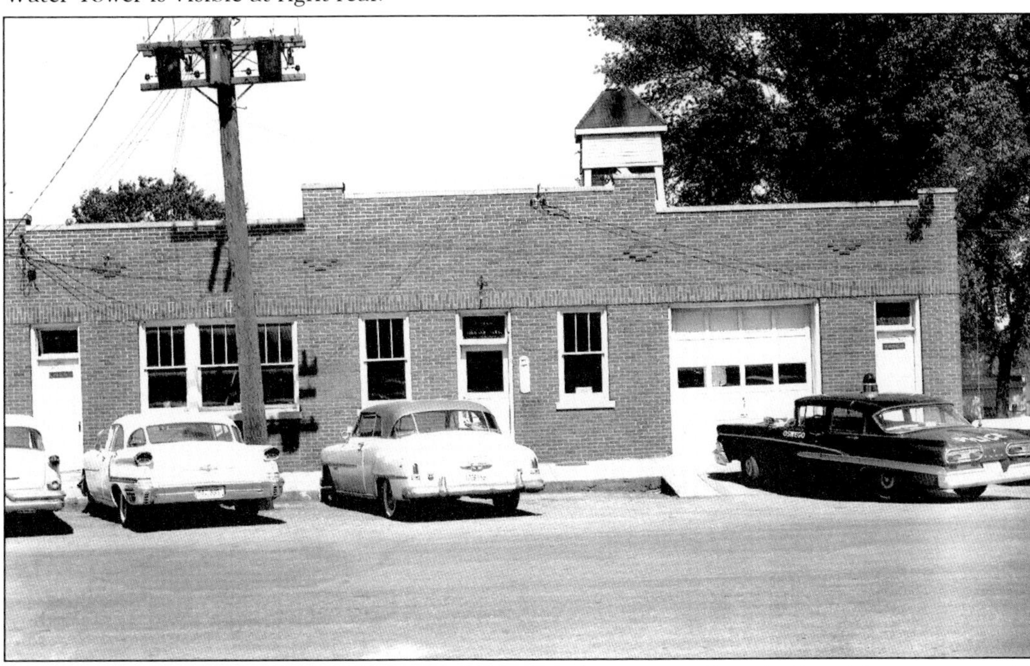

The current Oswego Village Hall was built as a combination village hall and fire station, with the Oswego Fire Protection District's truck stored in the garage on the right side of the building. The small roofed enclosure over the garage door protects the village's old fire siren.

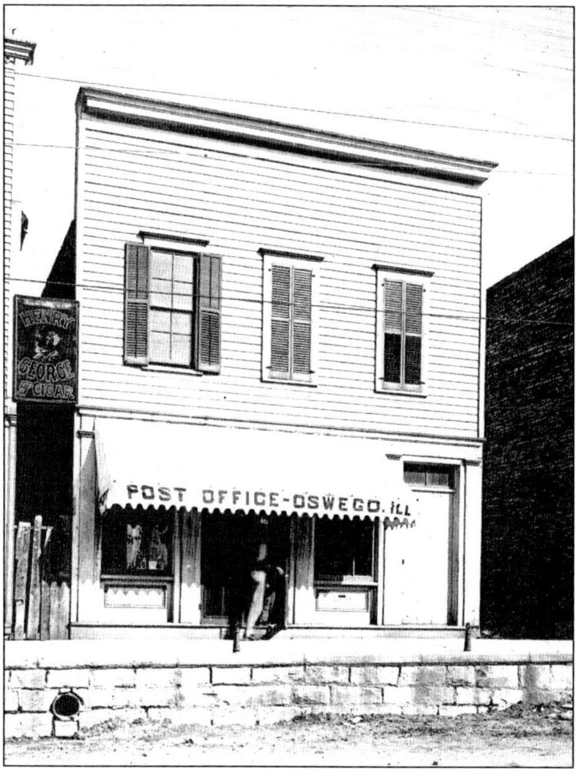

Oswego Postmaster Lorenzo Rank built this frame building—which still stands—in downtown Oswego as a post office and, upstairs, his living quarters. The post office occupied the building until 1911, when the office was moved to the new Burkhart Block on South Main Street. The old post office, donated to Oswego in Rank's will, became a library operated by the Nineteenth Century Club.

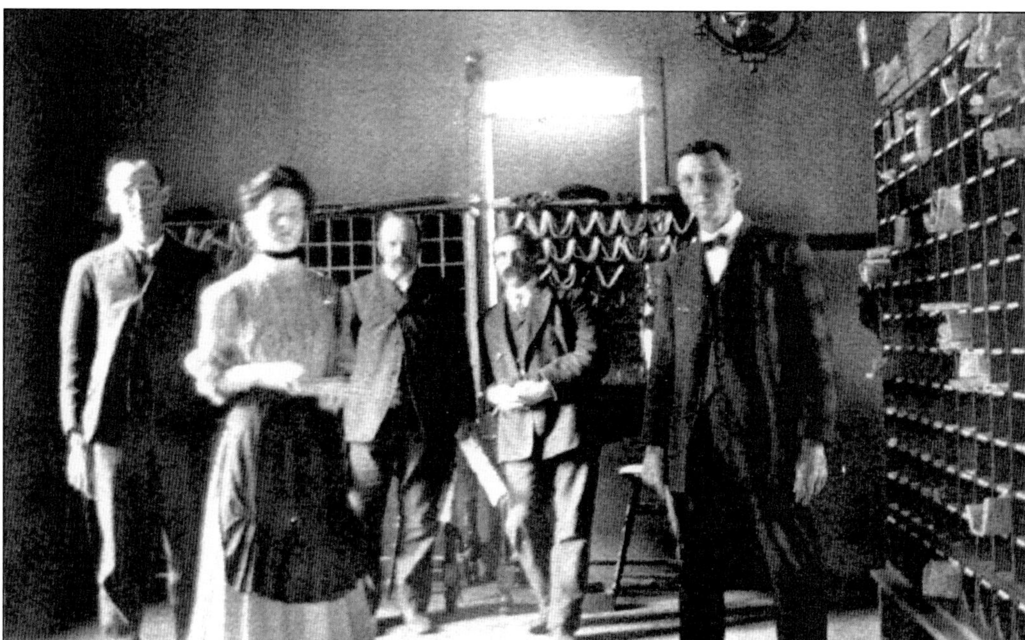

The interior of the Oswego Post Office is seen here as it appeared in the Rank Building about 1910. Postmaster Charles Cherry and worker Mayme Richards are seen here, along with local business owners George Crousehorn, Gus Weltz, and Harley Richards. Oswego was granted its first post office in January 1837. The first postmaster was one of Oswego's founders, Levi Arnold.

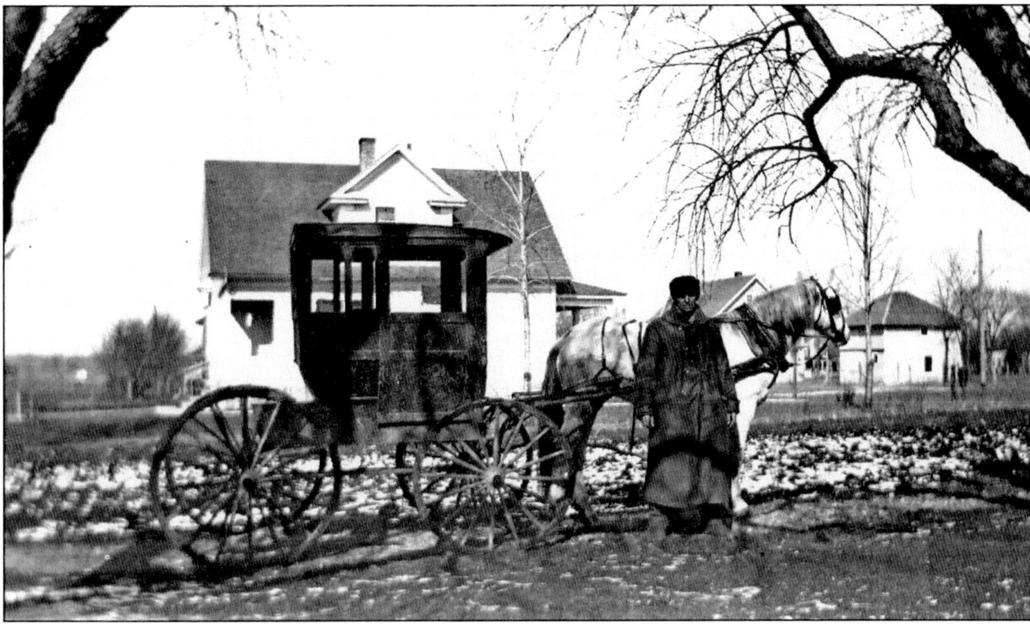

Oswego's rural mail carrier finishes up his rounds in this late spring photograph snapped along modern Chicago Road (U.S. Route 34) in Oswego around the beginning of the 20th century. Free delivery of mail in rural areas began in 1896 and soon led to the closure of the rural post offices that once dotted the countryside.

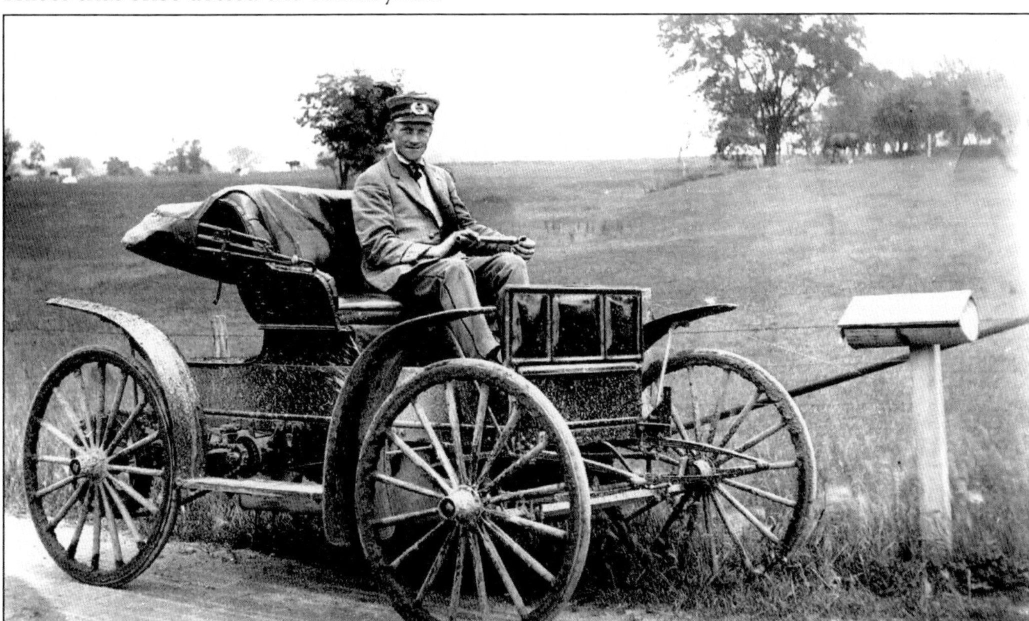

Oswego historian Paul Shoger identified this pleased mail carrier as Mr. Williams, who worked out of the Oswego Post Office carrying the mail with his Sears Automobile. The photograph was taken in 1902. Early automobiles, like the Sears, had the same high clearances as the old horse-drawn mail buggies, a must on the unpaved rural roads of the era that turned into seemly bottomless pits during wet spring weather.

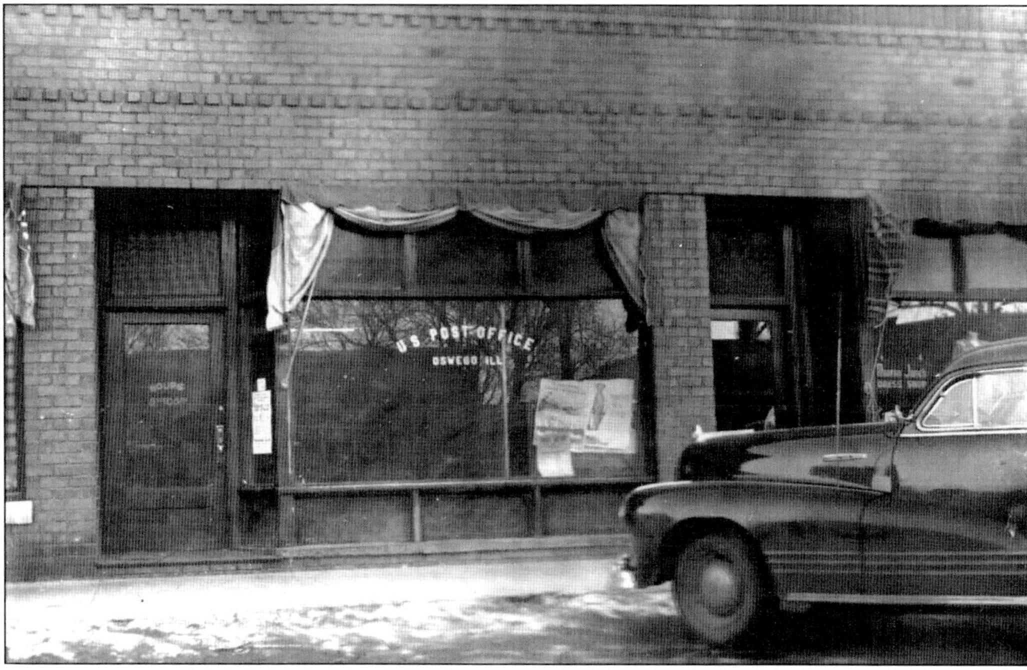

In 1911, the Oswego Post Office moved from its longtime home in the Rank Building on North Main Street to this space in the new Burkhart Block. The post office continued on at this location until about 1955 when it moved to the northwest corner of Main and Washington Streets. In January 1969, the current post office at Madison and Jackson Streets opened.

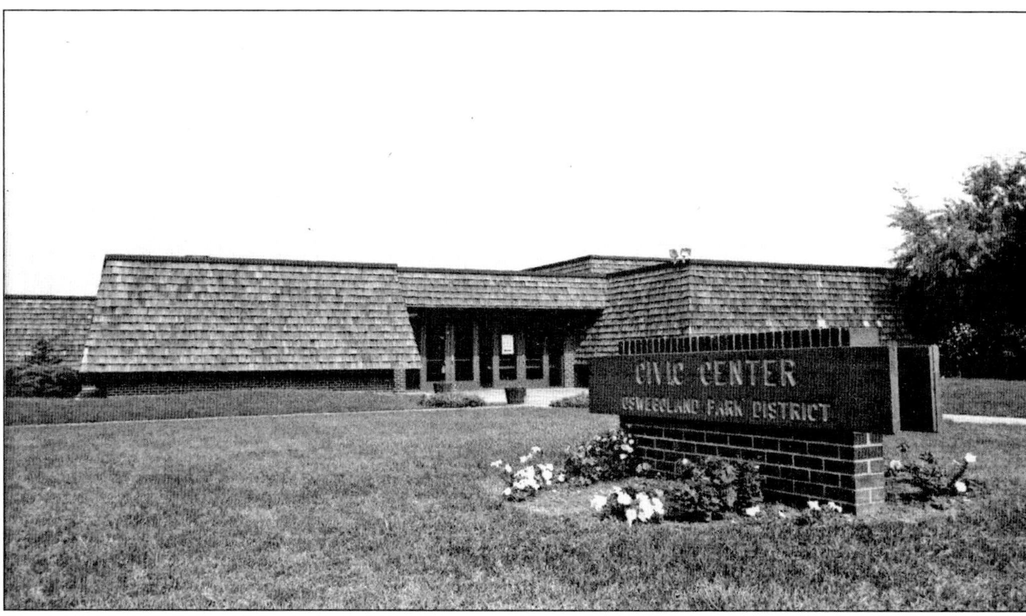

Although established by the voters in the spring of 1950, the Oswegoland Park District did not get its own building until the Oswegoland Civic Center opened in February 1969. The Civic Center and its adjoining pool offered public meeting and activity space for the first time. As of 2008, the park district has three activity centers and serves many thousands of area residents annually.

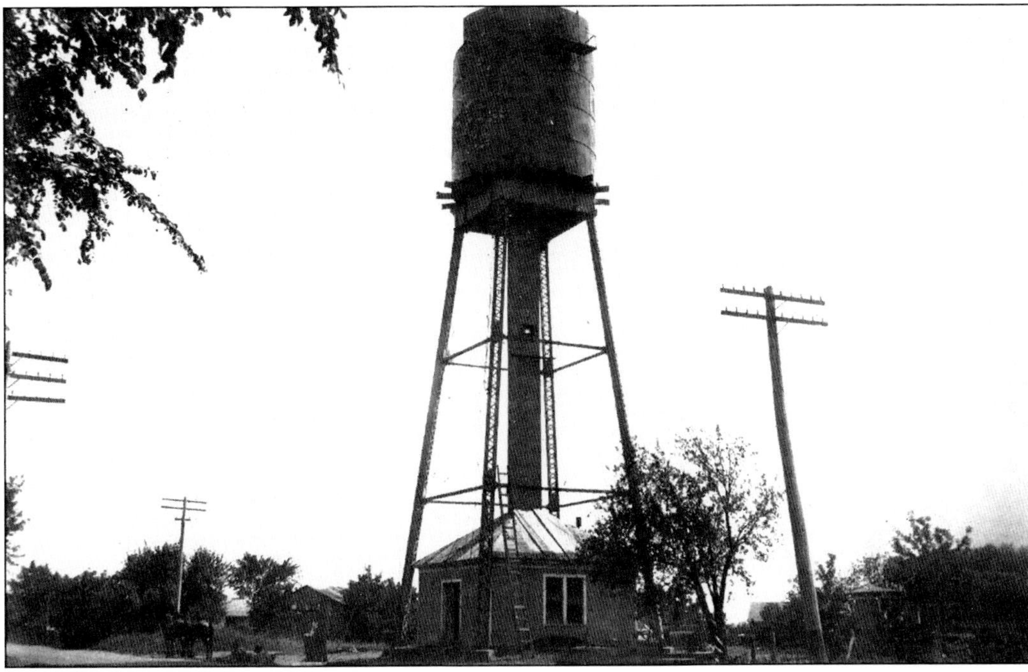

The original Oswego water tower was photographed by Charles Cherry under construction in 1895 at Van Buren and Washington Streets. The original tower featured a wooden water tank and provided Oswego's first pressurized water system.

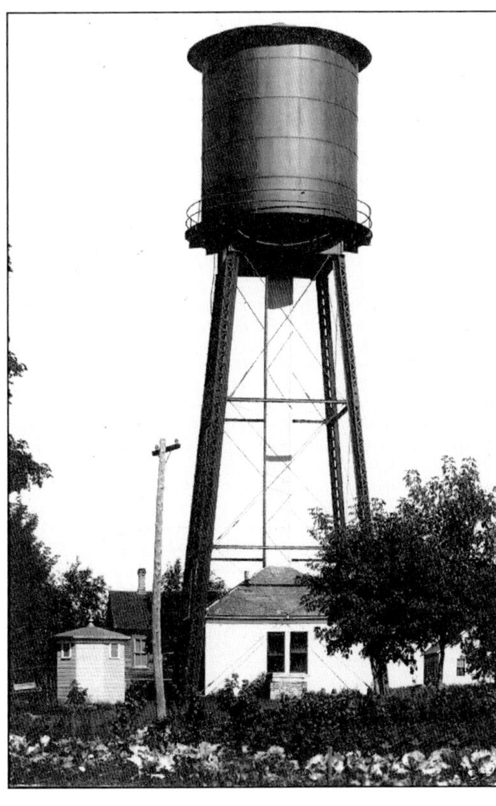

Oswego's first water tower after construction was finished. The electric pump that filled the tank with water had to be manually operated by a village employee. The old water tower was eventually replaced with a new, much taller and larger water tower at Madison and Douglas Streets in 1958.

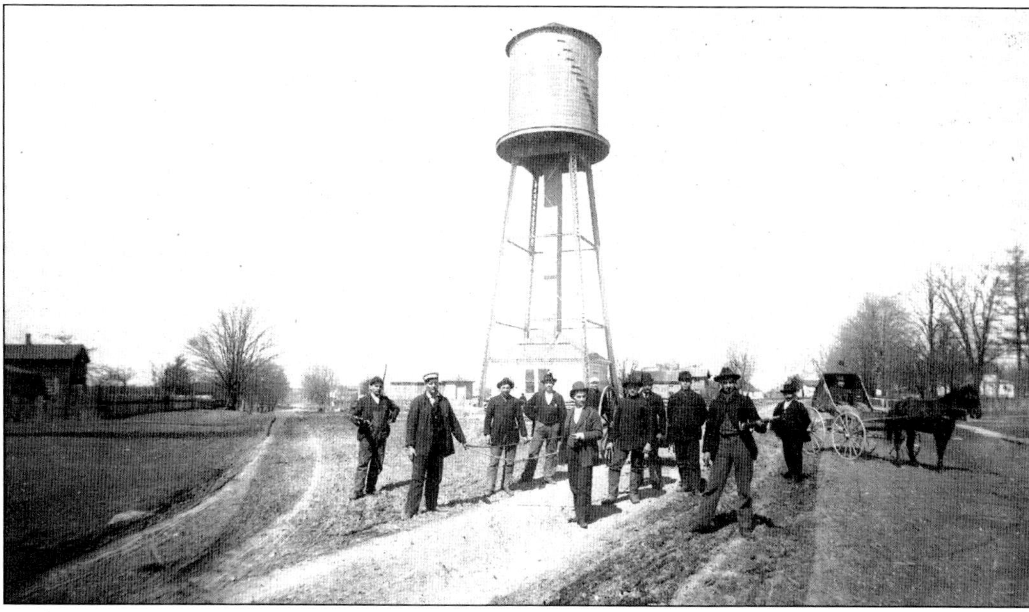

With a pressurized municipal water system, Oswego could finally have a fire brigade. A week after the system went into operation, the village bought several lengths of fire hose and a hose cart to carry it. The cart was pulled by village firefighters to nearby blazes. Seen above, the brigade poses on Washington Street in front of the new water tower with their hose cart.

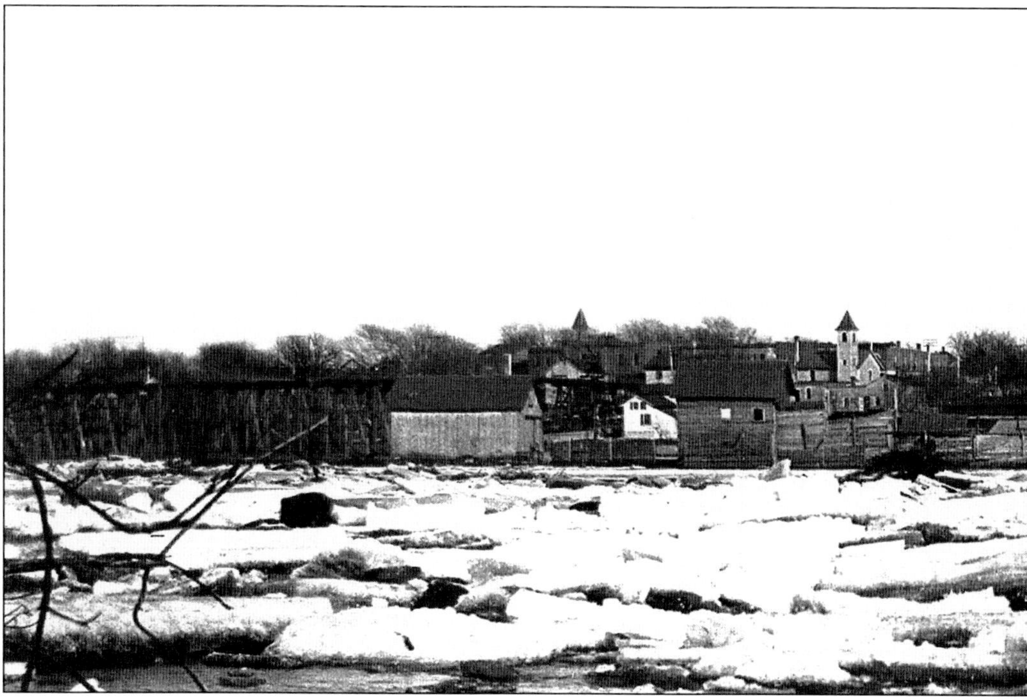

The hose cart and hose was stored in the Oswego Township Hall on Washington Street. This 1911 photograph shows the hall with its tall tower at right. The tower held the village fire bell and was used to dry the canvas fire hoses. The bell today sits in front of Fire Station One in downtown Oswego as a reminder of the Oswego Fire Protection District's long history.

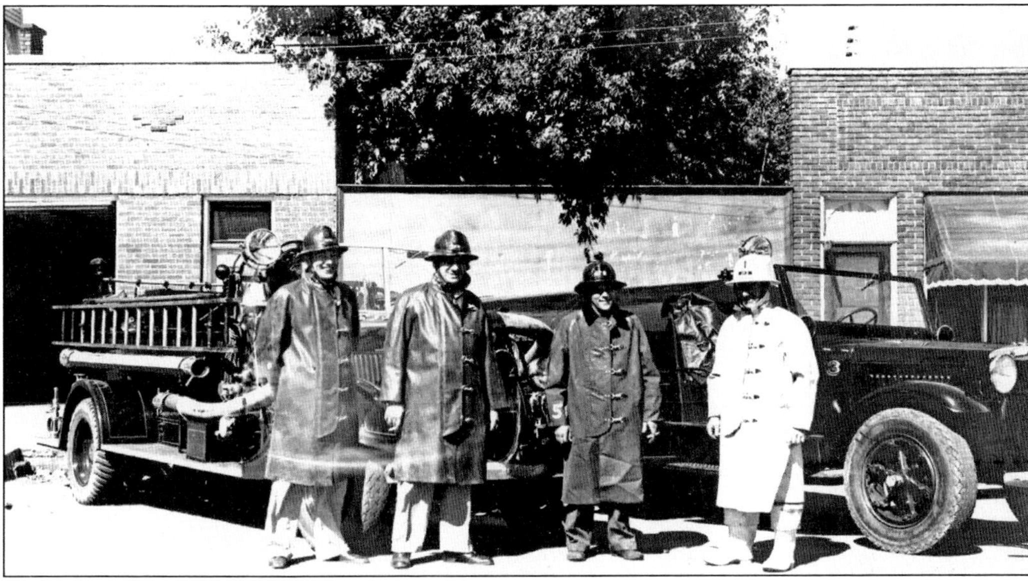

The Oswego Fire Protection District's personnel pose with their new and then innovative rural tanker in 1939 (right rear). The new truck was designed to provide enough water to fight rural fires. Firefighters here are, from left to right, Ed Inman, Ralph Johnson, Ralph Burkhart, and Fire Chief Kenneth Tripp.

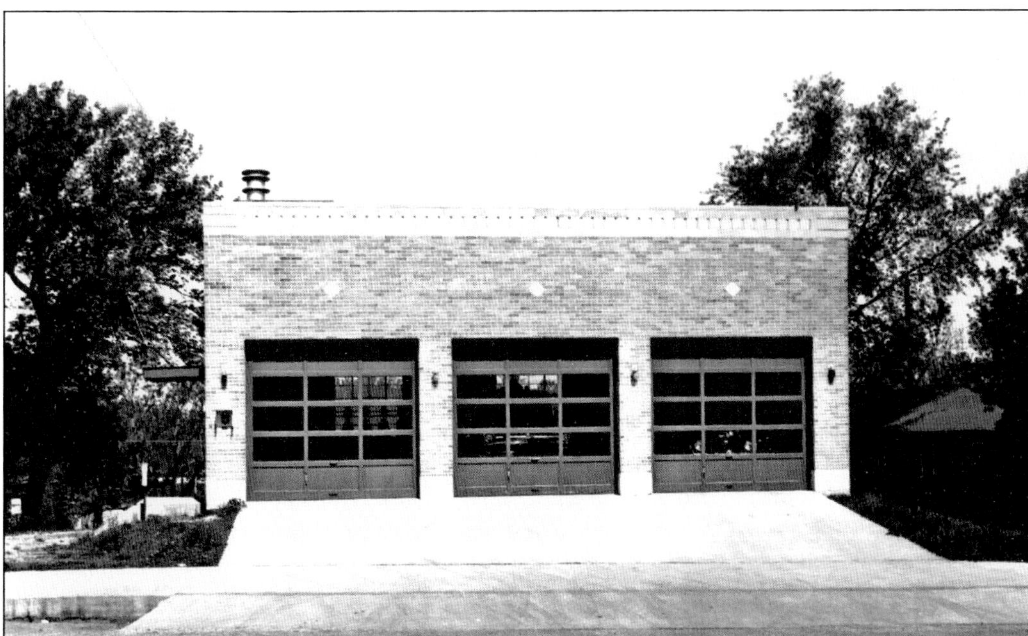

Having outgrown their small quarters at the Oswego Village Hall, the fire protection district opened this new fire station on Main Street in Oswego in 1954. Since then the station has been extensively enlarged to cope with the district's growth. As of 2008, the district has four fire stations, with construction on a replacement for the old Main Street station to begin on Woolley Road in the spring of 2008.

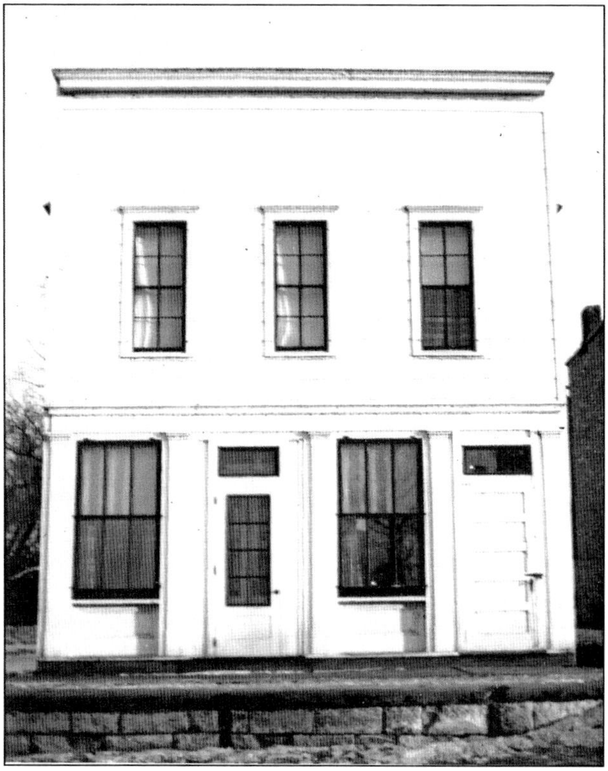

After being deeded to Oswego for use as a library by former postmaster Lorenzo Rank, the Nineteenth Century Club opened their privately funded lending library in the old post office building. This is how the building looked about 1940. In 2008, it housed the offices of the *Ledger-Sentinel*, Oswego's weekly newspaper.

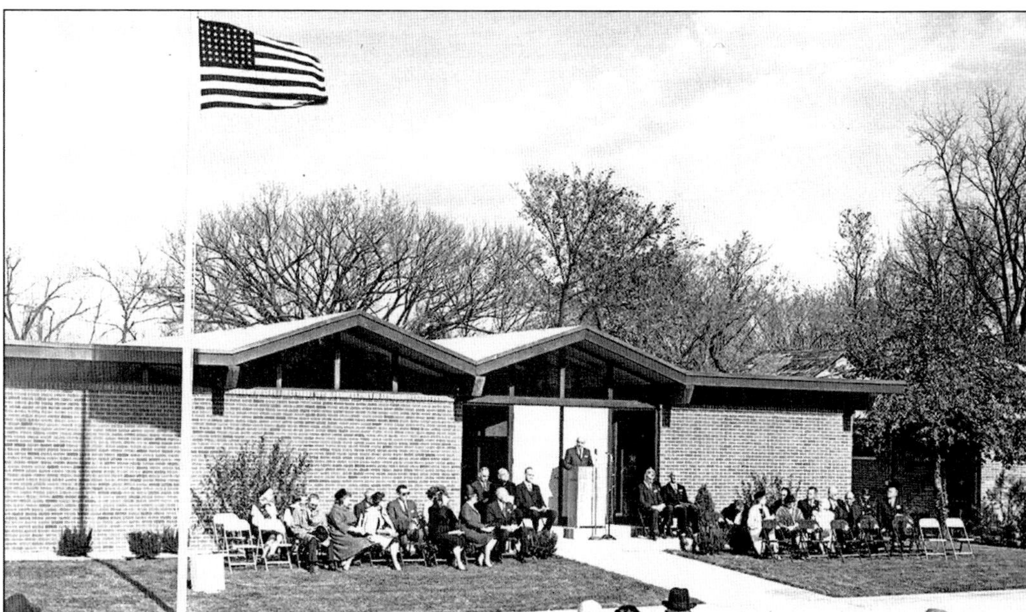

On October 18, 1964, the new tax-supported Oswego Township Library opened. Funds for the building had been raised by the Nineteenth Century Club, the Lions Club, and other community organizations, with the land being donated by the Oswegoland Park District. Today the Oswego Public Library District serves a population of some 50,000 residents in Kendall and Will Counties.

Oswego Village Marshall Jeff Rogerson gets ready for the Oswego Memorial Day Parade at his home on East Washington Street in this 1951 photograph. Until the 1960s, the village only had part-time officers. Rogerson's badge and handcuffs are on exhibit at the Little White School Museum.

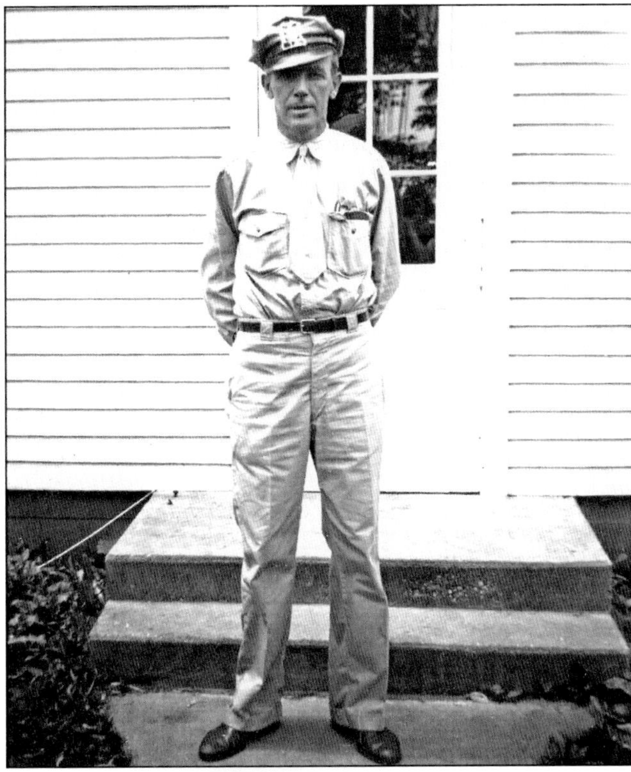

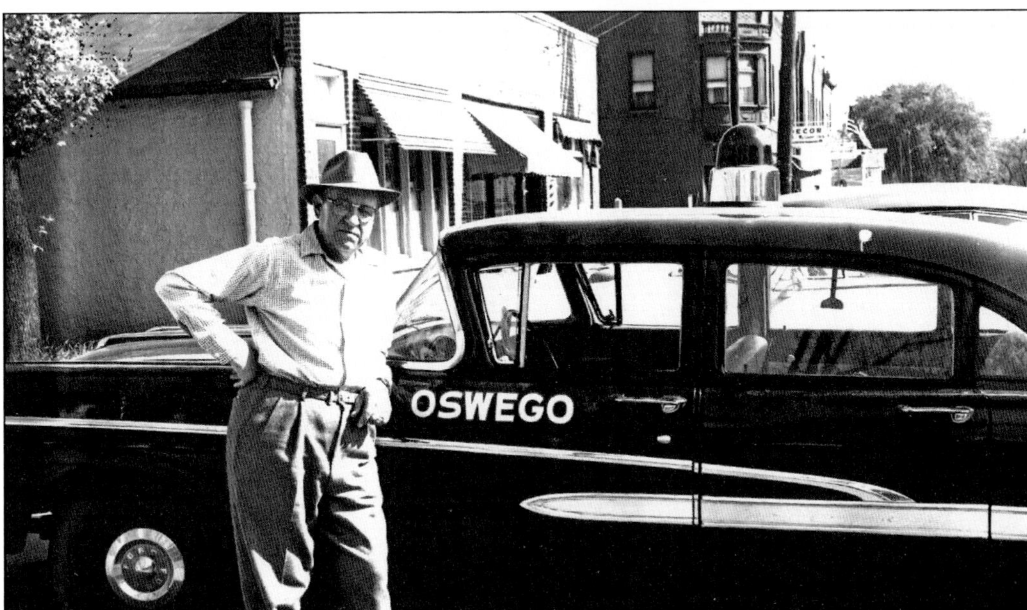

Paul Dwyre was one of Oswego's longest-serving police officers. In the image above, he shows off his new 1958 Ford squad car in this Homer Durand photograph. Although a former Illinois state police trooper, Dwyre was not only expected to do police duty in Oswego. He also maintained the village hall. Today the Oswego Police Department employs some 50 sworn officers, plus other personnel.

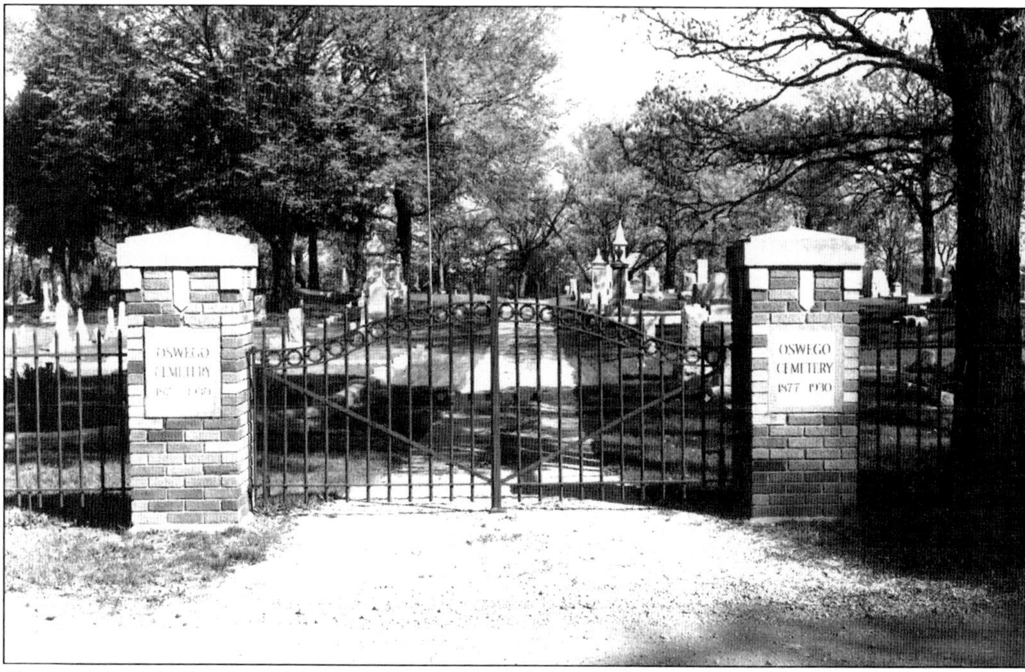

Oswego's original cemetery was located at Madison and Douglas Streets. About 1855, L. B. Judson created the Oswego Oak Grove Cemetery on property he owned, with the first lot sold to Jesse Holt. The graves from the old cemetery were moved to the new one, and in 1877, the Oswego Cemetery Association was established to manage it. Today, the scenic, historic cemetery is maintained by Oswego Township.

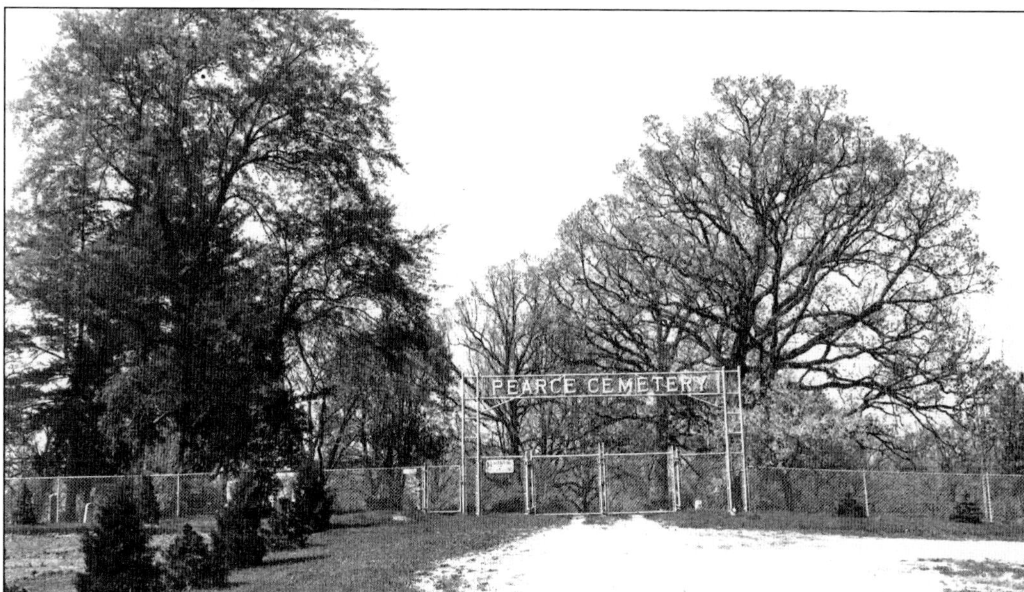

The old Pearce Graveyard, today's Pearce Cemetery, was established on the Daniel Pearce farm, with the first recorded burial, that of little Josephine Clark, taking place in September 1845. The old burying ground was typical of family plots established on many area farms. Today the Pearce Cemetery is owned and maintained by Oswego Township.

Eight

Faith on the Prairie

The Reverend Jesse Walker brought the first religious services to the Fox Valley after the settlement era began. Walker's Methodist co-missionary, the Reverend Stephen R. Beggs, rode a large circuit through northern Illinois holding services at pioneer cabins that drew crowds from miles around.

Walker had established the Fox River Mission in modern LaSalle County in 1825. The mission provided early settlers with the services of a blacksmith and gristmill, originally aimed to serve local Native American tribes.

In 1833, soon after they arrived from Ohio, Daniel and Sara Pearce hosted the township's first religious services at their cabin, with Beggs presiding.

When the Reverend Henry Bergen of the Rock Creek Congregational Church visited Oswego in 1842, he had to report that "Oswego . . . but it is a rather dark spot from a religious point of view. All they have is occasional Methodist preaching."

Bergen managed to persuade some receptive Oswegoans to establish a Congregational church in 1843, but it soon dissolved, possibly due to Bergan's somewhat negative assessment of the area. Meanwhile on the eastern edge of the Oswego Prairie, Stephen and Sybilla Wylie Findlay arrived from Scotland to settle and also held the first Presbyterian services at their new home.

In 1846, the Congregationalists formally established their church in Oswego, followed by the Baptists in 1848, and the German Albright Methodists out on the Oswego Prairie that same year.

By 1850, Oswego boasted two churches, one Methodist and one Congregational. During the rest of that decade, the Baptists, Presbyterians, and Lutherans built churches in town.

During the next century, congregations and their churches came and went. By 1950, the village had just two churches, the Federated and Oswego Presbyterian churches. Then in 1953, St. Mary's Catholic Church in Plano established a new mission in town that eventually became St. Anne's Catholic Church. During the next 50 years, the number of congregations of various faiths grew substantially.

Today the only remaining building from Oswego Township's pioneer days is the Little White School Museum in Oswego, built by the Methodists in 1850 and preserved as a living link with the community's pioneer religious past.

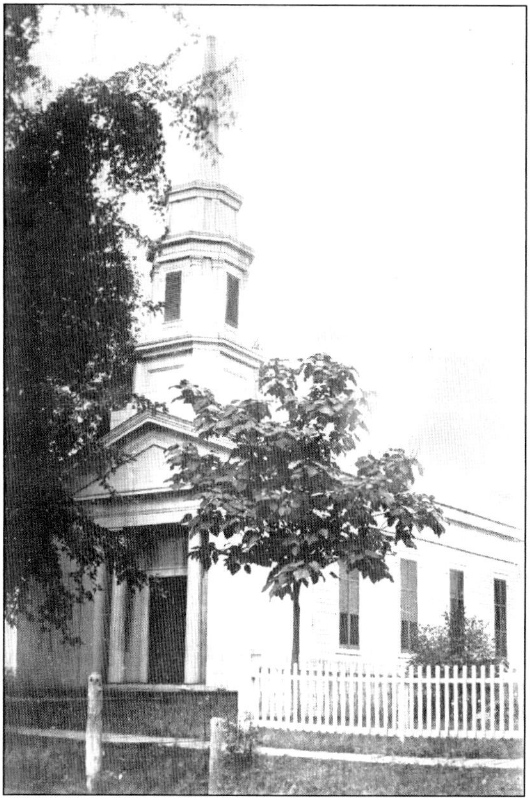

The Oswego Congregational Church at Main and Benton Streets copied the Greek Revival styling and towering steeple of New England churches of the same tradition. Members of the Congregational Church were also strong supporters of the Kendall County Anti-Slavery Society. The church burned to the ground in 1893.

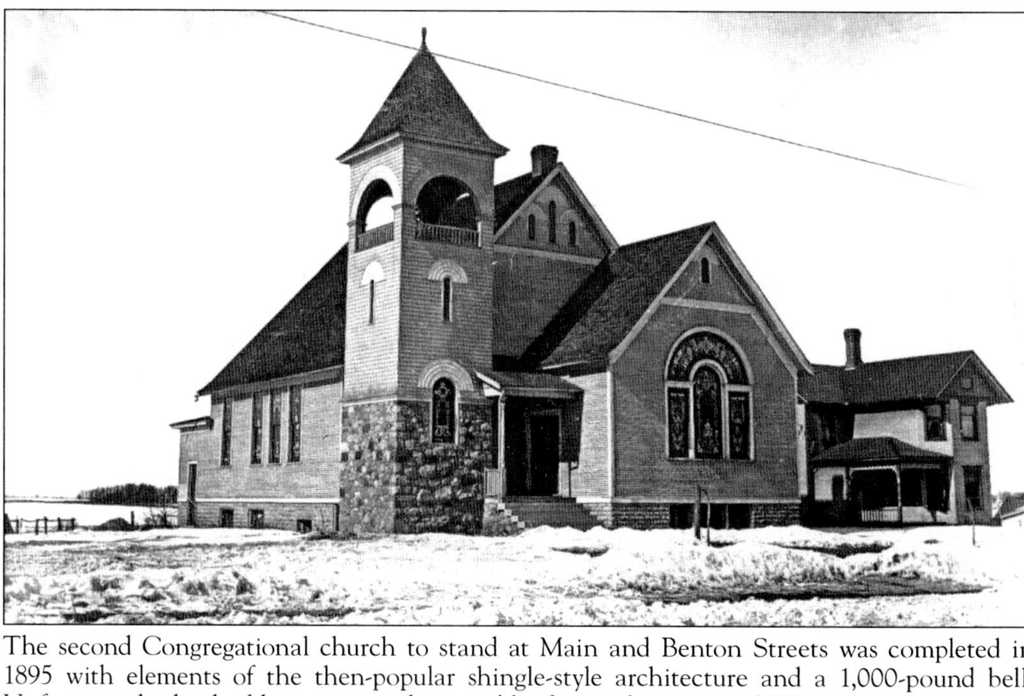

The second Congregational church to stand at Main and Benton Streets was completed in 1895 with elements of the then-popular shingle-style architecture and a 1,000-pound bell. Unfortunately this building too was destroyed by fire in the spring of 1920. After their second disaster, the Congregationalists decided not to rebuild.

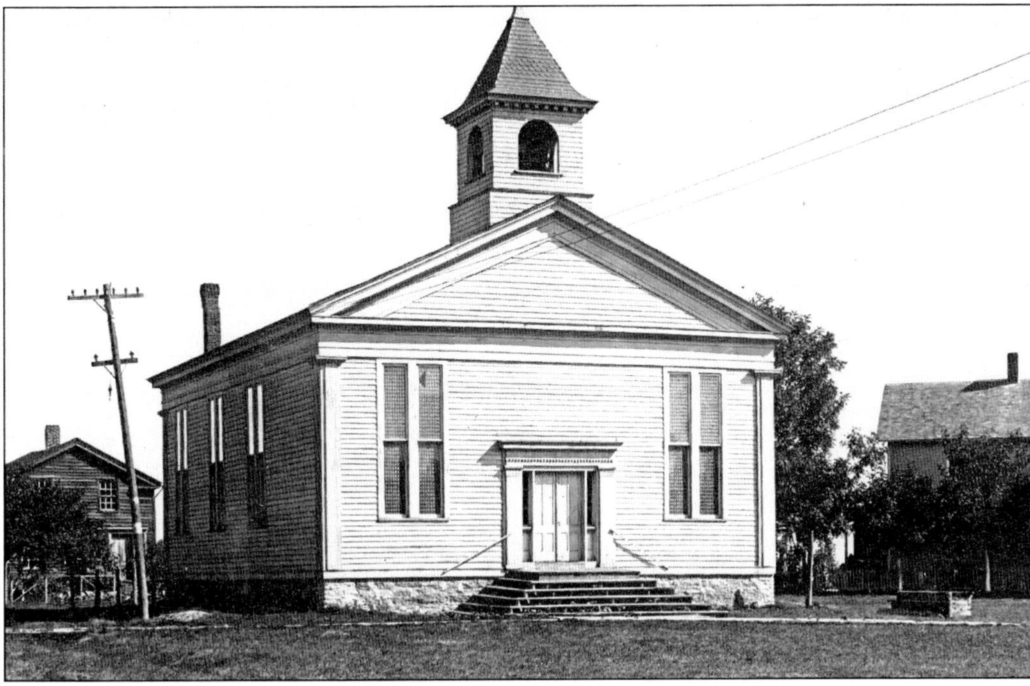

Oswego's Methodists completed this building in 1850 at Jackson and Polk Streets in Oswego. In 1901, Tirzah Minard, widow of the Reverend Henry Minard, donated the bell tower and bell to the building. In 1913, the congregation dissolved, and in 1915, the building was acquired by the Oswego School District. Today as the Little White School Museum, the building celebrates both the community's religious and educational history.

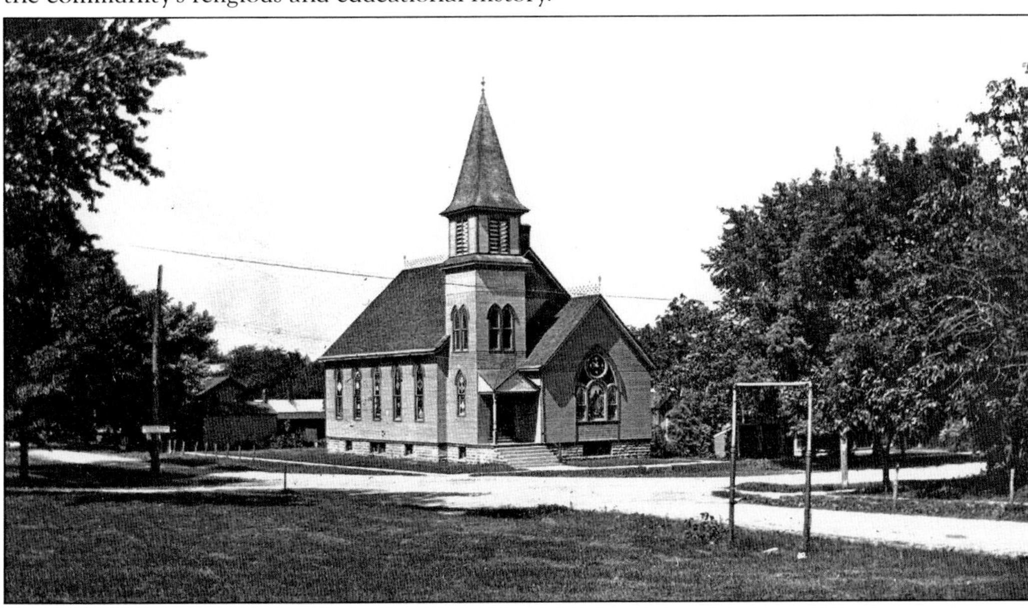

Built by Oswego's German Methodist Evangelicals, this landmark church at Washington and Madison Streets became the Federated Church with the addition of displaced Congregationalists, Baptists, Lutherans, and Methodists in 1920. In 1957, the congregation became the Church of the Good Shepherd United Methodist, its present name.

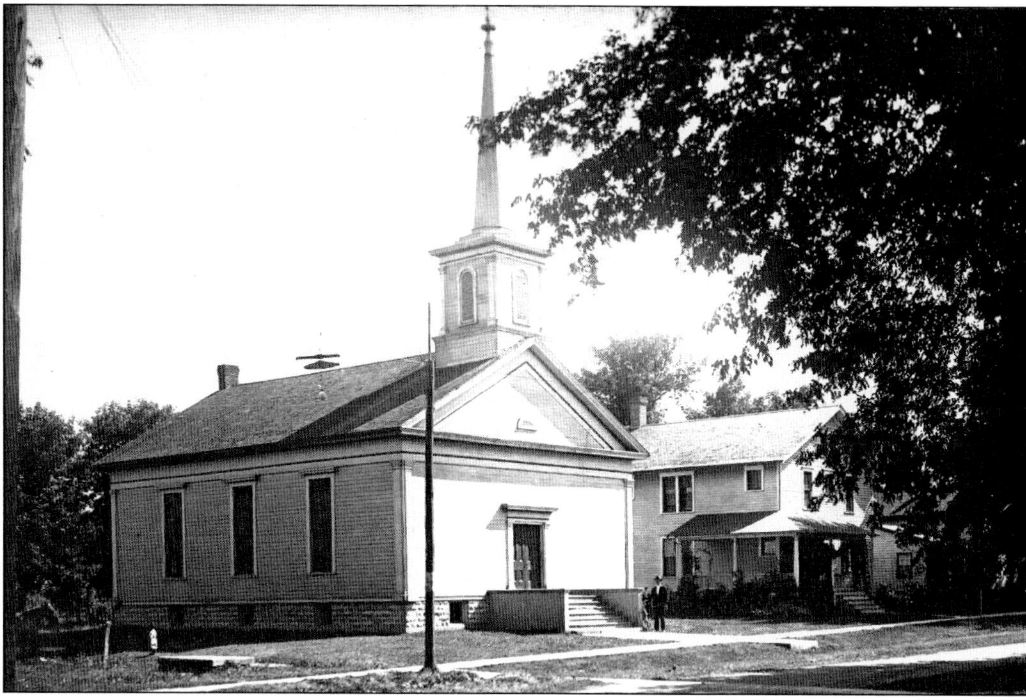

Oswego's Presbyterians built this Greek Revival church at Madison and Douglas Streets in 1857. In this photograph, it is shown after it was moved to Benton and Madison Streets in 1901. The parsonage, visible to the right, was added in 1905.

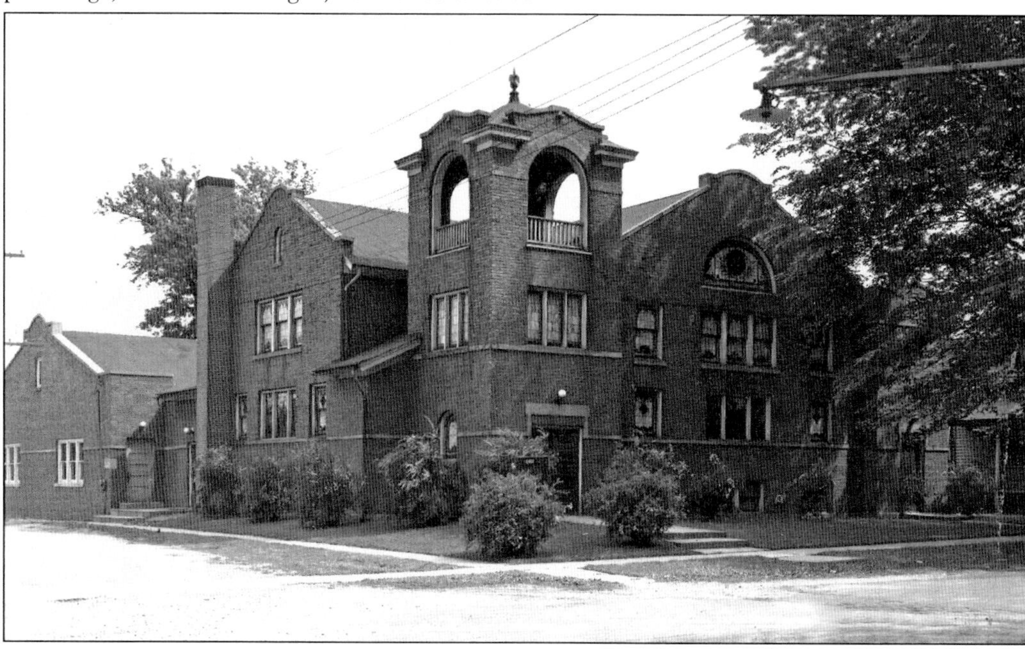

The Presbyterians completed a major expansion and remodeling of their building in 1913, changing it into this brick Romanesque church to serve the growing congregation. The education wing at left was added in 1938, and housed elementary public school classes during Oswego's early 1950s growth spurt. Its Baptist owners demolished the church building in 1980.

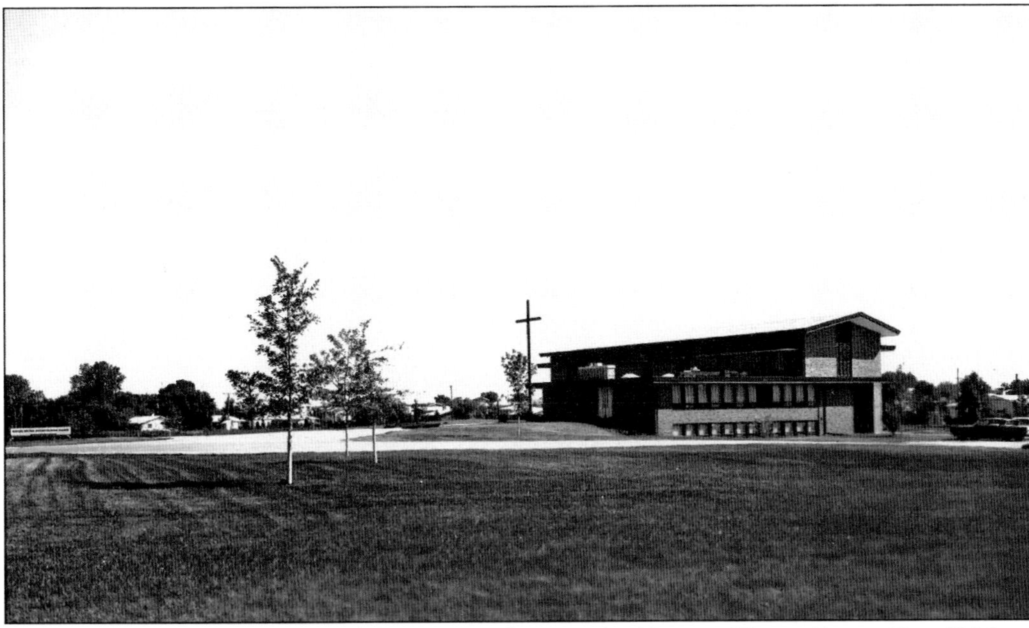

Oswego's Presbyterians dedicated this new modernistic building on Illinois Route 25 in 1966 and moved from their longtime location at Madison and Benton Streets after selling the building to the Oswego Baptist Church. In 2008, the congregation was planning a major expansion of their building.

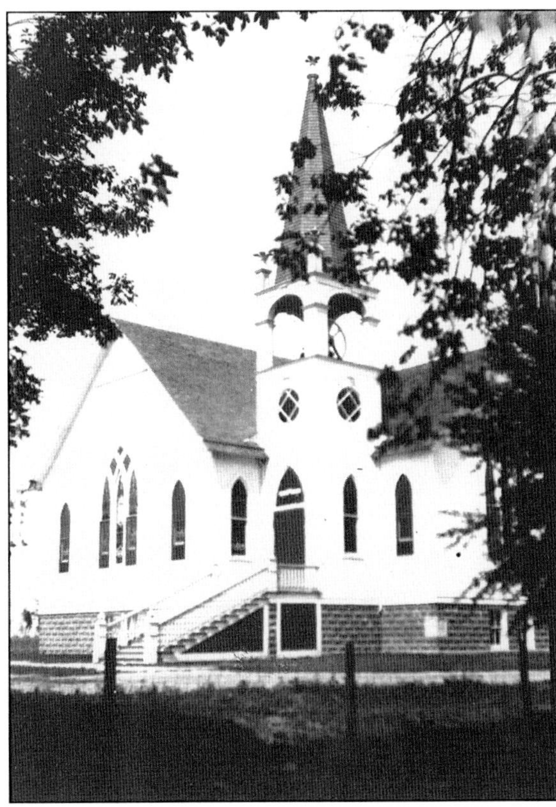

The Wheatland "Scotch" Presbyterian Church was built in 1906, replacing their old, smaller building on the same site. The congregation was founded by Scottish immigrants, mostly from the Ayrshire agricultural area of Scotland. The church is still attended by direct descendants of its founding family, Stephen and Sybilla Wylie Findlay.

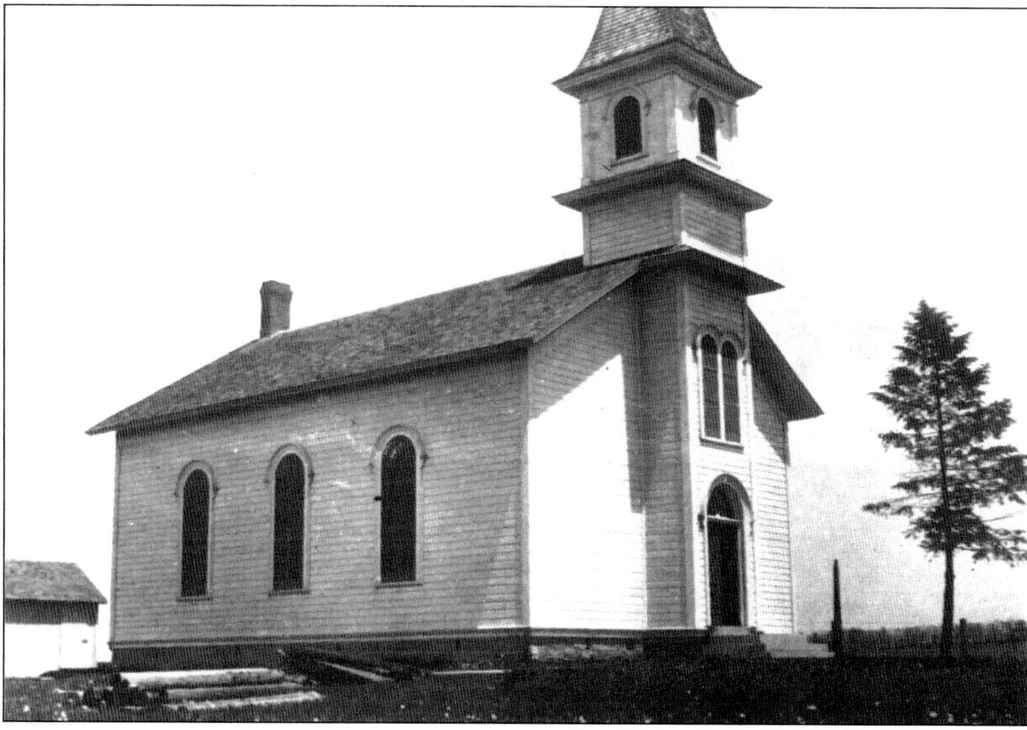

This 1871 building at Wolf and Roth roads was the second church built by the German Methodists on the Oswego Prairie east of Oswego. The 32-by-42-foot building with spire and bell cost $3,500 and was built on a site purchased from George Faust.

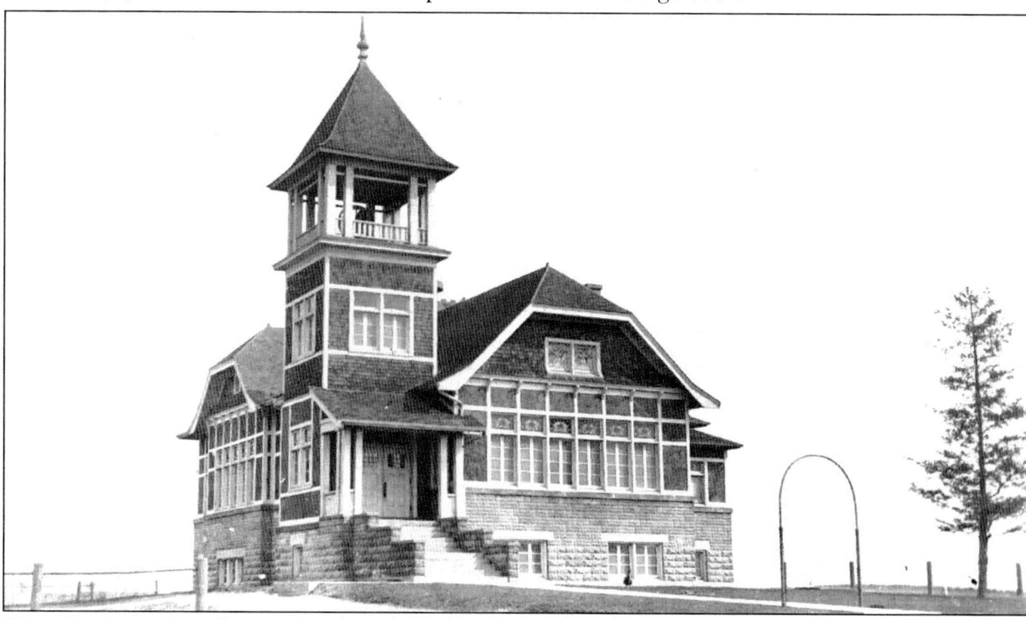

The third—and so far final—church built by the Oswego Prairie Methodist congregation was dedicated in 1910 on the site of the former 1871 building. A large education wing was added to the left of the building in 1960. Today many congregation members are descendants of the original German Albright Methodists who established the congregation in 1848.

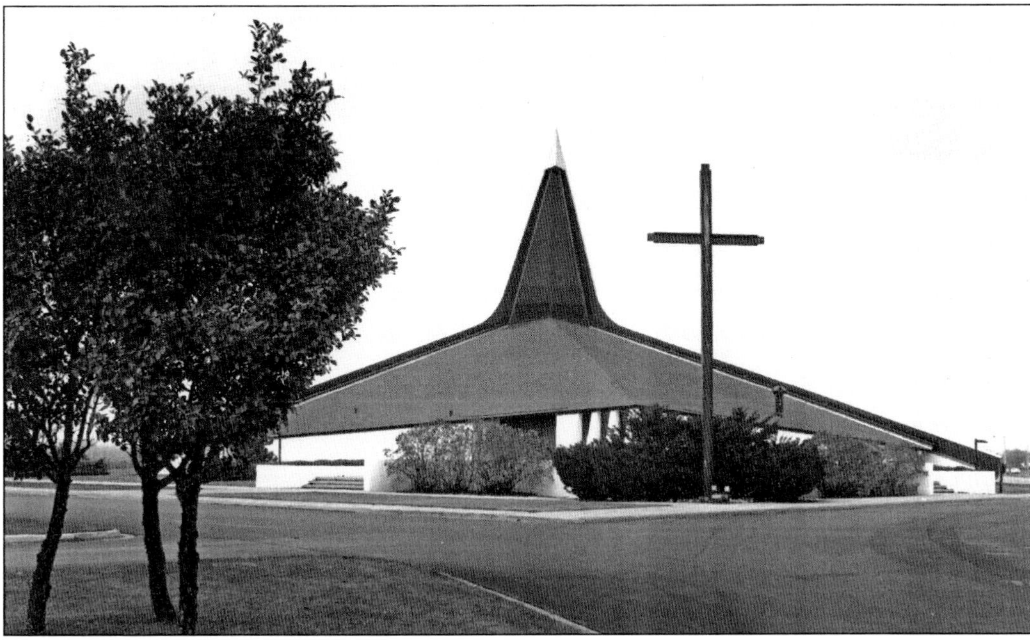

Established as a mission of St. Mary's Catholic Church in Plano in 1953, St. Anne's Parish in Oswego built this architecturally distinctive landmark church in 1969 on a site along Boulder Hill Pass just off U.S. Route 34. The Oswego landmark suffered a devastating fire on January 24, 2000, and has been replaced by a brick neo-Romanesque structure. The parish serves nearly 2,800 families.

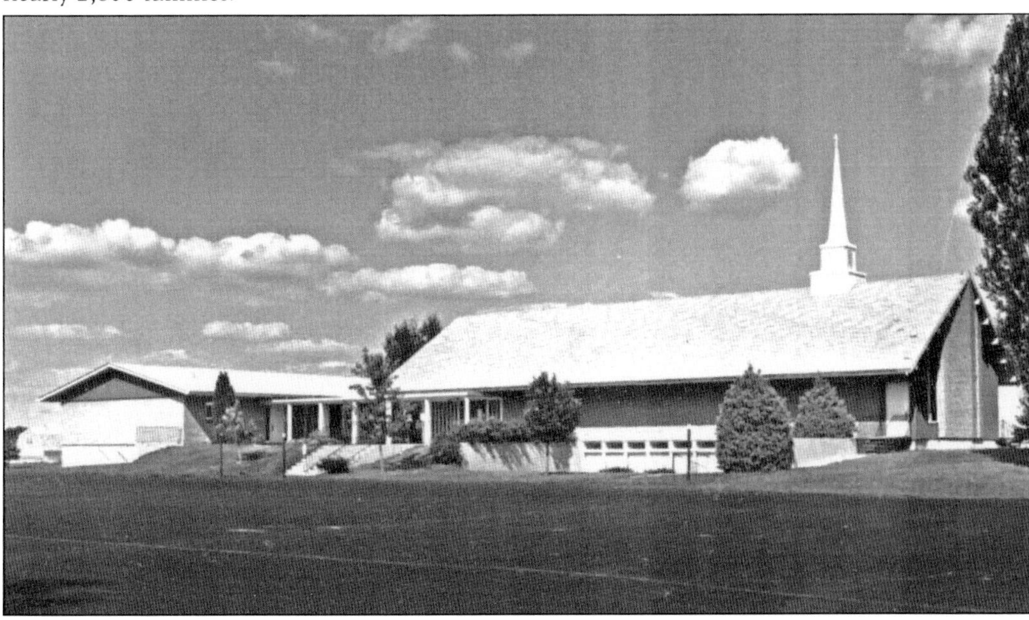

St. Luke's Lutheran Church began as a mission of St. Paul Lutheran Church in Aurora with the first service at Oswego High School—now Traughber Junior High—in November 1957. This modern church was completed on a site along Fernwood Road in Boulder Hill in 1963. The church has enjoyed consistent growth and now includes a school for grades kindergarten through eight.

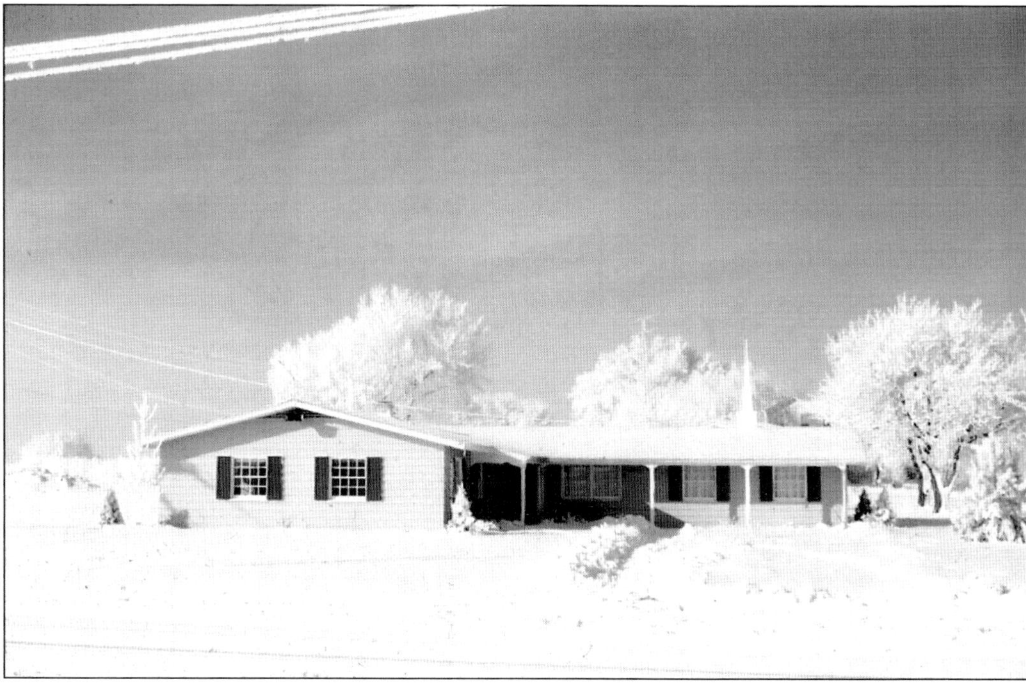

The Boulder Hill Neighborhood Church of the Brethren first held services in this new structure at 5 South Bereman Road in Boulder Hill in 1958. Designed to be converted into a home, interior walls were added, and it was turned into a home after the permanent church was completed on Boulder Hill Pass.

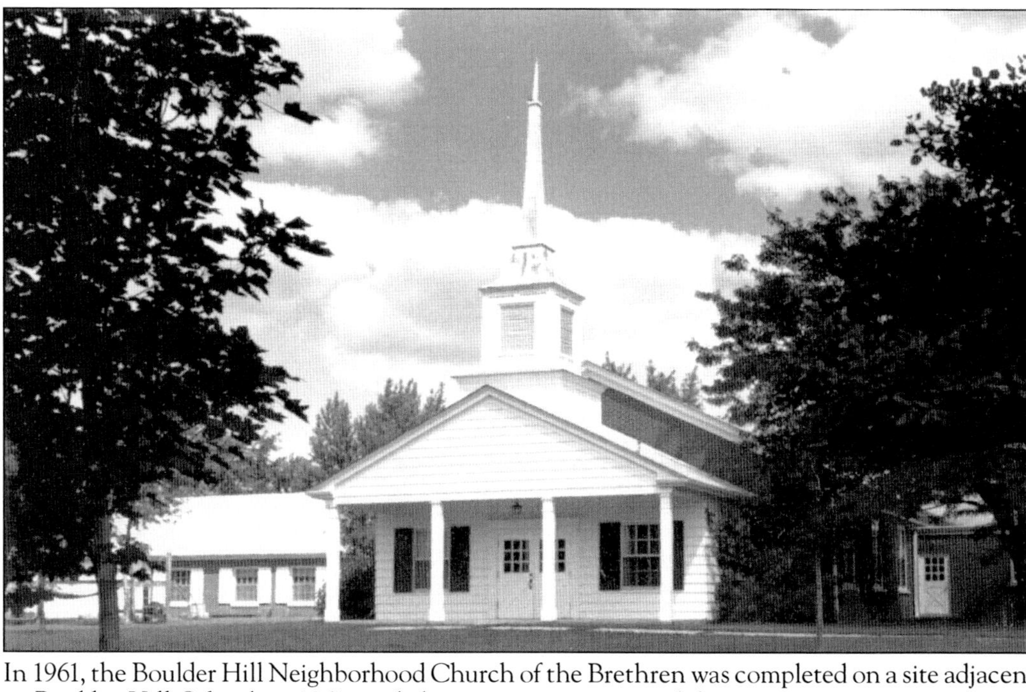

In 1961, the Boulder Hill Neighborhood Church of the Brethren was completed on a site adjacent to Boulder Hill School in 1961, and the congregation moved from its temporary quarters on Bereman Road. The church serves the Boulder Hill and surrounding community.

Nine

Time Out for Fun

Although the pioneers faced backbreaking labor in settling and then farming on the Illinois prairie, they knew, too, how to have fun.

In the earliest days, families gathered to help each other build cabins, houses, and barns. These impromptu cooperative work ventures usually turned into social gatherings, with potluck dinners and plenty of conversation and fun after the work was done.

That cooperative spirit continued as the pioneer era drew to a close and provided the basis for the churches and schools that, in turn, provided the foundation for the communities that exist to this day.

In Oswego Township, dancing was an important social outlet. The earliest invitation in the collections of the Little White School Museum is a small business card–sized 1864 invitation to a "Cotillion Party." While the card is the earliest invitation, the event it advertised was hardly the first of its kind. Nor was it the last. Community dances remained popular in the area through the 1930s. During that decade, square dances were held in the hall above stores on the east side of Main Street and even boasted entertainment that once or twice included singer and future movie star Gene Autry.

And, of course, the area's natural setting provided lots of opportunities for outdoor entertainment. Swimming and fishing in the Fox River and Waubonsie Creek, ice-skating, hunting, picnicking in the area's groves, and holiday celebrations were gradually joined by more organized entertainment. Riverview, later Fox River, Park in Oswego Township offered an exciting "shoot the chutes" attraction along with a roller coaster and hugely popular Chautauqua events that drew such speakers as William Jennings Bryant, along with professional entertainers.

Community sports teams became popular in the late 1800s, with keen baseball rivalries developing with nearby towns. Probably no other technological development resulted in more entertainment opportunities in the early 1900s than the automobile, as it ushered in the era of the Sunday drive.

Then in 1950, the establishment of the Oswegoland Park District started a tradition of community education and entertainment that continues to the present day, as Oswego Township residents always seem to take some time out for fun.

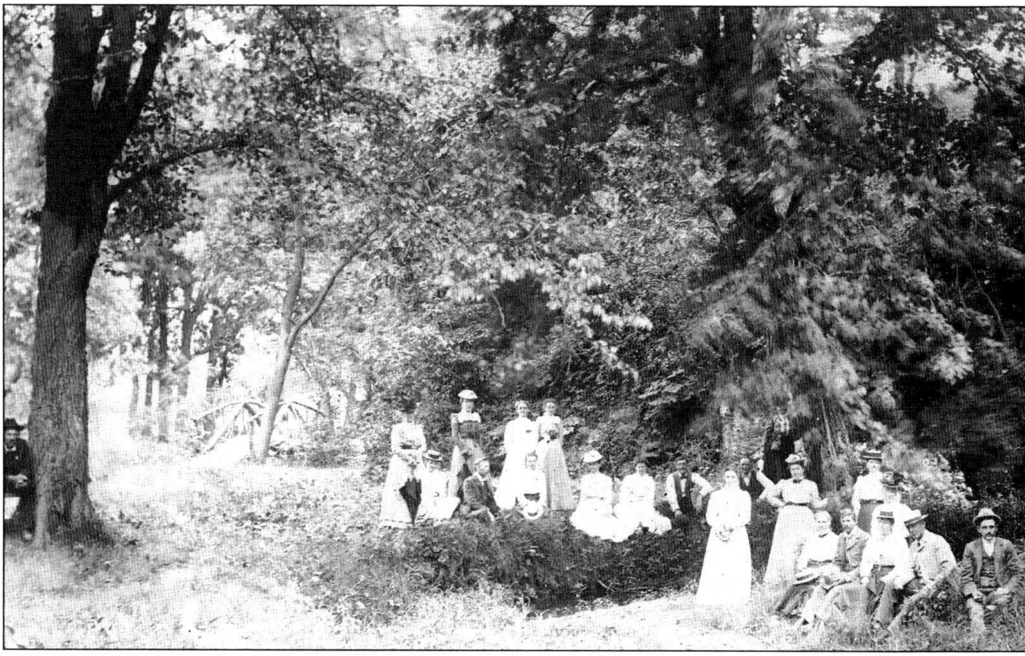

Picnics were as popular for family entertainment a century ago as they are now. In this photograph, probably taken about 1890, members of the Oswego Methodist Episcopal Church—now the Little White School Museum—enjoy an afternoon at Smith's Woods along Waubonsie Creek in Oswego.

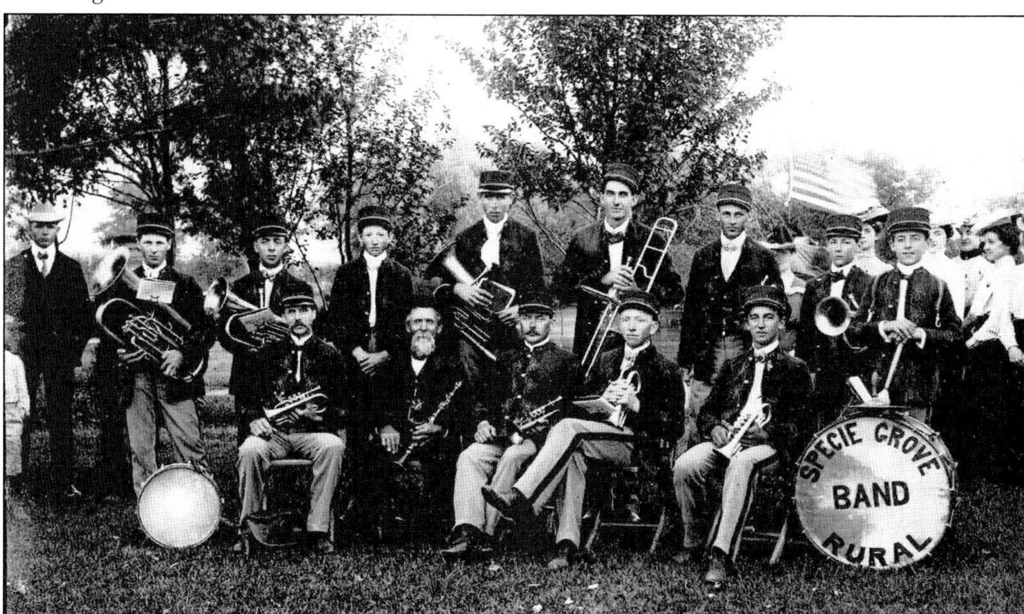

Rural bands were popular in the years after the Civil War. The Specie Grove Rural Band was made up largely of farmers from the Specie Grove area southeast of Oswego. Band members included A. J. Parkhurst, Fred Graham, James Gowran, Gilbert Collins, Ed Kusmaul, Albert Potts, Dwight Gowran, Winfield Clark, Watts Cutter, Arthur Lyons, Oren Gates, Reuben Parkhurst, Raymond Parkhurst, Charles Turpin, Tom Collins, and Clarence Parkhurst.

GRAND REUNION BALL,

On the evening of the 25th annual gathering of the

4th Ill. Cavalry,

FRIDAY, SEPTEMBER 24th, 1886,

AT OSWEGO, ILLINOIS.

Yourself and Ladies are Cordially Invited.

Good Music. General Put Howard's Full Band.

The Civil War created lifelong bonds between those who served as comrades in arms. Company A of the 4th Illinois Volunteer Cavalry was recruited largely in and around Oswego, and the unit's veterans sometimes held their annual reunions in the village. The 1886 reunion was typical of those events, most of which were held at the Star Roller Skating Rink on Main Street.

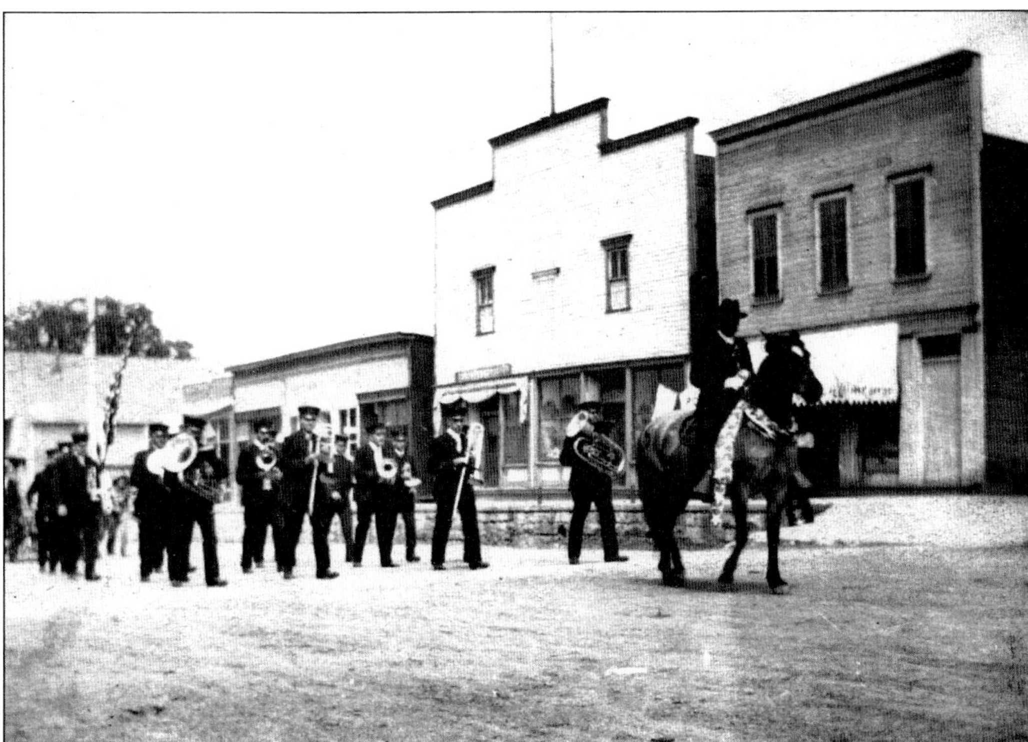

Decoration Day, now renamed Memorial Day, was established to honor the Civil War's dead and as a day of reflection. Here Capt. Charles Mann, formerly of the 4th Illinois Cavalry and a prominent Oswego horse breeder, leads a Decoration Day parade on its way to the Oswego Cemetery sometime in the 1880s. Note the Star Roller Skating Rink building to the left of the Rank Building housing the Oswego Post Office.

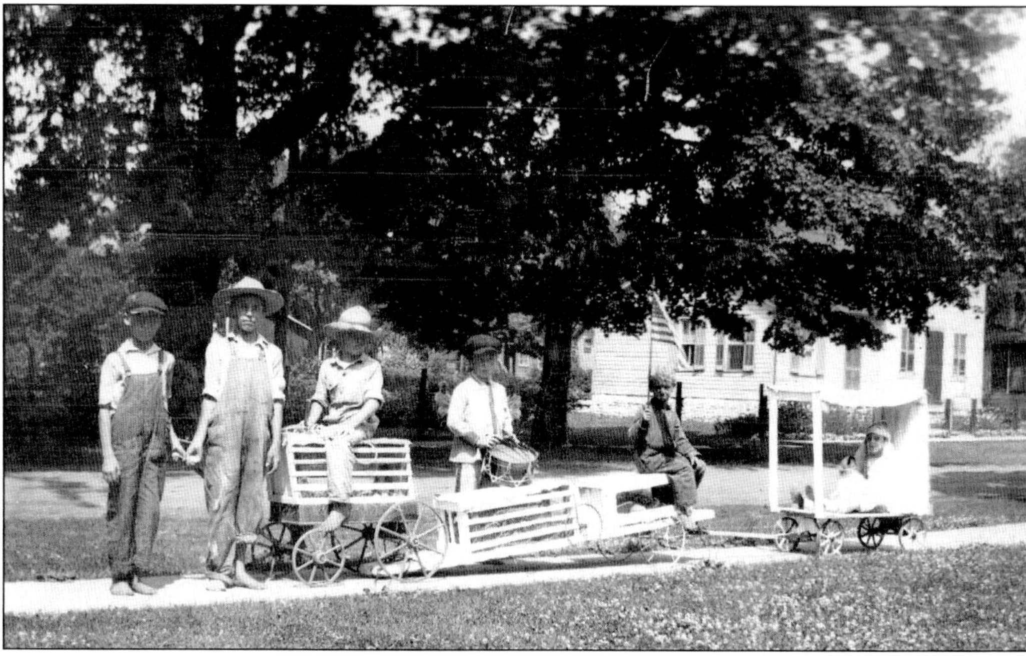

In small towns a century ago, children usually had to create their own entertainment. According to the September 26, 1906, *Kendall County Record*'s Oswego correspondent describing the event captured in the photograph above said, "A circus, Saturday, did not come to town but materialized right in it. . . . It was an affair of the small boys."

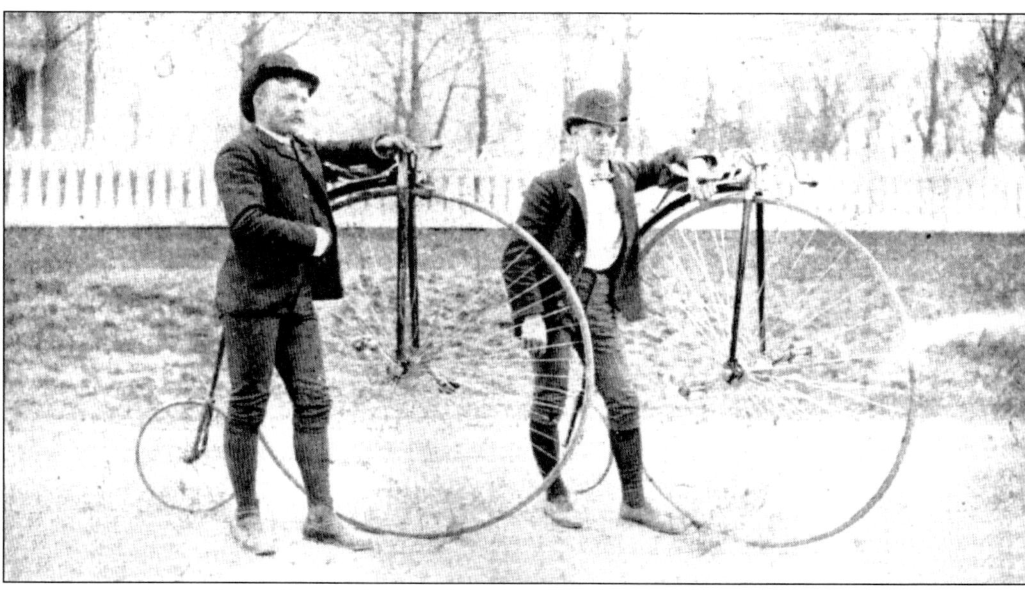

Oswego wheelmen Scott Cutter (left) and Joe Sierp look ready for a trip on their high-wheelers. A note in the August 20, 1880, *Kendall County Record* noted that the first bicycle ever seen in Oswego had passed through a couple days earlier. According to a note in the *Kendall County Record* in July 1885, "Joe Sierp of Oswego was one of the bicyclists of the great bicycle turnout on the Fourth at Ottawa."

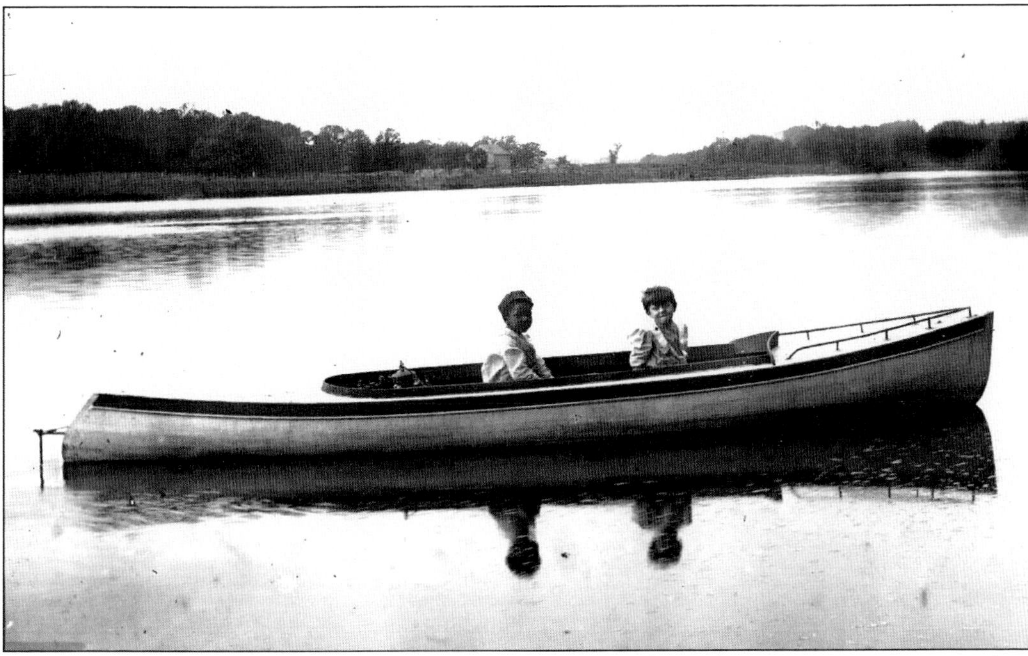

The Fox River has been both an economic and a recreation boost for Oswego since pioneer days. Here Carl White (left) and Ed Inman take a Fox River cruise in an early motorboat built by Lew Inman and Irvin Haines.

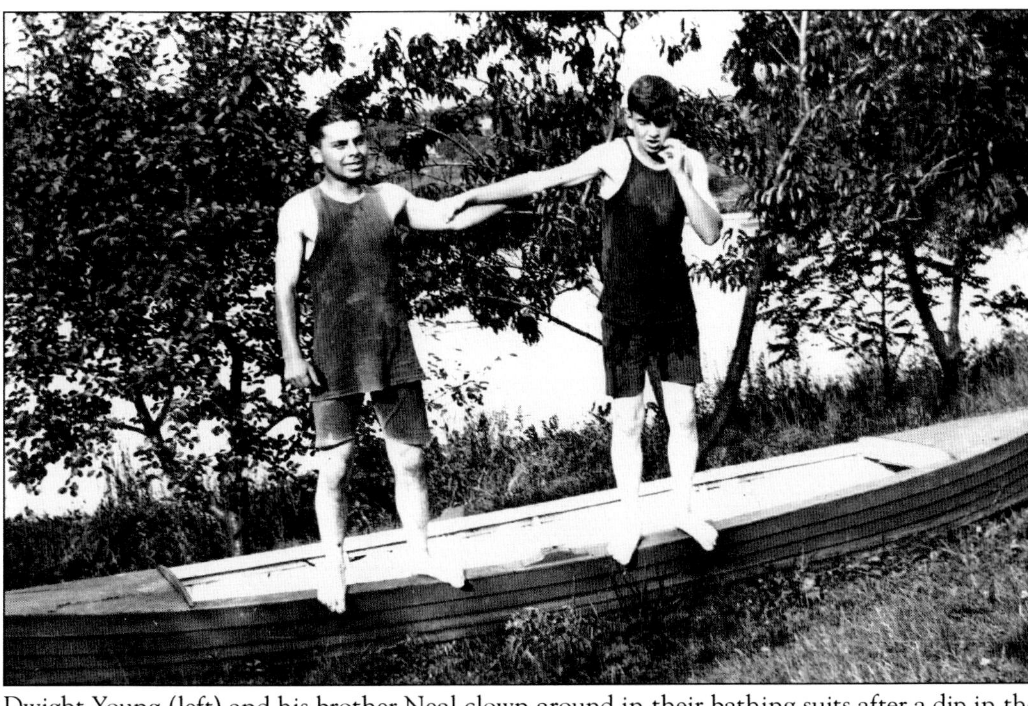

Dwight Young (left) and his brother Neal clown around in their bathing suits after a dip in the river behind their home, located just south of the Oswego Bridge on U.S. Route 34. Dwight used the speedy rowboat to snap some of the photographs in this book.

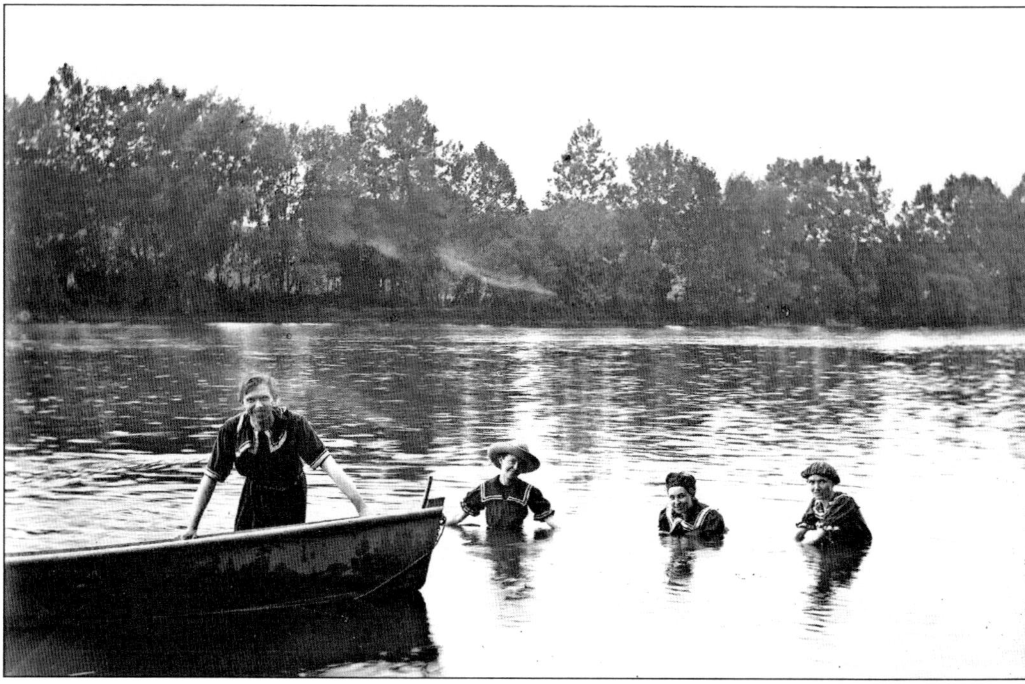

Swimming was not just for guys a century ago. This photograph was taken by Irvin Haines on the Fox River just above the Parker mills and dam around 1900 and clearly illustrates the difference between swimming attire of that era and today.

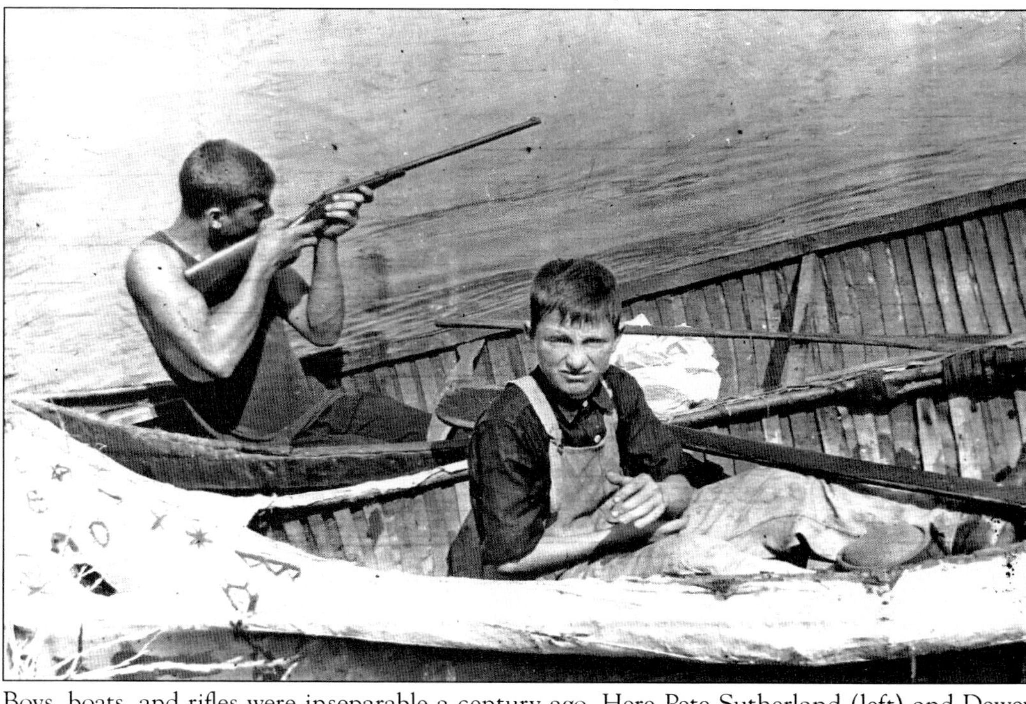

Boys, boats, and rifles were inseparable a century ago. Here Pete Sutherland (left) and Dewey Boyle pause during an expedition on the Fox River near Oswego about 1900 as Sutherland sights down the barrel of his Stevens Favorite .22 rifle.

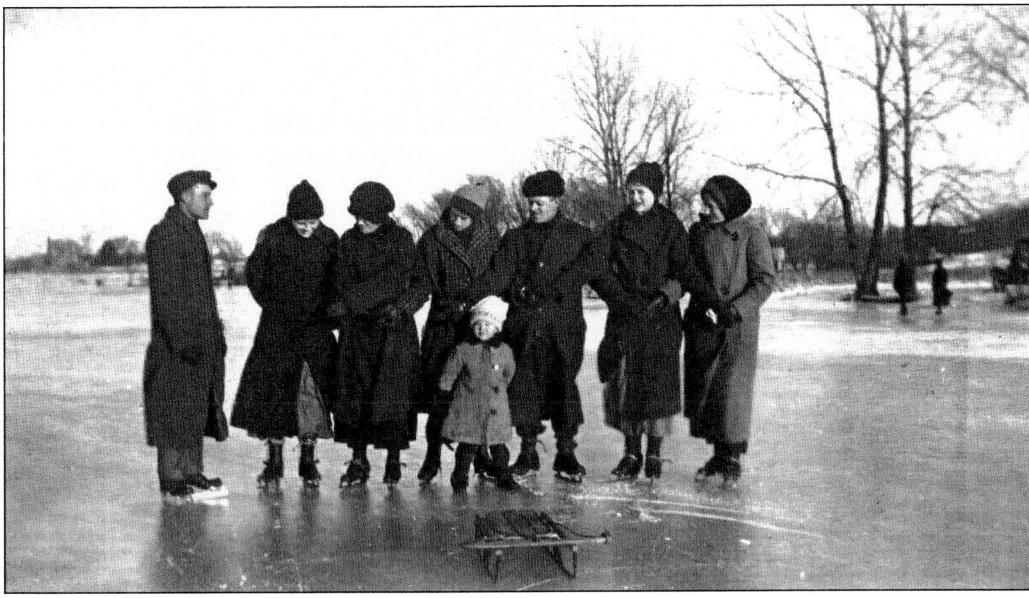

The Fox River did not lose its recreational potential during the winter months. Ice-skating, in the years before increases in population gradually warmed the river's water until it no longer froze solid in the winter, was a popular winter activity. Seen above, families pause on a cold winter day about 1915 while skating just above the Fox River Bridge in Oswego.

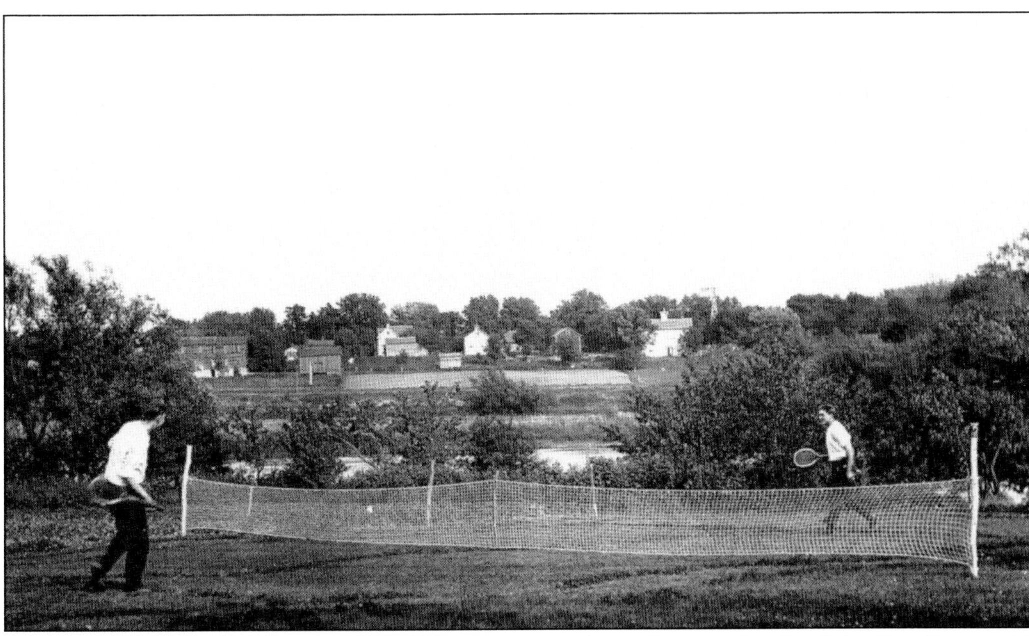

Dwight and Neal Young enjoy a bit of lawn tennis along the west bank of the Fox River with Oswego in the background. The building just visible at the far left is the old Armstrong Broom Factory that once stood along South Adams Street.

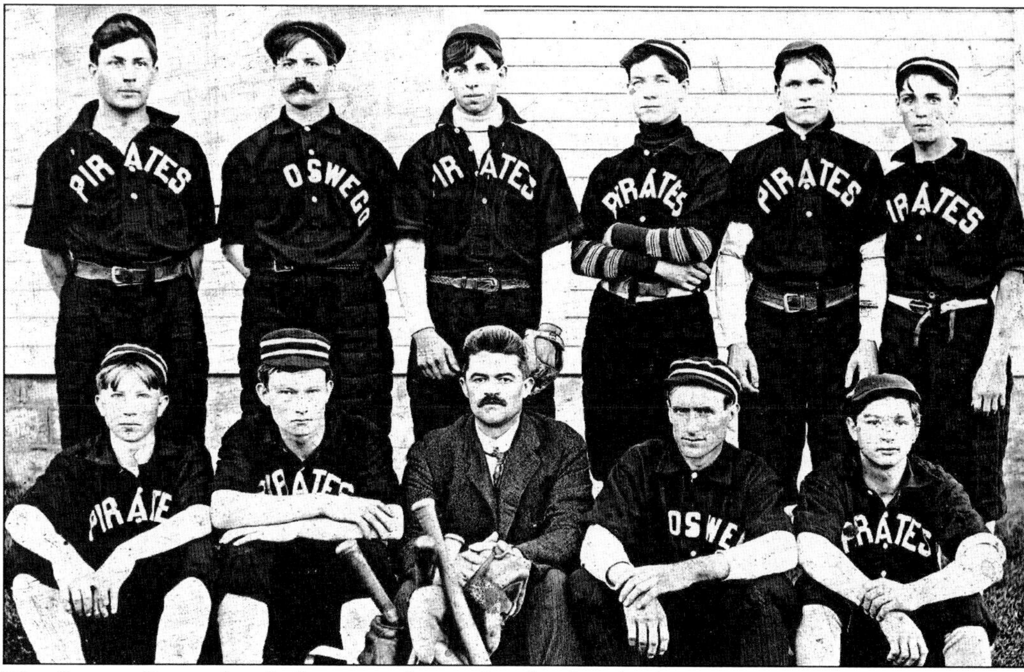

The Oswego Pirates baseball team is shown shortly after the beginning of the 20th century with their equipment neatly stacked. Team members include, from left to right, (first row) Guy White, Herman Young, manager Abner Updike, Arthur Roswell, and Grant Leigh; (second row) Clint Burkhart, Gus Wells, Ben Leigh, Chris Herren, Ben Beisemeier, and Joe Richards. The team drew most of its members from farmers living in east Oswego Township.

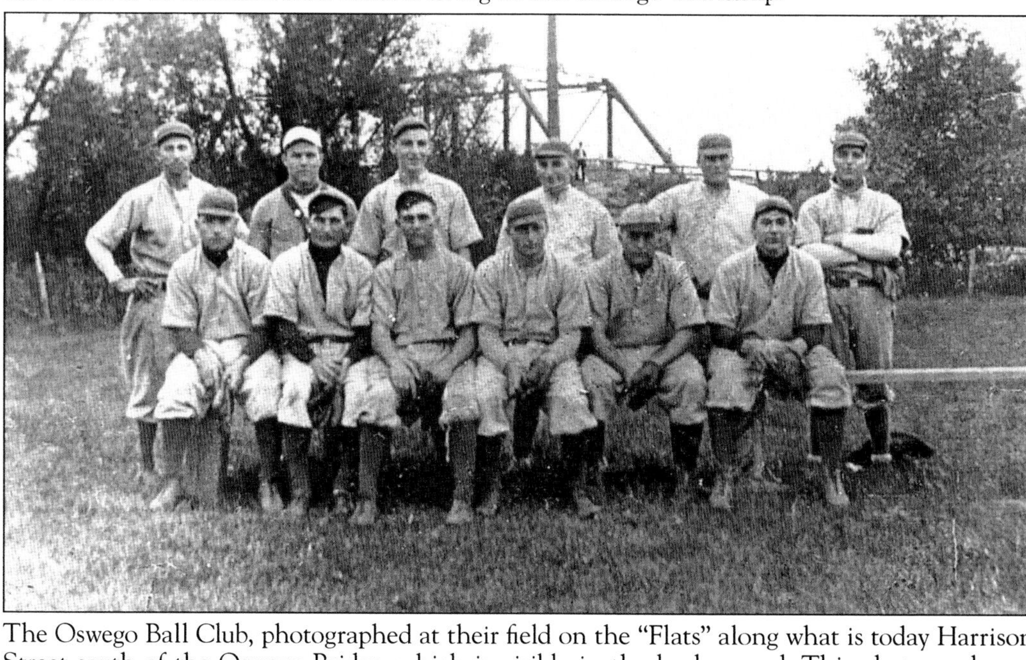

The Oswego Ball Club, photographed at their field on the "Flats" along what is today Harrison Street south of the Oswego Bridge, which is visible in the background. This photograph was taken about 1922 by Dwight Young as the team got ready for another game with a team from a nearby town. There was a particularly vigorous rivalry with Yorkville's ball team.

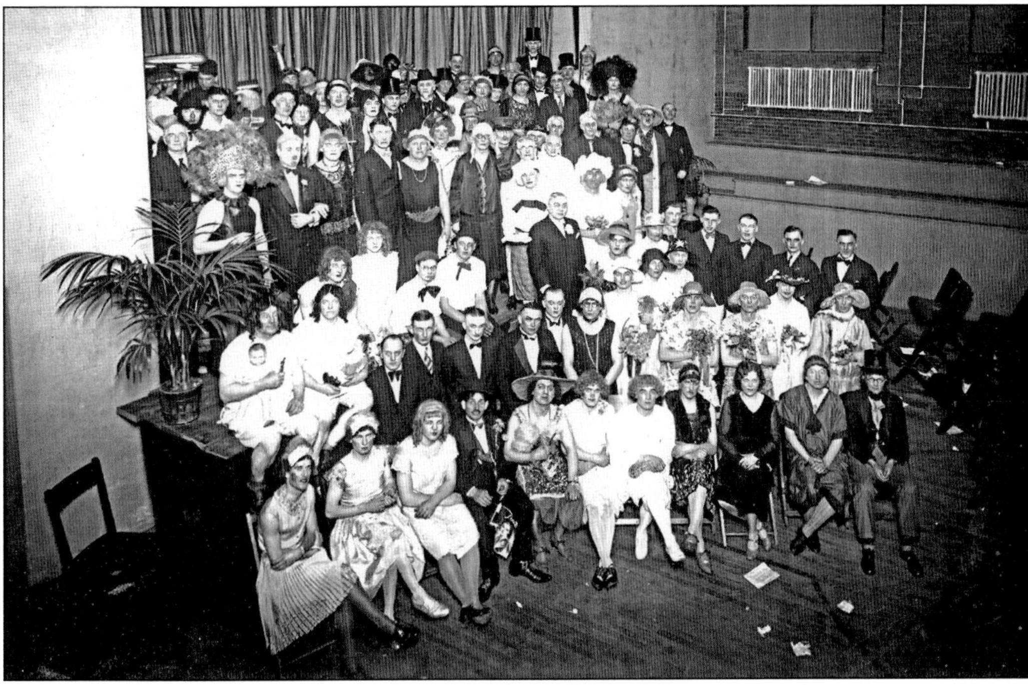

During the 1930s, entertainments where men dressed as women were popular community events, if somewhat unusual to modern eyes. The "Womanless Wedding" was one of the most popular events of that era. Held in the gym at the Red Brick School, it featured an all-male cast.

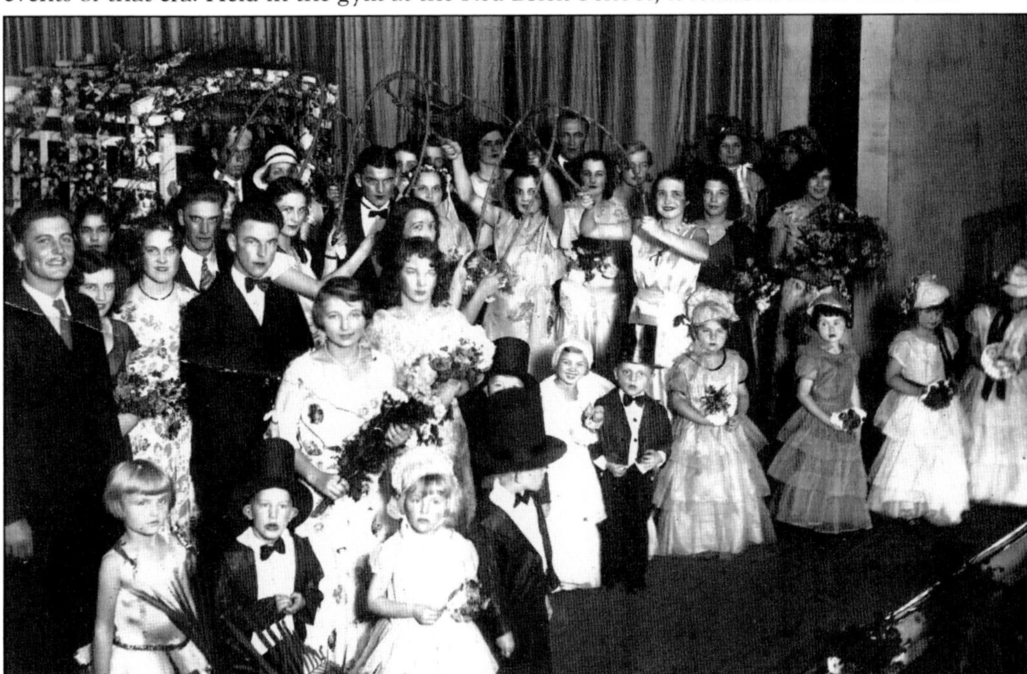

Children were not immune from the fascination with holding fictional weddings as entertainment. Here the young cast of the "Children's Wedding" pauses for a cast photograph on the stage in the Red Brick School gym about 1940.

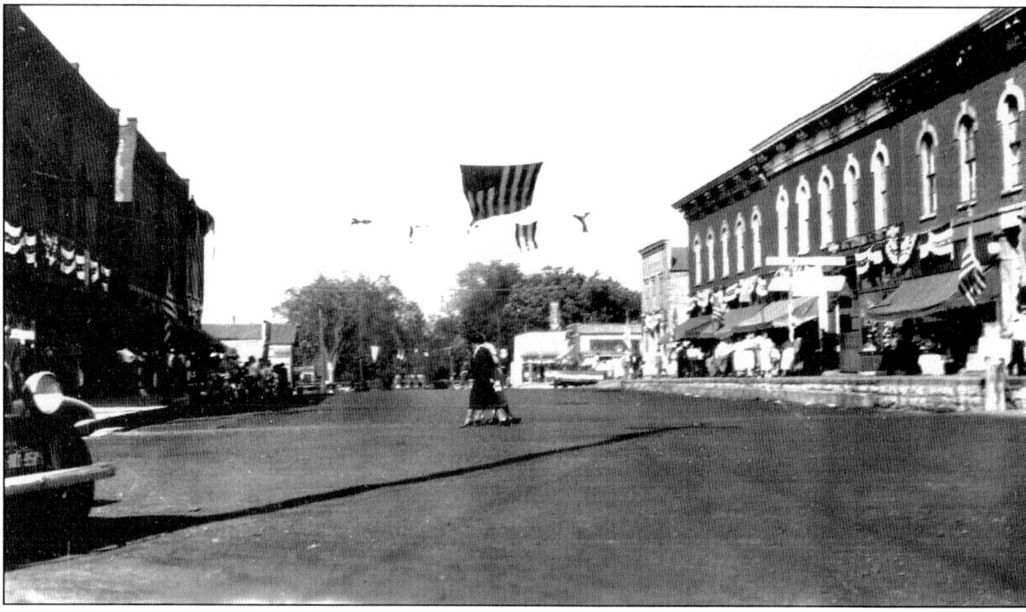

Oswego Township residents began looking back at their history in the 1930s. In 1933, the community held the centennial celebration of the township's settlement with parades and special events in the downtown business district. In the image above, spectators await the arrival of the centennial parade along a flag-bedecked Main Street.

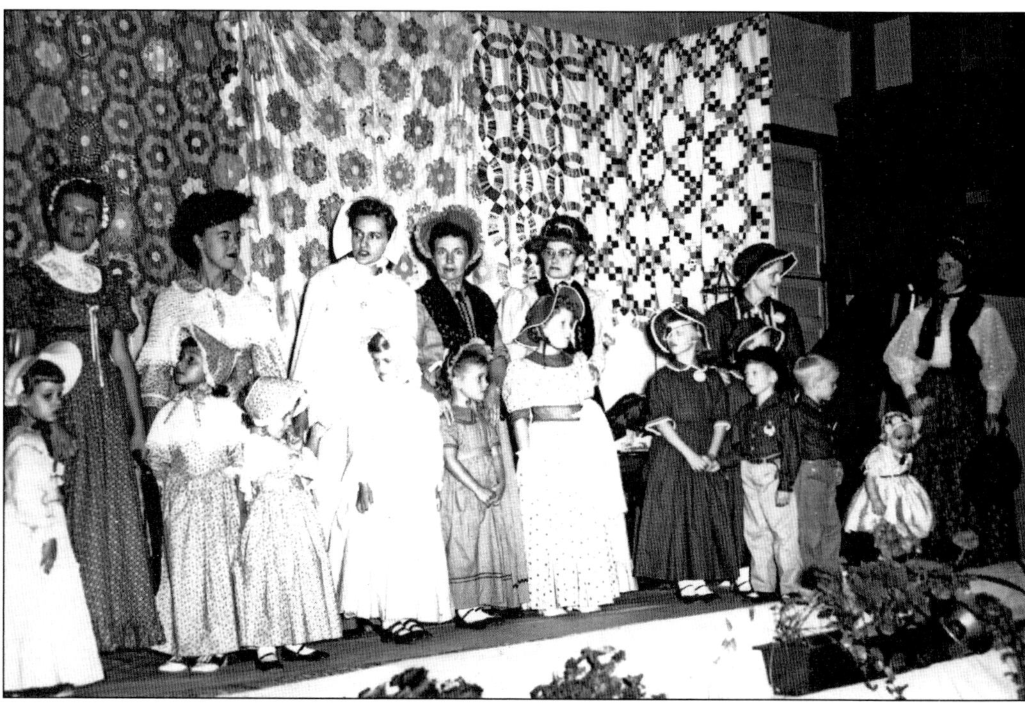

In 1958, the township celebrated its 125th anniversary with the Oswegorama celebration. Above some of the community's women, dressed in pioneer costumes, participate in the historical fashion show and tea held at the Red Brick School.

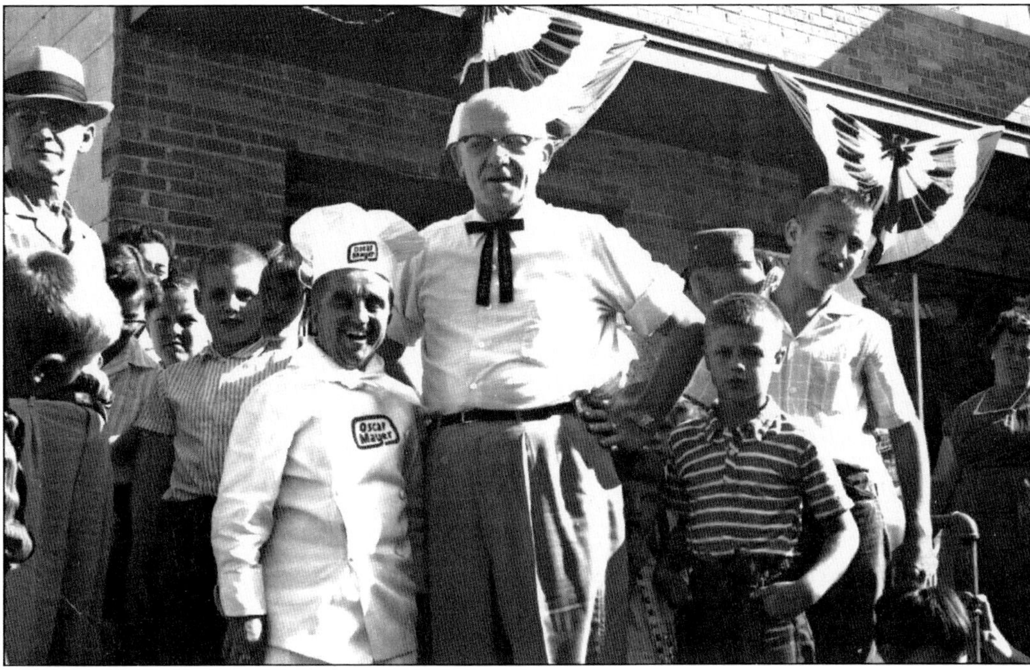

Little Oscar (left) and the famed Wienermobile visited Carl Bohn's store in 1958 as part of the Oswegorama events. Bohn poses with the hot dog icon as admiring Oswego youngsters look on. Also part of the celebration, an elaborate pageant involving many community residents and organizations was held nightly on a set built on the lighted football field at Oswego High School, now Traughber Junior High.

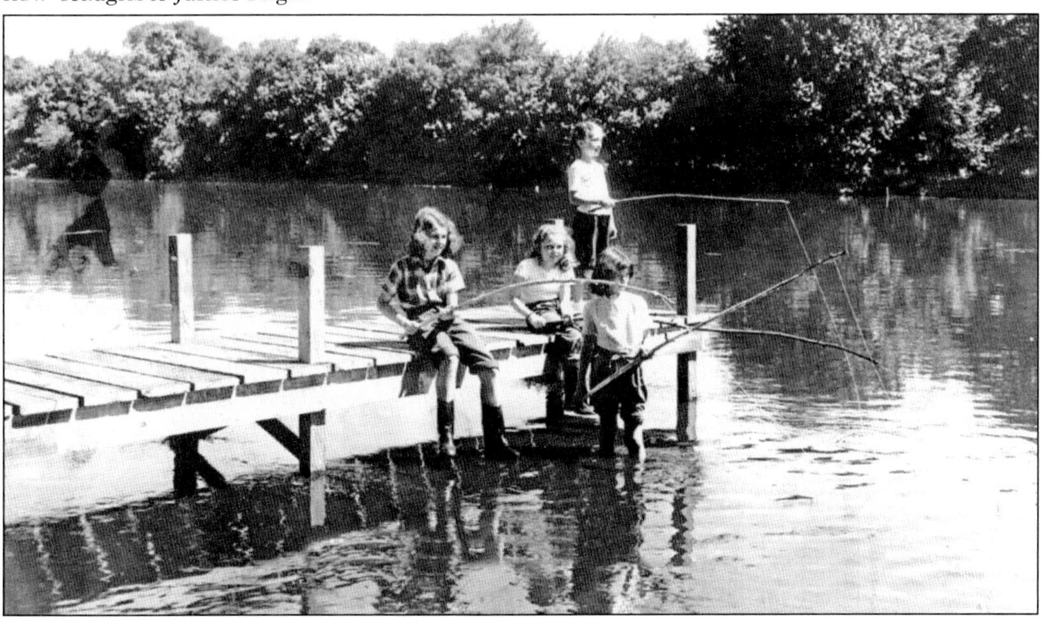

It was always possible to find a bit of quiet and a spot for some solitude along the banks of the Fox River. Above, campers from the YWCA's Camp Quarryledge, located along the river at the site of the old Wormley limestone quarry just north of Oswego, enjoy a quiet afternoon fishing in 1947.

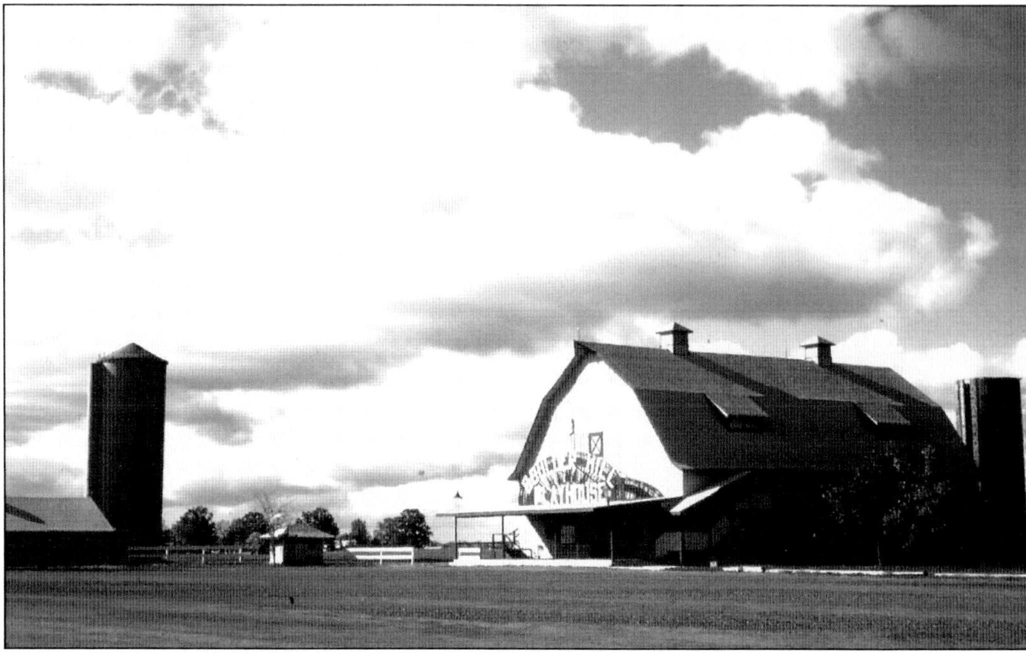

When Boulder Hill was developed on the old Bereman Boulder Hill Stock Farm, the barns were no longer needed for farming purposes. One of the largest of the barns was turned into the Boulder Hill Playhouse and featured an innovative revolving stage to allow quick scenery changes. The playhouse played to full houses until it was destroyed by fire in 1967.

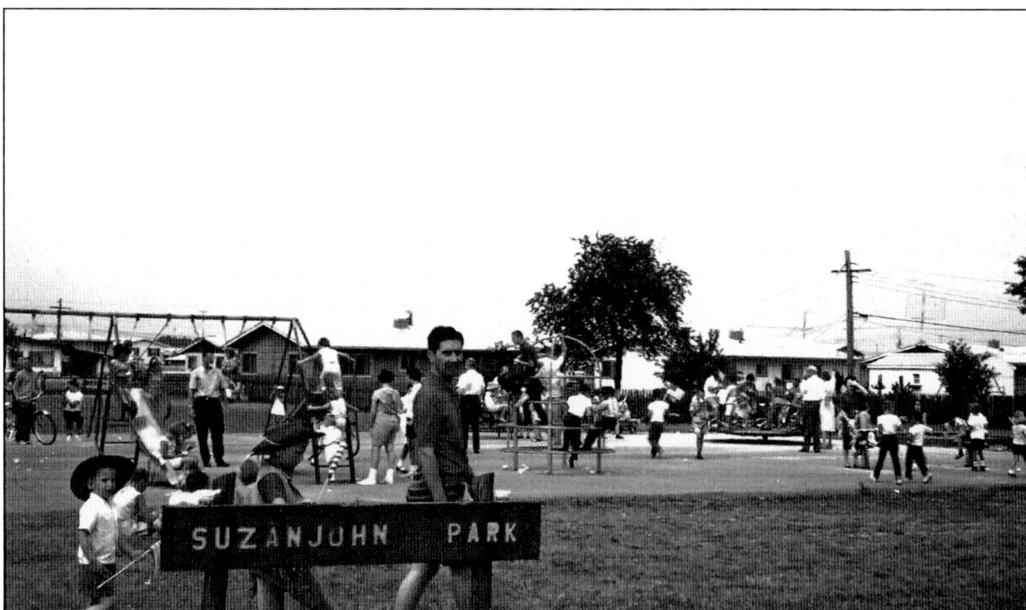

Started as an agency to provide summer recreation programs for Oswego area youth, the Oswegoland Park District was given its first park by Don L. Dise in 1960. Named SuzanJohn Park after Suzanne Dise and John Hyde, children of Dise and co-developer A. C. Hyde, the roughly one-acre parcel is situated between Hampton and Durango Roads in Boulder Hill. Today the park district owns 36 parks covering nearly 750 acres.

BIBLIOGRAPHY

Bateman, Newton and Paul Selby, eds. *Historical Encyclopedia of Illinois and History of Kendall County, Illinois*. Two volumes. Chicago: Munsell Publishing Company, 1914.

Farren, Kathy, ed. *A Bicentennial History of Kendall County, Illinois*. Yorkville: Kendall County Bicentennial Commission, 1976.

Hicks, Reverend E. W. *History of Kendall County, Illinois*. Aurora: Knickerbocker and Hodder, 1877.

Johnson, Oliver C. and Anna French Johnson. *Atlas and History of Kendall County, Illinois*. Elmhurst: Friendly Map and Publishing Company, 1941.

Matile, Roger, ed. *150 Years Along the Fox: The History of Oswego Township, Illinois*. Oswego: Oswego Sesquicentennial Days Steering Committee, 1983.